Progressive
Consumption Taxation

Progressive
Consumption Taxation

The X Tax Revisited

Robert Carroll
Alan D. Viard

The AEI Press

Publisher for the American Enterprise Institute

WASHINGTON, D.C.

Distributed by arrangement with the Rowman & Littlefield Publishing Group, 4501 Forbes Boulevard, Suite 200, Lanham, Maryland 20706. To order, call toll free 1-800-462-6420 or 1-717-794-3800. For all other inquiries, please contact AEI Press, 1150 Seventeenth Street, N.W., Washington, D.C. 20036, or call 1-800-862-5801.

NRI National Research Initiative

This publication is a project of the National Research Initiative, a program of the American Enterprise Institute that is designed to support, publish, and disseminate research by university-based scholars and other independent researchers who are engaged in the exploration of important public policy issues.

Library of Congress Cataloging-in-Publication Data

Carroll, Robert.
    Progressive consumption taxation : the X tax revisited / Robert Carroll and Alan D. Viard.
        p.   cm.
    Includes bibliographical references and index.
    ISBN 978-0-8447-4394-3 (cloth)—ISBN 0-8447-4394-1 (cloth)—
ISBN 978-0-8447-4395-0 (pbk.)—ISBN 0-8447-4395-X (pbk.)—
ISBN 978-0-8447-4396-7 (ebook)—ISBN 0-8447-4396-8 (ebook)
    1. Spendings tax—United States. 2. Value-added tax—United States. I. Viard, Alan D. II. Title.
    HJ5715.U6C28 2012
    336.2'7140973—dc23   2011050811

Printed in the United States of America

Contents

List of Illustrations

Figures

Tables

Acknowledgments

This book could not have been written without the financial support of the American Enterprise Institute's National Research Initiative. We are grateful to the NRI board—Christopher DeMuth, Kim Dennis, and the late James Q. Wilson—for approving this project. We thank NRI director Henry Olsen for his patient and steadfast encouragement of our work.

We are grateful to Alan Auerbach, Leonard Burman, Alex Brill, Julie Anne Cronin, Jane Gravelle, Chad Hill, J. Andrew Hipolit, Emily Lin, Jay Mackie, Susan Nelson, Thomas Neubig, Jim Nunns, Laura Power, Amy Roden, Jason Saving, Dan Shaviro, Andrew Smith, Eric Toder, David Weisbach, and George Yin for helpful comments and to Matt Knittel for providing data. We also thank Laura Harbold for her thorough and diligent work on this manuscript.

Introduction

The United States is alone among industrialized countries in having no broad-based consumption tax at the federal level. Yet, as we will explain in chapter 1, economic analysis reveals that consumption taxation has an economic advantage, relative to income taxation, because it does not penalize saving and investment. In recent years, a number of proposals to adopt some type of consumption tax have been advanced. As revenue needs increase due to the growth of Medicare, Medicaid, and Social Security in future decades, there is likely to be renewed interest in finding better ways to raise revenue, prompting further consideration of consumption taxes.

Several concerns have blocked a move to consumption taxation, however. On the key question of whether a consumption tax should replace all, or only part, of the income tax system, each approach has drawn strong objections. Partial replacement has been opposed by those concerned that having two revenue sources would fuel the growth of government spending, a concern reinforced by a common perception that the value-added tax (VAT)—the most likely candidate for a partial replacement—is a hidden tax that can function as a money machine. Also, partial replacement of the income tax would yield smaller economic gains than full replacement. On the other hand, full replacement has been opposed on the grounds that completely replacing the progressive income tax with a regressive VAT or sales tax would have unacceptable distributional implications, a concern heightened by the recent rise in economic inequality.

Although there may be other ways to address some of these concerns, we argue that the most appealing and comprehensive solution is to completely replace the income tax system with a *progressive* consumption tax. Progressive consumption taxation is not impossible or self-contradictory, although it does require the use of an unfamiliar tax system. In chapter 2, we describe the two leading forms of progressive consumption taxation, the X tax developed by the late David Bradford, and the personal expenditures tax (PET).

As we explain, the X tax modifies the VAT so that it no longer imposes a flat-rate tax on all consumption. The X tax splits the value-added tax base, which equals aggregate consumption, into two components, wages and business cash flow. Households are taxed on wages, and firms are separately taxed on business cash flow. Firms expense all investment in computing business cash flow so that the tax imposes a zero effective marginal tax rate on new investment. The business cash-flow tax falls on wealth accumulated prior to the reform and above-normal business investment returns.

The X tax system therefore imposes a household-level tax on consumption financed from wages and a firm-level tax on consumption financed from prereform wealth and above-normal returns. The first category of consumption is taxed at graduated rates, with higher tax rates for higher-wage workers. The second category of consumption, which is largely enjoyed by affluent households, is taxed at a high flat rate, equal to the tax rate on the highest-wage workers. This rate structure makes the X tax progressive.

We compare the X tax to the PET, which is a household-level graduated-rate tax on income minus net saving. While recognizing that the PET has some advantages, we argue that they are outweighed by the simplicity and other benefits of the X tax. We therefore propose that an X tax be adopted to completely replace the individual and corporate income taxes and the estate and gift tax, as well as the Unearned Income Medicare Contribution tax slated to take effect in 2013. Because concerns about whether the X tax can be satisfactorily implemented have helped block its acceptance, we devote the remainder of the book to addressing those concerns.

In chapter 3, we further discuss the progressivity of the X tax. We explain how to measure the distributional effects of moving to the X tax and address misconceptions about those effects. We discuss the possible tax rate structure and examine related issues, such as the tax treatment of the family and the averaging of wages across different tax years.

In chapter 4, we discuss the treatment of employer-provided health insurance and other fringe benefits under the X tax and the impact of tax reform on Social Security and other transfer payments. We discuss the timing rules that should apply to the taxation of defined-benefit pensions and other employer savings accounts. We propose that the X tax disregard public and private transfer payments, with no tax on the recipient and no deduction for the payer. We discuss options for the tax treatment of charitable giving. We recommend that the Social Security and Medicare payroll taxes be maintained alongside the X tax, to preserve earmarked funding for Social Security and Medicare Part A and the tax-benefit linkage in the Social Security program. We also discuss how to modify means tests for antipoverty programs to operate in a world without an income tax.

In chapter 5, we examine the taxation of business firms. We propose to sweep away the complex and artificial distinctions between partnerships, S corporations, and C corporations that afflict the current income and payroll and self-employment tax systems. We recommend unified treatment of all types of business organizations, apart from a few special rules designed to offer simplification for sole proprietorships. We generally propose that firms be required to pay reasonable compensation to owners who work for the firm. Firms would deduct this compensation under the business cash-flow tax, and the workers/owners would pay household wage tax and payroll tax on this amount. We also emphasize the importance of providing tax relief for firms with negative cash flows, noting that the denial of such relief may result in positive effective tax rates on investment. We therefore propose that firms with negative cash flows be allowed five-year carryback and unlimited carryforward with interest.

In chapter 6, we discuss the tax treatment of financial intermediaries. We explain that, contrary to some claims, this issue can be handled at least as easily under the X tax as under an income tax. We endorse, and elaborate on, proposals to tax financial intermediation transactions under a cash-flow method that integrates real and financial payments. By offering a unified regime for almost all financial intermediaries, this approach largely obviates the need to distinguish among different intermediaries, although it requires that intermediaries be distinguished from other businesses. Although this real-plus-financial cash-flow method requires unfamiliar, or even counterintuitive, calculations by some intermediaries, the calculations are simple to implement, and tax computations by the intermediaries' customers are unaffected. We also discuss tax accounting issues that arise under the X tax.

In chapter 7, we discuss the taxation of international transactions, often considered a major challenge for the X tax. While VATs throughout the world are border adjusted to rebate tax on exports and impose tax on imports, international trade agreements are likely to be interpreted as prohibiting border adjustment of the X tax. Although the United States might be able to persuade the international community to modify this prohibition, we conclude that it would be better to simply refrain from border adjusting the X tax. We review the well-established economic finding that border adjustment offers none of the "competitiveness" advantages imagined in popular discussions. We also emphasize the little-understood point that the transition to a border adjustment would transfer several trillion dollars of wealth from Americans to foreigners. We conclude that we should not pressure other countries to modify trade agreements solely for the privilege of giving our wealth to their citizens. We also endorse, and elaborate on, a proposal by David Bradford to address the transfer-pricing challenges that the X tax will face without a border adjustment.

In chapter 8, we discuss the transition to the new tax system, a significant issue for any tax reform. Without transition relief, the adoption of a consumption tax imposes a significant burden on existing wealth accumulated prior to the reform, although the accompanying repeal of the income tax offers some offsetting gains to existing wealth. We propose a policy that offers significant, but limited, transition relief to existing business capital. Our proposed policy can be administered at the firm level in a way that does not require detailed tracking of depreciation allowances and that does not encourage inefficient changes in firms' behavior. We also discuss transition policies for other specific issues.

In chapter 9, we discuss the tax treatment of the nonbusiness sector, including owner-occupied housing, consumer durables, governments, nonprofit institutions, and household employers. We show that, contrary to common myths, the treatment of housing and durables is much simpler under consumption taxation than under income taxation. While income tax principles require the taxation of imputed rent, consumption taxation can employ a prepayment method that need not measure or tax imputed rent. (Ironically, the current "income tax" system, which exempts imputed rent from tax, largely follows consumption tax principles in this area.) We explain that the prepayment method effectively exempts homes and durables from the business cash-flow tax, thereby allowing existing homes and durables to escape the transition burden that the X tax imposes on existing business capital. We conclude that sparing homes and durables from this burden is appropriate, particularly because these assets will still decline in value to some extent due to income tax repeal. We similarly propose to exempt the federal, state, local, and tribal governments and nonprofit institutions from the business cash-flow tax while requiring their employees to pay household wage tax on the same terms as other workers. We also consider the conformity of state and local tax systems to the federal X tax and the treatment of state, local, and tribal taxes and municipal bonds.

In chapter 10, we examine an alternative policy under which a VAT is adopted as a partial replacement of the income tax. Reviewing the recent interest in the VAT, we note that this outcome is more likely than, though economically inferior to, the complete replacement of the income tax by the X tax that we propose. We consider the extent to which different taxes could be replaced by a VAT and discuss measures to combat the regressivity of the VAT and to prevent it from fueling spending growth.

Because the X tax is a modification of the VAT, we also discuss the extent to which our analysis could be applied to a partial-replacement VAT. Our proposed treatment of financial transactions, owner-occupied housing, and consumer durables under the X tax could be applied under a VAT with little change. One major difference from the X tax, though, is that the VAT would surely be border adjusted, triggering a wealth transfer abroad that our proposal would avoid. Some issues could be handled more easily under a partial-replacement VAT than under the X tax, including the treatment of owners who work for firms and the treatment of firms with negative cash flow, as well as the administration of antipoverty programs. In other respects, though, a partial-replacement VAT would actually cause more disruption than a complete-replacement X tax. Most prominently, the VAT would likely prompt the Federal Reserve to permit a one-time increase in consumer prices. Also, politically sensitive changes to Social Security would be necessary, and economic neutrality would require the imposition of an employer payroll tax on state, local, and tribal governments and nonprofit institutions. Due to the border adjustment, the increase in consumer prices, and administrative differences, the VAT would also require a different transition policy than the X tax, with transition relief provided at the household level.

We hope that this book will prompt renewed consideration of the X tax's potential to achieve a complete replacement of income taxation by progressive consumption taxation.

1

Why Tax Consumption?

Economic theory suggests that consumption taxation is economically superior to income taxation, with simulations suggesting that the complete replacement of the U.S. income tax system by a consumption tax would increase long-run output by several percent. Every other industrialized country raises a significant part of its revenue from consumption taxation, as do most of the U.S. states. A shift from income to consumption taxation in the federal tax system therefore warrants careful consideration.

In this chapter, we explain the economic advantages of consumption taxation, emphasizing how it promotes economic efficiency by removing the income tax's penalty on saving and investment.

Removing the Income Tax Penalty on Saving

The primary economic advantage of consumption taxation is that, unlike income taxation, it does not penalize saving. The savings penalty, which is a penalty on late consumption and early work, causes economic inefficiency.

Penalty on Late Consumption. We illustrate the income tax's penalty on saving with an example drawn from Carroll, Viard, and Ganz (2008). Consider two individuals, Patient and Impatient, each of whom earns $100 of wages today. Impatient wishes to consume only today; Patient wishes to consume only "tomorrow," which is decades later than today. Savings are invested by firms in machines that produce output tomorrow. The marginal rate of return on machines—the additional return available if one more machine is constructed—is 100 percent. If financial markets are competitive, the rate of return that firms pay to savers must be equal to the marginal rate of return on machines.

In a world with no taxes, Impatient consumes $100 today. Patient lends her $100 of wages to a firm, which buys a machine that yields the 100 percent marginal rate of return and therefore provides a $200 payoff tomorrow. The firm pays Patient back her $100 loan with $100 interest, allowing her to consume $200 tomorrow.

What happens in a world with a 20 percent income tax? Impatient pays $20 tax on his wages and consumes the remaining $80, which is 20 percent less than he consumed in the no-tax world. Patient also pays $20 tax on her wages and lends the remaining $80 to the firm. On her $80 loan, she earns $80 interest and is therefore repaid $160 by the firm. However, a $16 tax is imposed on the $80 interest. Patient is left with $144 to consume tomorrow, which is 28 percent less than the $200 she consumed in the no-tax world.

The income tax has reduced Patient's consumption by 28 percent, compared to a mere 20 percent reduction in Impatient's consumption. Under the income tax, Patient faces a higher percentage tax burden than Impatient solely because she consumes later. In other words, she is penalized because she saves for future consumption rather than engaging in immediate consumption. Another way to understand the penalty is to note that the income tax reduces the after-tax rate of return on saving. Because Patient sacrifices $80 of consumption today to obtain $144 tomorrow, she receives an 80 percent after-tax return, which falls short of the 100 percent before-tax return.

In contrast, consumption taxation yields a neutral outcome if the tax rate remains constant over time. For simplicity, consider a 20 percent consumption tax that is imposed directly on individuals, with the tax being applied to income minus saving (or plus dissaving). This tax can be viewed as a personal expenditures tax, a tax that we will discuss in chapter 2. Although the X tax has a different design, we will verify in chapter 2 that it produces the same results when applied to this example.

After earning $100 of wages, Impatient consumes $80 and pays $20 tax, the same outcome as under the income tax. Patient lends her entire $100 to the firm and owes no tax because she has not yet consumed; she reports $100 of income, with an offsetting deduction for $100 of saving. On her $100 loan, she earns $100 interest, accumulating $200. She consumes $160 tomorrow and pays $40 tax; her tax is 20 percent of $200, equal to her $100 interest income plus $100 of dissaving. Each worker's consumption is reduced by 20 percent relative to a world with no taxes. Because both workers face the same percentage tax burden, the consumption tax does not distort the choice between current and future consumption.

The neutrality of this constant-rate consumption tax is confirmed by the fact that Patient earns an after-tax return of 100 percent on her savings, identical to the before-tax rate of return. When Patient makes the $100 investment, she gives up only $80 of consumption today; if she had not invested, she would have paid $20 tax and consumed only $80. Her sacrifice of $80 today provides her with $160 of consumption tomorrow, a 100 percent rate of return.

Because the after-tax rate of return is equal to the before-tax rate of return under the consumption tax, the effective marginal tax rate on saving is zero. In contrast, the income tax imposed a 20 percent effective marginal tax rate on savings, because the 80 percent after-tax rate of return was 20 percent lower than the 100 percent before-tax return.

The example assumes that the consumption tax rate remains constant over time. Consumption taxation ceases to be fully neutral if the tax rate varies over time; it penalizes saving if the tax rate rises over time and rewards saving if the tax rate falls over time. It is important to realize, though, that the income tax inescapably penalizes saving, even if the tax rate remains constant over time.

Penalty on Early Work. So far, we have described the income tax's penalty on saving as a penalty on late consumption. But it is also a penalty on early work, as can be seen from a variant of the above example. Consider two other individuals, Young Worker and Old Worker. Young Worker earns $100 of wages today, and Old Worker earns $200 of wages tomorrow. As before, the interest rate between today and tomorrow is 100 percent. Both Old Worker and Young Worker wish to consume only tomorrow. In a world with no taxes, Young Worker saves her $100 of wages, earns a $100 return, and consumes $200 tomorrow. Old Worker earns $200 of wages tomorrow, which he immediately consumes.

What happens with a 20 percent income tax? Young Worker pays $20 tax on her wages today and saves the remaining $80. She earns an $80 before-tax return, on which she pays $16 tax, and consumes $144 tomorrow. In contrast, Old Worker pays $40 tax tomorrow on his $200 of wages and consumes $160. The results fit the previous pattern, as the individual who saves (in this case, Young Worker) is hit with a 28 percent tax burden, while the individual who does not save (Old Worker) bears only a 20 percent tax burden.

As before, consumption taxation with a constant 20 percent rate results in neutral treatment. Young Worker saves her $100 of wages and earns $100 interest, which allows her to consume $160 tomorrow after paying $40 tax. With his $200 of wages tomorrow, Old Worker also consumes $160, after paying $40 tax.

Saving occurs when individuals consume later than they work. The income tax's penalty on saving therefore creates artificial incentives both to consume earlier and to work later.

Understanding the Penalties. Because the heavier tax on saving under the income tax arises from the imposition of two taxes—one on wages and one on the return to savings—it is sometimes referred to as the "double taxation of saving." Others object to the double-taxation terminology, arguing that no single event is taxed twice, as the earning of wages and the receipt of interest income are separate events.

Fortunately, we need not resolve this semantic dispute. The relevant economic reality is that income taxation places a higher effective tax rate on future consumption than on current consumption and on current work than on future work. It is irrelevant whether the higher effective tax rate arises from one event being taxed twice or from two events being taxed; it is even irrelevant that it arises from the collection of two taxes rather than from a single larger tax. All that matters is that the tax burden on future consumption and current work is larger, in percentage terms, than the tax burden on current consumption and future work.

It is sometimes thought that neutrality is attained through equal taxation of all income, whether from capital or labor, as occurs under a well-designed income tax. But that is not the case. Economic neutrality requires uniform taxation of all uses of resources, not of all income. Although someone who consumes later than she works earns additional income, that fact provides no justification for imposing additional tax.

Gains from Reform

Ending the income tax penalty on saving would improve economic efficiency and promote simplicity.

Efficiency Gains. By eliminating the penalty on saving, consumption taxation offers efficiency advantages. The consumption tax's neutral treatment of work and consumption at different dates allows individuals to choose the most efficient allocation of work and consumption across their lifetimes. Under broad assumptions about preferences, consumption taxation involves lower deadweight loss or excess burden than income taxation, as the incentive effects of consumption taxation prompt households to work later and consume earlier, thereby increasing saving.

A common argument holds that, for any given amount of revenue, consumption taxation imposes a heavier tax on work than does income taxation. Because consumption is smaller than income (in an economy with positive saving), a consumption tax generally requires a higher statutory tax rate than an income tax to raise the same revenue. Proponents of this argument assert that this higher tax rate increases work disincentives. Moving from income to consumption taxation is said to amplify work disincentives even as it eliminates saving disincentives, with the net impact on economic efficiency reflecting a trade-off between these two effects.[1]

Although this argument has superficial appeal, a deeper examination reveals it to be invalid, as explained by Auerbach (1997), Bankman and Weisbach (2006, 1417–30), Viard (2006), Toder and Reuben (2007, 103), Shaviro (2007b, 759–60), Weisbach (2007), and others. A revenue-neutral move to consumption taxation does increase the tax rate on working to consume today. But it reduces the effective tax rate on working to consume tomorrow, which, under income taxation, is hit with both a wage tax and a tax on income from saving. The revenue-neutral shift therefore leaves overall work disincentives roughly the same under consumption taxation as under income taxation. We explain this point further in the "Trade-off Fallacy" box (pages 18–19).

A long-standing body of literature considers the role of consumption taxation in an optimal tax system. The starting point is the result of Atkinson and Stiglitz (1976), which establishes that different consumer goods should be taxed at a uniform rate when consumers' choices among the various goods are separable from their decisions about how much to work. If this separability condition holds, uniform taxation of consumer goods is desirable even if policy makers place a strong emphasis on redistribution, because such redistribution can be advanced more efficiently by increasing tax rates on all goods rather than by singling out some goods for higher taxes than others. As Kaplow (2008b, 221–24) and others have explained, this result can be applied to the choice between income and consumption taxation by treating consumption at different dates as different goods. If consumers' choices about when to consume are separable from their decisions about how much to work, then the Atkinson-Stiglitz result states that consumption at different dates should be taxed at a uniform rate. As we demonstrated in the Patient-Impatient example, consumption taxation with a constant tax rate achieves such uniformity, whereas income taxation does not.

Of course, the separability condition is unlikely to hold precisely, and the stylized Atkinson-Stiglitz model omits some relevant features of real-world tax policy. In a more general framework, it may well be optimal to deviate from a policy of taxing consumption at all dates at exactly the same rates. But such deviations are likely to be minor and difficult to identify precisely. Moreover, the deviations may go in either direction; depending on various factors, it may be optimal to tax late consumption at either slightly lower, or slightly higher, rates than early consumption. The general analysis therefore offers little support for abandoning the uniformity achieved by consumption taxation and adopting the income-tax policy of imposing markedly higher tax rates on late consumption. Kaplow (2008b, 225–48), Bankman and Weisbach (2006), and Auerbach (2008) discuss these issues.

A number of economic simulations report substantial long-run economic gains from replacing income taxation with consumption taxation, although the size of the gains is sensitive to economic assumptions and to the design of the reform. We defer a discussion of the magnitude of the gains from reform to the concluding chapter.

Simplicity Advantages. As Slemrod (1995), Edwards (2003), and others emphasize, consumption taxation also offers powerful simplicity gains.

Whereas consumption taxation requires the measurement of consumption, which is relatively observable, income taxation faces the inherently more complex task of measuring the return on saving and investment to determine the change in the household's wealth.

Income taxation must either measure accrued gains and losses or (like the current tax system) defer taxation until gains and losses are realized, a policy that penalizes asset sales and requires the tracking of cost basis. A host of tax shelters seek to realize losses without realizing associated gains or to manipulate the allocation of cost basis across assets. Income taxation must also distinguish between principal and interest on loans, requiring complicated original-issue-discount, market-discount, and imputed-interest rules. Firm-level income taxation requires rules on capitalization and amortization, depreciation, and inventory accounting. Because these complexities are inescapably required by income tax principles, they cannot be avoided even in well-designed income tax systems. All these complexities are eliminated under consumption taxation.

The U.S. Supreme Court has recognized the inherent complexity that the income tax system faces in distinguishing between capital expenditures that should be amortized and current business expenditures that should be immediately deducted. In 1933, in an opinion by Justice Benjamin Cardozo, the Court said, "One struggles in vain for any verbal formula that will supply a ready touchstone. The standard set up by the statute is not a rule of law; it is rather a way of life. Life in all its fullness must supply the answer to the riddle" (*Welch v. Helvering,* 290 U.S. 111, 115 [1933]). Consumption taxes allow all business expenditures to be immediately deducted, avoiding any need to seek guidance from "life in all its fullness."

To be sure, no tax can be completely simple in a complex economy. Consumption taxation *retains* many complexities that are present under income taxation, including the need to distinguish between consumption and costs of earning income and the need to measure the consumption services provided by financial intermediaries. But consumption taxation removes the complexities discussed above without introducing any significant complexities that are absent under income taxation, except a few complications arising from the fact that tax rate changes are more disruptive under consumption taxation than under income taxation.

Of course, any tax can be complicated by poor design. It is surely true that any actual consumption tax will be more complex than a textbook consumption tax. By the same token, though, the actual income tax is vastly more complex than a textbook income tax, adding many extraneous complications (such as the distinction between debt and equity and the distinction between corporate and noncorporate firms) to the unavoidable income-tax complexities listed above. There is no reason to expect more such extraneous complications under a consumption tax than under the current income tax.

A balanced comparison reveals that consumption taxation is significantly simpler than income taxation.

Fallacious Arguments. The real advantages of consumption taxation, as outlined above, are sometimes overshadowed by invalid arguments offered by some consumption tax supporters.

One argument assumes that consumption taxes can and will be imposed on imports and rebated on exports and concludes that a switch to consumption taxation permanently reduces the trade deficit by making domestic producers more "competitive." Despite its superficial appeal, economists have long recognized that this argument is invalid, as we will discuss in chapter 7. As explained in that chapter, we actually recommend that the X tax *not* be imposed on imports or rebated on exports.

Another argument holds that consumption taxes do not penalize work because tax is triggered by consuming rather than working. This claim is invalid, because individuals work in order to consume, either in the present or the future. Accordingly, as Metcalf (1996, 99), Cnossen (2009, 690), and others note, income and consumption taxes both penalize the decision to work and consume rather than to enjoy leisure. As discussed above and in the "Trade-off Fallacy" box (pages 18–19), the two tax systems impose roughly the same penalty on work at any given revenue level. Consumption taxation removes income taxation's penalty on saving, but not its penalty on work.

Still another argument holds that consumption taxation is desirable because it taxes people on what they take out of the economy rather than what they put into the economy. It is not entirely clear what this means, because budget constraints require that what each individual takes out of the economy be equal, in present discounted value, to what the individual puts into it. The actual flaw of income taxation is that it induces economic inefficiency by penalizing people for taking late consumption, rather than early consumption, out of the economy and for putting early work, rather than late work, into the economy.

A final argument holds that consumption taxation is less prone to evasion than income taxation. In reality, both systems offer the same fundamental opportunities and incentives for evasion, including the use of cash transactions and personal expenditures disguised as business expenditures. The level of evasion is likely to vary to some extent across different forms of consumption and income taxes, but there is no inherent reason why it should be smaller under consumption taxation.

These fallacies should not obscure the real efficiency and simplicity advantages of consumption taxation.

Consumption-Tax Features in the Current Income Tax System

Some observers have noted that the current U.S. income tax system has certain features that alleviate the tax burden that a pure income tax would impose on saving. As detailed below, many of these features are similar to those found in consumption tax systems. The presence of these features in today's tax system may suggest that today's system already provides many of the advantages of consumption taxation, thereby diminishing the urgency of a full-fledged switch to consumption taxation.

The actual policy implications are somewhat different. Although the current tax system includes some features that resemble consumption taxation, these features provide only limited relief from the problems of income taxation, and they add problems of their own. Moreover, other features of the tax system actually increase the tax burden on saving beyond that which would be imposed by a pure income tax system.

One consumption-tax feature of today's tax system is the provision of tax-preferred savings accounts and retirement plans. Reflecting a fundamental ambivalence about taxing saving, Congress has created more than twenty types of tax-preferred savings plans and accounts, each of which is subject to different contribution limits, eligibility rules, and restrictions on withdrawals.[2] The National Taxpayer Advocate (2004, 423–32) and the Joint Committee on Taxation (2001, 149–54, 163) document the complexity that these accounts have added to the tax system. The Advocate noted a study in which 30 percent of workers choosing not to participate in 401(k) plans cited complexity as the principal reason.

While adding complexity, these accounts play only a limited role in reducing the tax burden on saving. Although the accounts shield about 36 percent of household financial assets from taxes, according to the President's Advisory Panel on Federal Tax Reform (2005, 22), they probably do much less to promote saving than would a 36 percent across-the-board reduction in tax rates on saving. Tax-preferred accounts are inferior ways to encourage saving because taxpayers can reduce their tax liabilities by shifting money from taxable to tax-preferred accounts without doing additional saving. Also, the accounts offer no marginal incentive to save for those households that bump up against the maximum contribution limits, who are likely to be the households in the best position to increase their saving.

Sheppard (2011) and others have pointed to the availability of tax-preferred accounts to argue that the current tax system functions as a consumption tax for most Americans. In reality, though, the current system does not offer the simplicity advantages of consumption taxation to most Americans, as they can avoid taxes on their saving only if they comply with the intricate restrictions governing tax-preferred accounts. Moreover, the current system does not function like a consumption tax for those Americans who do most of the saving, so the economic advantages of consumption taxation remain largely unattained.

The income tax system also allows some investments to be expensed, which, as we will explain in chapter 2, effectively removes the marginal tax burden on those investments. Other investments receive accelerated depreciation, which reduces, but does not eliminate, the marginal tax burden. Also, as we will discuss in chapter 9, imputed rent on owner-occupied homes and consumer durables is not taxed, which is consistent with consumption-tax principles. But these provisions are selective and limited in scope, inefficiently favoring some investments over others. Similarly, the deferral of tax on capital gains until they are realized lowers the effective tax rate on gains but introduces a new distortion by encouraging asset holders to postpone asset sales.

Meanwhile, other features of the tax system amplify the basic saving penalty imposed by the income tax. Notably, the corporate income tax imposes an additional tax burden on investment done through C corporations, although the additional burden is partly offset by preferential individual income tax rates for dividends and capital gains. Estate and gift taxes also impose an additional tax burden on saving to pass wealth on to the next generation. At the state and local levels, individual and corporate income taxes, property taxes, sales taxes on capital goods, and inheritance taxes further penalize saving; because our proposal does not directly alter the state tax system, it may not eliminate these disincentives. Also, the current tax system does not correct for inflation in its measurement of the income from saving. For example, a taxpayer who receives 5 percent interest, when inflation is 2 percent, has real interest income of only 3 percent, but the full 5 percent of nominal interest income is taxed. The tax system also fails to correct for inflation in the measurement of taxable capital gains and depreciation allowances, which also amplifies the tax penalty on saving and investment. As Hubbard, Skinner, and Zeldes (1995) observe, the means tests used in many transfer payment programs also create saving disincentives by reducing or eliminating benefits based on the asset holdings of potential recipients; as we will discuss in chapter 4, some of these disincentives will remain in place under our proposal.

Recent laws and proposals point to an increased tax burden on saving in upcoming years. Under the March 2010 health care reform law, a new 3.8 percent Unearned Income Medicare Contribution tax on interest, dividends, and capital gains received by high-income households is slated to take effect in 2013. In late 2011, five bills that would have imposed surtaxes, ranging from 0.5 to 5.6 percent, on the adjusted gross income, including interest, dividends, and capital gains, of millionaires received majority support in the Senate, but did not win the sixty votes required for passage. President Barack Obama has also proposed that the 2001 and 2003 tax cuts be allowed to largely expire for high-income households at the end of 2012, which would increase marginal tax rates on those households' capital incomes by several percentage points (more than twenty percentage points for dividends). Moreover, the projected growth in federal spending over the upcoming decades, detailed by the Congressional Budget Office (2011b), is likely to create pressure for additional taxes on saving, pressure that may be difficult to forestall unless the United States makes a full-scale move to consumption taxation.

In summary, the current tax system includes some selective, complex, and ineffective features that ease the tax penalty on saving and other features that actually amplify that penalty. A full consideration of the current system makes clear that a move to consumption taxation is the only effective way to address the penalty on saving.

Conclusion

Economic theory suggests significant economic gains from moving toward consumption taxation. In this book, we explain how a particular type of consumption tax, the Bradford X tax, offers a progressive and relatively simple form of consumption taxation, and we recommend that the United States adopt this tax.

Except in chapter 10, we focus on proposals to adopt a consumption tax as a complete replacement for the federal taxes that penalize saving and investment, namely, the individual and corporate income taxes (including the individual and corporate alternative minimum taxes), the estate and gift tax (including the generation-skipping tax), and the Unearned Income Medicare Contribution tax. Complete replacement offers larger efficiency gains than partial replacement. And only complete replacement offers real simplicity gains; if the income tax remains in place as even part of the overall tax system, its complexity is still present.

We do not propose, however, to replace other federal taxes that pose little or no penalty on saving. As we will explain in chapter 4, we propose that the Social Security and Medicare payroll taxes be maintained; as we will explain in chapter 5, we recommend that the self-employment tax system be folded into the payroll tax system. We do not propose that excise taxes or customs duties be modified as part of the move to consumption taxation.

We reject the notion of allowing taxpayers to choose between the current income tax system and the new X tax system. Allowing taxpayers a choice between tax systems preserves some of the complexity of the current tax system and also makes it more difficult to meet revenue targets. Moreover, a consumption tax system generates the proper incentive effects only if all taxpayers are subject to it in all years.

In chapter 2, we survey the different types of consumption taxes and explain our preference for the X tax.

Box
THE TRADE-OFF FALLACY

The trade-off fallacy can best be understood through an analogy. Consider an economy in which people choose between leisure, apples, and oranges. The "general" tax rate is 20 percent, but oranges are subject to an 8 percent surtax, so apples are taxed at 20 percent and oranges at 28 percent. Economists note that the surtax inefficiently favors apples over oranges and propose moving to a uniform 24 percent tax, which is revenue neutral if half of wages are spent on each fruit. A critic acknowledges that the proposed reform eliminates the bias in favor of apples over oranges, but contends that it increases the bias in favor of leisure over work by raising the general tax rate from 20 percent to 24 percent. The critic perceives a trade-off between increased efficiency in the fruit market and decreased efficiency in the labor market.

The critic's analysis is flawed. Because apples and oranges are both alternatives to leisure, work disincentives depend on the tax rates on both fruits; the oranges surtax, no less than the general tax, penalizes work. It is true that the proposed reform increases the bias in favor of leisure relative to apples by raising the tax rate on apples from 20 percent to 24 percent. At the same time, though, the proposal reduces the bias in favor of leisure relative to oranges by lowering the tax rate on oranges from 28 percent to 24 percent. The net effect on work incentives is ambiguous.

Similarly, in the Patient-Impatient example, a 20 percent income tax imposes a 20 percent tax rate on consumption today and a 28 percent tax rate on consumption tomorrow, effectively imposing an 8 percent surtax on the latter. Just as the oranges surtax increased the bias in favor of leisure over oranges and thereby added to work disincentives, so this surtax increases the bias in favor of leisure over consumption tomorrow and thereby adds to work disincentives. A person who works to consume tomorrow must pay both the wage tax and the tax on capital income, and both taxes therefore discourage work.

If half of wages are consumed today and half are saved, replacing the 20 percent income tax with a 24 percent consumption tax is revenue neutral in present-value terms. The tax rates on consumption today and consumption tomorrow are then both 24 percent. How are work disincentives affected? Although the bias in favor of leisure relative to consumption today rises from 20 percent to 24 percent, the bias in favor of leisure over consumption tomorrow falls from 28 to 24 percent. The net effect on work incentives depends on consumer preferences.

If the two types of consumption are equally complementary to leisure, the revenue-neutral switch to consumption taxation has no net effect on work incentives. If consumption today is relatively complementary to leisure, a revenue-neutral move to consumption taxation actually reduces work disincentives and increases labor supply. On the other hand, if consumption tomorrow is relatively complementary to leisure, a revenue-neutral move to consumption taxation increases work disincentives and reduces labor supply. In any case, the net change in work disincentives is likely to be small. The largest efficiency effect of the switch to consumption taxation is the gain from the removal of the saving disincentive.

In summary, the trade-off argument is invalid. Although taxing income rather than consumption permits a lower tax rate on wages, doing so does not substitute a saving disincentive for a work disincentive. Instead, it adds a saving disincentive while maintaining a roughly unchanged work disincentive. Under almost all types of consumer preferences, income taxation is less economically efficient than consumption taxation.

2

The Case for the X Tax

In this chapter we discuss the leading types of consumption taxes—the retail sales tax, the value-added tax, the flat tax, the Bradford X tax, and the personal expenditures tax—and explain our preference for the X tax. Part of this discussion is drawn from Viard (2011a, 185–95).

The Retail Sales Tax and the Value-Added Tax

The retail sales tax is the type of consumption tax that is most familiar to Americans, and the VAT is the type with the most widespread international use.

Retail Sales Tax. A retail sales tax is easily recognized as a consumption tax because, in its pure textbook form, it is imposed only on retail sales to consumers. Sales from one business firm to another are excluded from the tax base. Although a general sales tax has never been used at the federal level in the United States, forty-five states and the District of Columbia currently impose sales taxes, as do many local governments. Unfortunately, as we will discuss in chapter 10, most state and local sales taxes diverge significantly from this pure textbook design, exempting significant amounts of consumer purchases while taxing a substantial amount of sales between business firms.

The retail sales tax is a real-based tax, which means that it applies only to the sale of real goods and services and does not tax, or provide deductions for, financial transactions such as loans and stock purchases. Also, firms do not deduct payments of wages or other employee compensation in computing their sales tax base.

The discussion of the sales tax offers a useful opportunity to clarify the distinction between the tax-exclusive and tax-inclusive methods of quoting tax rates. For example, consider a sales tax system that imposes a $20 tax on a consumer good that costs $80 before tax so that the total price paid by the consumer is $100. The tax-exclusive rate is 25 percent, because the $20 tax is 25 percent of the $80 net-of-tax price. This method of quoting the tax rate is called tax-exclusive because the tax payment is excluded from the tax base to which the rate is applied; here, the $20 tax payment is excluded from the $80 tax base to which the 25 percent rate is applied. The tax-inclusive rate in this example is 20 percent because the $20 tax is 20 percent of the $100 total price. Under the tax-inclusive method, the tax payment is included in the base to which the rate is applied; here, the $20 tax payment is included in the $100 base to which the 20 percent rate is applied.

Sales tax rates are usually quoted in tax-exclusive form, and income tax rates are usually quoted in tax-inclusive form. (An individual who pays $20 tax on $100 before-tax income is usually viewed as paying a 20 percent tax rate, not a 25 percent rate on her $80 after-tax income.) Because the tax-exclusive rate is always higher than the corresponding tax-inclusive rate,[3] this practice artificially makes sales tax rates look higher than income tax rates. Nevertheless, deviating from common practice by quoting sales tax rates in tax-inclusive form can cause confusion.

At the federal level, the most prominent sales tax proposal is the FairTax plan, put forward by Americans for Fair Taxation. The plan would replace the individual and corporate income taxes, payroll and self-employment taxes, and the estate and gift tax with a retail sales tax featuring a 29.87 percent tax-exclusive (23 percent tax-inclusive) rate. The FairTax plan has repeatedly been introduced in Congress but has never emerged from committee. The FairTax bills in the 112th Congress, H.R. 25 and S. 13, have attracted sixty-seven sponsors in the House of Representatives and nine sponsors in the Senate.

Value-Added Tax. The VAT can be viewed as a modification of the sales tax. Durner, Bui, and Sedon (2009) report that more than 145 countries have a VAT; they tabulate each country's tax rate and the year in which the tax was introduced.

A VAT, like a retail sales tax, applies to goods and services sold to consumers. But unlike a retail sales tax, which is collected once on the final sale to a consumer, a VAT is imposed and collected at every stage in the production and distribution of a good or service. This collection structure helps prevent the tax from being evaded at the retail level.

Like the retail sales tax, the VAT is a real-based tax that disregards financial transactions. Also like the sales tax, it does not allow a deduction for wages or other employee compensation. Like sales tax rates, VAT rates are usually quoted in tax-exclusive form.

For simplicity, the discussion below focuses on a subtraction-method VAT. (As we will explain in chapter 10, most actual VATs use the distinct, but highly similar, credit-invoice method.) Under a subtraction-method VAT, the tax base for each firm is receipts from sales of real goods and services minus purchases of real goods and services, including capital goods, from other firms. Sales minus purchases measures the firm's valued added, which is the contribution of the firm to the overall value of output.

For the economy as a whole, the base of a VAT is sales of real goods and services to consumers, because sales from one business to another are subject to offsetting inclusion and deduction and therefore do not comprise part of the net tax base. So, the aggregate VAT tax base is equal to consumption, which is also the aggregate sales tax base.

Figure 2-1 illustrates the relationship of the VAT to the sales tax in an economy with two firms and two individuals. Firm A produces a machine that it sells for $100 to Firm B and pays $70 of wages to Jones, its employee. Firm B buys the machine for $100, pays $40 of wages to its employee Smith, and produces $150 of consumer goods. Jones buys $90 of the consumer goods, and Smith buys the remaining $60.

Under a retail sales tax, tax is collected from firm B on the $150 of consumer goods that it sells. Under a VAT, tax is collected from firm A on the sale of the $100 machine and from firm B on its $50 value added ($150 sales to consumers minus $100 machine purchase). Because the sale of the machine nets out, the VAT has the same $150 aggregate tax base as the sales tax.

The Regressivity Problem. As we will discuss in chapter 10, a number of recent proposals call for the adoption of a VAT alongside the income tax. Except for the FairTax plan mentioned above, however, policy makers have shown little interest in completely replacing the income tax with a sales tax or VAT.

The most important reason for this lack of interest is that such complete replacement would result in politically unacceptable regressivity. Without

FIGURE 2-1
FOUR WAYS TO TAX CONSUMPTION

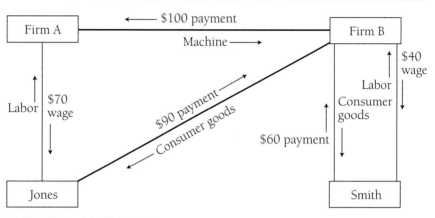

$150 TOTAL CONSUMPTION

Retail Sales Tax: B $150
VAT: A $100, B $50
Flat Tax/X Tax: A $30, B $10, Jones $70, Smith $40
PET: Jones $90, Smith $60

SOURCE: Example drawn from Viard (2011a).

any modification, the sales tax or VAT is regressive because all consumers pay tax equal to a fixed fraction of their consumer spending. The importance of the regressivity concern has been amplified by the rise in economic inequality during the last few decades; the Congressional Budget Office (2011c) reports that the top 20 percent of households received 59.9 percent of national income before taxes and transfers in 2007, up from 49.6 percent in 1979.

The regressivity problem can be addressed to some extent by providing rebates (as the FairTax plan does), expanding transfer payments, or exempting necessities while taxing luxuries at higher rates. Unfortunately, these solutions fall short of fully addressing the problem. Rebates and transfer payments provide only a limited offset to regressivity, leaving a politically unacceptable share of the fiscal burden on the middle class. Taxing different goods at different rates creates complexity and economic inefficiency and also provides only a limited offset to regressivity.

Accordingly, any sales tax or VAT that is adopted is likely to serve as only a partial replacement of the income tax, with an income tax retained to provide progressivity. Given our interest in complete-replacement options, we set the sales tax and VAT aside for most of this book, although we will discuss in chapter 10 how a partial-replacement VAT could be designed if complete replacement cannot be achieved.

We therefore turn to more progressive consumption taxes, beginning with the flat tax and the X tax. These taxes, which differ only in their rate schedules, both use the same tax base, which is obtained by splitting the VAT tax base, value added, into two parts. Before discussing the rate schedules of the flat tax and the X tax, we discuss the two-part VAT tax base design that both taxes share, explaining why, despite its initial appearance, this design yields a consumption tax rather than an income tax.

The Two-Part VAT

To alleviate the regressivity of the VAT, the Hall-Rabushka flat tax and the X tax split the VAT base, value added, into two components, wages and business cash flow, and tax them separately.

Household Wage Tax and Business Cash-Flow Tax. Robert Hall and Alvin Rabushka (1983) proposed to split the VAT into two taxes, one imposed on business firms and the other imposed on households. Business firms compute value added, as they would under a subtraction-method VAT, but deduct their wage payments. The resulting tax base is called business cash flow. Households are taxed on their wages but not on their investment income. The total tax base is the same as under a VAT and therefore the same as under a retail sales tax; the only difference from a VAT is that wages are taxed to workers rather than to firms.

Throughout this book, we will refer to the components of the two-part VAT as the "household wage tax" and the "business cash-flow tax." The tax rates under both components of the two-part VAT are generally quoted in tax-inclusive form, as income tax rates are usually quoted. This practice makes the tax rates look artificially lower than sales tax and conventional VAT rates, but does not lower the true level of the rates.

Figure 2-1 shows the application of the two-part VAT in the simple economy. Firm A is taxed on its $30 cash flow ($100 value added minus $70 wage payment), and Firm B is taxed on its $10 cash flow ($50 value added minus $40 wage payment). Smith and Jones are taxed on their wages.

Although its aggregate tax base is equal to national consumption, the two-part VAT looks more like an income tax than a consumption tax, at least at first glance. After all, it includes a household tax on wages, a major component of income, and it does not appear to include any tax on consumers. Adding to the confusion, the name of the two-part VAT's first incarnation, the "flat tax," offers no clue that it is a consumption tax. Many early descriptions of the flat tax were ambiguous about the nature of the tax; Zelenak (1999, 1180–82) describes how the status of the flat tax as a consumption tax has been obscured in the popular debate. Further confusion occurs when supporters of a flat-rate income tax refer to that quite different levy as a flat tax or even, as in Laffer (2010), as a "true flat tax." The name of the two-part VAT's later incarnation, our preferred "X tax," avoids misleading income-tax connotations, but also fails to reveal that it is a consumption tax.

No Tax Penalty on Saving. One way to see the proper classification of the two-part VAT is to introduce it into the Patient-Impatient example that we used in chapter 1. If wages and business cash flow are both taxed at 20 percent, do Patient and Impatient ultimately receive the same treatment that they experienced under the 20 percent consumption tax, or do they instead receive the treatment that they experienced under a 20 percent income tax?

Little information can be gleaned by considering Impatient. Under both the income tax and consumption tax considered in chapter 1, he paid $20 tax on his wages and consumed the remaining $80. The two-part VAT also yields that same result, because Impatient pays $20 tax on his wages. Moreover, his consumption results in no firm-level tax being collected. If we imagine a firm paying workers $80 to produce the consumption goods sold to Impatient, the firm is taxed on the $80 sale proceeds and deducts the $80 wage payment, leaving no net tax.

The litmus test is the treatment of Patient. Does the 20 percent two-part VAT cause her to consume $144 tomorrow (the income-tax result) or $160 (the consumption-tax result)? Under the two-part VAT, Patient pays $20 tax on her wages today and lends the remaining $80 to the firm. So far, this looks like an income tax, because Patient has paid tax on her wages, even though she has not yet consumed anything. The picture changes, though, as we walk through the remaining steps.

With the $80 obtained from Patient, the firm buys a machine with a before-tax cost of $100. Under the two-part VAT, a $100 machine costs only $80, because the firm immediately deducts the $100 cost of the machine under the business cash-flow tax, reaping a $20 tax savings. If the firm produces the machine itself, it deducts the $100 wages paid to its workers; if the firm buys the machine from another firm, it deducts the $100 purchase cost.

The $100 machine yields a $200 payoff tomorrow, on which the firm pays $40 of business cash-flow tax. With the remaining $160, the firm pays Patient her $80 principal plus an $80 return. Patient then consumes the entire $160; she makes no tax payment because investment income is exempt from the household tax.

As with the direct consumption tax considered in chapter 1, Patient bears only a 20 percent burden, the same as the burden on Impatient, and is not penalized for her decision to save. Because the defining characteristic of the consumption tax is that it does not penalize saving, this outcome confirms that the two-part VAT is a consumption tax. It is easy to see why the household component of the two-part VAT does not penalize saving, as the tax applies only to wages and exempts income from saving. The question of why the firm-level component of the two-part VAT, the business cash-flow tax, does not penalize saving is a little more complicated, with the answer turning on the fact that this tax allows investment to be expensed.

The Importance of Expensing. Although a tax on a firm's net income, such as the current corporate income tax, penalizes saving, a tax on the firm's business cash flow does not. The difference between the two approaches is the manner in which the firm deducts the costs of its business investments. Under a net income tax, the firm depreciates the cost of the investment over its useful life; under a business cash-flow tax, as under a VAT, the firm immediately deducts, or expenses, the investment costs. This subtle difference has dramatic implications.

Under a 20 percent firm-level net income tax, the firm would have been able to buy only an $80 machine with Patient's $80 of savings because there would be no tax deduction at the time of purchase. When the machine yields $160 tomorrow, the firm would deduct the full $80 cost as depreciation because the machine would then be worthless. The firm would pay $16 tax on its $80 net income, leaving only $144 to be paid over to Patient for her to consume. A 20 percent firm-level tax on net income therefore penalizes saving in the same way and to the same extent as the 20 percent individual income tax we considered in chapter 1.

The two-part VAT avoids that outcome because it taxes firms on business cash flow rather than net income, allowing firms to expense their investments up front. Under the business cash-flow tax, the firm immediately deducts the cost of the $100 machine and reaps an immediate $20 tax saving, which is why it can buy a $100 machine with only $80 of Patient's funds. When the machine delivers its $200 payoff, the entire cash inflow is taxable, so the firm pays $40 tax, leaving $160 to be paid to Patient.

Although the investment triggers a $40 tax on the firm tomorrow, it also triggers a $20 tax saving for the firm today, which is precisely the effect that saving had on Patient's tax liability under the direct consumption tax discussed in chapter 1. Here, as there, the immediate tax savings and the subsequent tax payment cancel out in present value, leaving no net tax penalty on investment.

This neutrality result applies to expensing in general. By definition, the future cash flows from a marginal investment have a present discounted value equal to the cost of the investment. Provided that the tax rate remains constant (always a prerequisite for the neutrality of consumption taxation), the tax on the marginal investment's future cash flows has the same present value as the tax savings from the up-front expensing deduction. As a result, the marginal effective tax rate on saving and investment is zero.

Is the Tax Paid by Consumers? Although the two-part VAT has an aggregate tax base equal to national consumption and does not penalize saving, readers may still resist the conclusion that it is a consumption tax. After all, it looks like a tax on workers and firms rather than a tax on consumers. In figure 2-1, the sales tax and VAT, although remitted by the firms, are universally understood to ultimately be paid by the final consumers (Firm B's customers), with Jones ultimately taxed on $90 and Smith on $60. The two-part VAT has the same $150 aggregate tax base, but the allocation of tax payments across individuals and firms looks completely different.

The Patient-Impatient example features a similar discrepancy in the timing of payments under the two-part VAT. Today, Impatient is taxed on $100, Patient is taxed on $100, and the firm deducts $100, leaving a net aggregate tax base of $100, which equals today's aggregate consumption, all of which is done by Impatient. Tomorrow, the firm is taxed on $160 with no tax on Patient and Impatient, yielding an aggregate tax base of $160, which equals tomorrow's aggregate consumption, all of which is done by Patient. As in figure 2-1, the tax base is always equal to consumption in the aggregate, but the allocation of tax payments across individuals and firms does not line up with the allocation of consumer spending. Splitting the VAT in two appears to completely change who pays the tax, breaking any link between tax payments and consumption.

Economic theory reveals, however, that these differences in allocation are illusory. According to long-standing principles of public finance economics, the tax burden on a transaction depends on the combined tax of the parties to the transaction, not on the tax liability of either party. Moreover, the manner in which the two parties share the real economic burden of the tax does not depend on the amount of tax liability legally assigned to each party. In the Patient-Impatient example, the two-part VAT imposes zero tax on Patient's saving, just as any good consumption tax should. Yes, Patient pays tax on the $100 that she saves, but the firm to whom she lends her saving claims an offsetting $100 deduction. Moreover, the two-part VAT taxes the $160 consumed by Patient tomorrow, just as a consumption tax should. Although no tax is imposed on Patient, the full $160 is taxed to the firm that pays her the money that she consumes.

A True Consumption Tax. Appearances notwithstanding, the two-part VAT is a consumption tax. It has an aggregate tax base equal to national consumption and, assuming that the tax rate remains constant over time, it imposes a zero effective marginal tax rate on saving and therefore does not penalize saving. It also imposes a combined tax on each transaction equal to that imposed by a conventional VAT, although the legal allocation of the payment between parties to the transaction is different than under a conventional VAT.

Recall that the combination of two key features makes the two-part VAT a consumption tax. First, the household tax applies only to wages. All returns to saving, including interest, dividends, and capital gains, are exempt from the household tax. Second, firms are allowed to immediately expense, rather than depreciate, their investments. Both of these features are crucial to the design of the tax.

The X Tax: A Progressive Two-Part VAT

The above discussion establishes that a two-part VAT with a 20 percent tax on households' wages and a 20 percent tax on business cash flow is economically equivalent to a 20 percent conventional VAT. Because the conventional VAT is far easier to explain, though, there seems to be little to recommend the two-part VAT. Indeed, if the goal is to tax all consumption at the same proportional rate, the conventional VAT is the way to go.

The purpose of splitting the VAT in two, however, is precisely to tax different components of consumption at different rates, something that cannot be done under the conventional VAT. As explained below, both incarnations of the two-part VAT—the flat tax and the X tax—tax business cash flow more heavily than wages and tax different workers' wages at different rates, an arrangement that promotes progressivity.

Under the flat tax proposed by Hall and Rabushka (1983), firms are taxed at a single flat rate—say, 25 percent—on business cash flow. Workers are taxed at that same rate on wages, but only above a substantial exemption amount. This exemption amount ensures some degree of progressivity across workers and lowers the overall tax rate on wages, relative to the rate on business cash flow. Ironically, this makes the "flat" tax more progressive, and hence less flat, than a conventional VAT or sales tax, casting additional doubt on the utility of its name.

To further promote progressivity, Bradford (1986, 81–82) proposed that the Hall-Rabushka flat tax be modified to feature a full set of graduated rates for the household wage tax. Under this approach, the tax rate on business cash flow is relatively high (as explained in chapter 3, we will use an illustrative value of 38.8 percent throughout this book), and workers with the highest wages pay a marginal tax rate equal to that rate. But workers with lower earnings face lower rates, and those below the exemption amount continue to pay no tax. If desired, refundable tax credits can be provided to low-wage workers. Bradford (1988) referred to this modified approach as an "X tax."

Taxing higher-wage workers at higher rates clearly allows the flat tax and X tax to promote progressivity in ways that the conventional VAT does not. The other distinctive feature of the flat tax and X tax, though, is that business cash flow is taxed more heavily than wages. This is true even under the flat tax, which allows a fixed exemption amount under the wage tax but not under the business cash-flow tax. The X tax goes further, taxing all business cash flow at the top rate, a rate that applies to the wages of only the highest-paid workers. As explained below, this heavier taxation of business cash flow further promotes progressivity, because the burden of the cash-flow tax largely falls on well-off households.

Role of the Business Cash-Flow Tax. In the current form of the Patient-Impatient example, the business cash-flow tax is irrelevant, and only the 20 percent household wage tax matters. Patient would have the same $144 consumption tomorrow if the 20 percent business cash-flow tax did not exist. As previously discussed, thanks to the expensing of investment, the business cash-flow tax results in a $20 tax saving when Patient saves today and a $40 tax payment when Patient consumes her investment proceeds tomorrow. The government enjoys no net revenue gain because the $40 tax payment it collects tomorrow is the same as what it could have obtained by investing the $20 tax payment forgone today at the 100 percent marginal return available in the economy. As discussed above, this zero-present-value feature is precisely why the business cash-flow tax does not penalize saving. Indeed, there would still be no net revenue gain and no saving penalty if the cash-flow tax were imposed at a 50 or 99 percent rate, as the tax would then yield a $50 or $99 tax saving today, followed by a $100 or $198 tax tomorrow.

But the actual economy differs in important ways from this example. Under more realistic assumptions, the business cash-flow tax raises some revenue from saving, even though it still imposes no penalty on new saving on the margin. This revenue arises from two sources, existing capital that is in place when the tax is introduced and above-normal returns.

The first source of revenue is associated with the introduction of the tax. In the above example, suppose that there is no tax of any kind today and that the business cash-flow tax is unexpectedly introduced between today and tomorrow. Impatient consumes $100 today and is unaffected by the subsequent introduction of the tax. Patient saves $100 today, expecting to consume $200 tomorrow, but ultimately consumes only $160 due to the unexpected $40 tax liability.

The unexpected tax leaves Patient with only a 60 percent after-tax rate of return on her investment, which is actually lower than the 80 percent return she would have cleared under the income tax and far below the 100 percent before-tax rate of return. The problem is one of timing. If the business cash-flow tax is in place all along, Patient's decision to save gives her a $20 tax savings today, offset by a $40 tax tomorrow (all at the firm level, of course). But with the business cash-flow tax introduced in midstream, Patient gets the worst of both worlds. She pays the $40 tax tomorrow, but does not receive the $20 tax savings today because the business cash-flow tax is not in effect today to provide those savings.

So, the business cash-flow tax raises revenue from the savings already put in place before it is adopted and imposes an unexpected penalty on that saving. But this penalty applies only to savings that Patient has already done. The tax does not impose a penalty on *new* saving and therefore does not discourage future saving, unless it creates fears of future unannounced levies on savings already in place. The unexpected burden on past saving does raise fairness and other concerns, which we will discuss in chapter 8. Although most consumption tax proposals respond to these concerns by offering some transition relief, none of them, including our proposal, offer sufficiently generous relief to completely eliminate the tax on capital that is in place when the reform is introduced.

Second, some investments yield above-normal returns, also called rents or pure profits. In the above example, Patient's investment was assumed to be in a machine that yielded the 100 percent marginal rate of return. But some machines may yield a rate of return higher than the marginal machine, perhaps due to innovation or the exercise of market power. Suppose that Patient has access to a specific investment opportunity with a 120 percent return, a machine that yields $220 tomorrow. Under the business cash-flow tax, her decision to invest triggers a $44 tax payment tomorrow. If she had not saved, the government would have collected $20 tax today, which could have been invested (at the 100 percent marginal yield available on additional investment) to yield $40. So, the government collects $4 of net revenue tomorrow, which is equal to 20 percent of the $20 above-normal return on Patient's investment.

Here, too, the business cash-flow tax appears, at first glance, to impose a penalty on this investment. After all, the tax reduces Patient's consumption by 22 percent, compared to the 20 percent reduction suffered by Impatient.

But the higher tax applies only to the above-normal returns, returns over and above the return on the marginal investment. There is no penalty on a marginal investment, one that yields a 100 percent return. And any investment that yields a before-tax return greater than the marginal return also earns an after-tax return greater than the marginal return. So long as investors are willing to buy machines that yield the marginal return of 100 percent, they must also be willing to buy any that yield more than 100 percent. The business cash-flow tax therefore does not penalize saving and investment *on the margin*. Yet, it raises revenue by taxing above-normal returns, those that exceed the required rate of return on the marginal investment.

In the presence of uncertainty, the cash-flow tax also has other effects, collecting positive tax from lucky investments and negative tax from unlucky ones. We defer a discussion of those effects, which are much less significant than they initially appear, to chapter 3.

Because the business cash-flow tax applies to savings that have already been done and to savings with above-normal returns that will continue to be done even in the face of the tax, it should not cause households to save less. Because the business cash-flow tax does not cause a change in behavior, it cannot be shifted to other people. The burden of the tax therefore falls on those who own capital at the time the tax is introduced and those who are able to invest at above-normal returns.

Because those groups are generally likely to be well-off, the heavy taxation of business cash flow under the X tax promotes progressivity. Under the X tax, therefore, high tax rates apply to high-paid workers, owners of existing wealth, and recipients of above-normal investment returns, while lower tax rates apply to lower-paid workers. This pattern makes the X tax a progressive two-part VAT.

The President's Advisory Panel on Federal Tax Reform (2005) adopted two different tax reform proposals in its final report. Although one plan would have merely reformed the income tax system, the other plan, called the Growth and Investment Tax Plan, would have largely replaced the income tax system with an X tax, featuring a 30 percent tax rate on business cash flow and the wages of the highest earners. This plan would have retained one vestige of the income tax system, a 15 percent flat rate tax on capital income. The panel considered, but did not adopt, a Progressive Consumption Tax Plan that would have completely replaced the income tax system with an X tax, featuring a 35 percent top tax rate. More recently, Hubbard (2011) urged policy makers to consider replacing the income tax with the X tax.

Comparing the X Tax to the Personal Expenditures Tax

The PET offers another way to achieve progressive consumption taxation. Under this tax system, each household files an annual tax return on which it reports income, deducts all saving (deposits into savings accounts, asset purchases, amounts lent to others, and payments made on outstanding debts), and adds all dissaving (withdrawals from savings accounts, gross proceeds of asset sales, amounts borrowed from others, and payments received on outstanding loans). The resulting measure equals the household's consumption, which is taxed at graduated rates. The direct consumption tax considered in the Patient-Impatient example in chapter 1 can be viewed as a PET.

The PET was proposed by Kaldor (1955) and extensively analyzed by Andrews (1974). The tax briefly received attention in the policy arena in 1995 when Senators Sam Nunn (D-Georgia) and Pete Domenici (R-New Mexico) introduced the Unlimited Savings Allowance (USA) plan, which would have replaced the individual and corporate income taxes with a PET, accompanied, oddly enough, by a VAT. Due to various problems in its design, the USA plan never received serious consideration in Congress. Robert Frank of Cornell University (2005, 2008) and Edward McCaffery of the University of Southern California Law School (2002) advocate the PET. Andrews (1980), Seidman and Lewis (2009), and Thuronyi (2011) propose levying a PET on high-consumption households as a supplement to the current tax system. Landsburg (2011) also suggests consideration of a PET. A budget plan recently released by the Heritage Foundation (2011, 36–38) would replace income and payroll taxes with a PET, although the plan imposes a flat rate of 25 to 28 percent on consumer spending above an exemption amount, rather than using graduated tax rates.

Given that the X tax and the PET can each generate progressivity and serve as a complete replacement of the income tax system, which is superior? It is certainly easier to explain that the PET is a consumption tax than it is to offer the corresponding explanation for the X tax. That, along with other features, may give the PET an optical advantage. Yet, as discussed in the "Optics of the X Tax and the PET" box (page 39), some optical issues cut in favor of the X tax. In any case, we favor the X tax on balance because of the simplicity offered by its real-based nature. Of course, either the X tax or the PET would be a dramatic improvement over the income tax system.

Advantage of Real-Based X Tax. Because the key differences between the X tax and the PET arise from how the two taxes treat financial transactions, it is useful to review the relationship of real production and financial transactions. Firms and workers engage in real production by using labor and capital to produce goods and services, generating wages for workers and capital income for firms. Two sets of financial transactions determine which households ultimately receive the cash flow and income generated by the real production.

One set of financial transactions initially allocate the income and cash flow generated by production to households. Firms obtain funds from households by issuing stock and bonds, pay funds to households in the form of interest and dividends, and retain funds on behalf of stockholders. These transactions do not change the total cash flow or income generated by the firms' real production.

A second set of financial transactions, such as borrowing and lending, occur between households. These transactions further rearrange cash flow and income, but also result in zero aggregate net cash flow and income. For example, when a lending household receives interest income, the borrowing household incurs negative interest income (interest expense).

A real-based tax system tracks only the production activity of firms and workers, whereas a real-plus-financial tax system also tracks financial transactions. Either system can measure the aggregate income and business cash flow in the economy, but only the real-plus-financial system can measure the income and consumption ultimately enjoyed by specific households. Because the real-based system does not track capital income or business cash flow to the final recipients, it can tax those items only at a flat rate at the firm level. To employ graduated rates based on a household's annual income or consumption, as the PET and the current individual income tax do, we need a real-plus-financial approach that tracks all flows to the final household recipients.

At one extreme, the real-based nature of the VAT eliminates the need for any household tax returns, but it forces all consumption to be taxed at a single flat rate. At the other extreme, the real-plus-financial nature of the PET permits graduated tax rates tied directly to annual consumer spending, but requires households to file annual tax returns reporting a wide array of financial transactions. The X tax follows an intermediate strategy, adopting the real-based approach of the VAT, but taxing wages at the household rather than the firm level. The X tax achieves much, but not all, of the simplicity of the VAT and largely matches the progressivity of the PET.

First, the X tax is almost as simple as the VAT. Although households must file tax returns, they report only their wages, the type of income that is easiest to measure. Like the current individual income tax, the household wage tax would be collected through withholding. As they do today, most households would obtain the necessary information to report their wages from their W-2 forms. Households would not report interest or other capital income and would not deduct interest expense. Few households would need to make quarterly estimated tax payments. The X tax undertakes the relatively simple task of tracking wages to their final recipient, while avoiding the far more difficult task of tracking business cash flows to their final recipients.

Second, the X tax achieves progressivity, but in a less refined manner than the PET. The X tax system taxes wages at graduated rates tied to annual wage income and imposes a high flat tax rate on business cash flow, which largely accrues to the well-off. This progressivity is not as finely calibrated as that achieved by the PET, in which graduated rates are tied directly to annual consumer spending. For example, households that are not affluent may hold a little wealth accumulated prior to the tax reform and may earn a little in above-normal returns. Under the X tax, such households face the high flat tax rate on the business cash flow that they receive, even though this high rate is not appropriate for their economic circumstances. This outcome is avoided under the PET, which links tax rates directly to spending levels. But the PET achieves this finer calibration only by tracking all financial flows and requiring households to report all of their saving and dissaving. We view the additional refinement of the PET to not be worth the associated complexity. If a small number of disadvantaged households are adversely affected by the business cash flow tax, the best solution is to provide them with targeted relief within the X tax system.

Front-Loaded versus Back-Loaded Treatment of Saving. The difference between the treatment of financial transactions under the PET and under the household wage tax in an X tax system can be most easily understood with an analogy to the treatment of different types of tax-preferred accounts under the current tax system.

The PET treatment of financial transactions matches the current treatment of pensions and conventional IRAs, in which savings receive front-loaded tax breaks. Each household deducts inflows into these savings vehicles and pays tax on subsequent withdrawals. In contrast, the treatment of financial transactions under the household wage tax in an X tax system matches the current tax treatment of Roth IRAs, in which savings receive back-loaded tax breaks. Households do not deduct inflows and do not pay tax on withdrawals.

As economists have long known, the two approaches are equivalent for investments with marginal returns if the household remains in the same tax bracket over time. As we showed in our discussion above of the role of the cash-flow tax, the up-front deduction and the inclusion of the proceeds offset each other in present value. Because each household's financial transactions have zero expected market value, the present value of the outflows equals the value of the inflows. If the tax rate remains constant, a tax on the outflows must have a present value equal to the tax savings from deducting the inflow. As we will explain in chapter 3, this result also holds for risky investments.

Of course, the equivalence of front-loaded and back-loaded treatment breaks down if tax rates are not constant. The conventional front-loaded approach used by the PET is more generous if the household is in a higher tax bracket when it saves than when it withdraws; the Roth back-loaded approach used by the household wage tax in an X tax system is more generous if the household is in a higher tax bracket when it withdraws than when it saves.

The issue at hand, though, is not which approach is more generous, but whether the PET's use of the front-loaded approach at the household level provides social gains that warrant the complexity of reporting savings and withdrawals on tax returns. On balance, we think not. If the household remains in the same tax bracket over time, the front-loaded approach has no net effect and financial transactions are tracked for no purpose. If the household moves between different brackets over time, the front-loaded approach actually disrupts the neutrality that could be achieved with constant-rate consumption taxation, as taxpayers are encouraged to save in high-bracket years and to withdraw savings in low-bracket years.

The advantage of using the front-loaded approach at the household level is that it achieves a finer calibration of progressivity for households that have highly variable wages but relatively smooth consumption. This advantage does not seem to warrant the complexity of tracking financial transactions, particularly because, as we will discuss in chapter 3, the X tax can partially attain this advantage by allowing households with highly variable wages to average their wages across different years.

Although the household wage tax in an X tax system adopts a Roth back-loaded approach to saving, the overall X tax system, no less than the PET, adopts the conventional front-loaded approach, with a deduction for savings and a tax on outflows. Rather than implementing the deduction and the tax at the household level as the PET does, the X tax implements them at the firm level through the business cash-flow tax as firms deduct their business investments and are taxed on the proceeds of the investments. The business cash-flow tax is simple because it is imposed at a flat rate and does not track financial flows to individual recipients.

The choice between the X tax and the PET is a close call. But for the reasons described above, we judge the X tax to offer the better combination of simplicity and progressivity. Nevertheless, the X tax poses some challenges that must be addressed before it can be accepted as a replacement for the income tax.

Challenges Facing the X Tax. The X tax faces four major difficulties. In the remainder of this book, we will present solutions to these difficulties and discuss other aspects of X tax implementation.

One problem concerns individuals who work for firms while also providing capital to the firms, such as sole proprietors and some partners and S corporation shareholders. There is no simple way to divide payments that such individuals receive from the firm into wages and business cash flow. This division is critical under the X tax because business cash flow is taxed more heavily than wages. We will discuss this issue in chapter 5.

A second problem under the X tax concerns the significant number of firms that are likely to have negative business cash flow in particular years. The neutrality of the X tax requires that each firm immediately deduct its investment outlays, something that it may be unable to do if excess deductions are not refunded in cash. We will also discuss this issue in chapter 5.

A third problem concerns the tax treatment of financial institutions, whose real activities are often mislabeled as financial transactions in the marketplace. Because the X tax is a real-based tax, it runs the risk of not taxing these transactions properly. In chapter 6, we will present a relatively simple solution that separates real and financial activities in expected market value.

A fourth problem concerns international trade. The X tax does not readily fit into the trade rules adopted by the international community, which were written with the VAT in mind. We will address this issue in chapter 7.

In other chapters, we will discuss the transition to the new tax system and the treatment of pensions and fringe benefits, transfer payments, owner-occupied housing and consumer durables, nonprofit organizations, and state and local governments.

In addressing these challenges, we often exploit the flexibility offered by consumption taxation. As explained above, we generally prefer the basic X tax design, which *includes* a firm-level business cash-flow tax that imposes zero present-value tax on marginal investments, and generally *excludes* financial transactions, which also have zero present value. But because these features have zero present value, we can, when appropriate, deviate from the basic X tax design in specific areas without untoward consequences. For example, we choose not to extend the business cash-flow tax to the nonbusiness sector, and we choose to include financial transactions in the tax base for financial institutions and for transactions between U.S. firms and their foreign affiliates. This mixing and matching allows us to capture the advantages that the basic X tax design offers in most applications while avoiding the disadvantages that it poses in selected areas.

Conclusion

We conclude that the X tax is the best consumption tax to use for a wholesale replacement of the income tax system. In the next chapter, we will examine the degree of progressivity that can be achieved under the X tax.

BOX
OPTICS OF THE X TAX AND THE PET

The PET has an optical advantage over the X tax because it satisfies the political demand for a visible tax on households living off of capital income. Of course, no consumption tax system imposes a marginal tax on capital income from new saving; that is done only by income tax systems. But consumption taxes do tax above-normal returns and existing wealth held on the reform date. The PET makes those levies visible because households report their capital income on a tax return while deducting their new saving. In contrast, the X tax imposes no household-level tax on those with capital income, while imposing a highly visible tax on households with labor income. Under the X tax, above-normal returns and existing wealth are taxed much less visibly, at the firm level through the cash-flow tax.

On the other hand, the PET faces an optical challenge with respect to the tax treatment of borrowing. In accord with income tax principles, the proceeds of borrowing are currently not taxed. In contrast, the PET taxes households on the proceeds of borrowing, but then allows the borrower to deduct all subsequent payments, principal and interest, on the loan. Although those deductions cancel out the initial tax in expected market value (if the household remains in the same tax bracket), the tax on borrowing is still likely to be unpopular. The X tax avoids this optical problem by not tracking financial flows; although consumption by borrowers is taxed, the tax is collected at the firm level.

Also, the X tax may have an optical advantage over the PET because Americans generally prefer that business firms "remit" or "pay" part of the tax burden. Although individuals rather than firms ultimately pay taxes, the X tax's inclusion of a cash-flow tax on firms may be politically popular.

3

Maintaining Progressivity

In this chapter, we discuss potential tax rate schedules under the X tax and confirm that the X tax can largely replicate the progressivity of the current tax system. We also discuss how to assess the distributional effects of moving to the X tax, emphasizing some shortcomings of conventional distributional analysis.

Tax Rate Schedule

Tax rates under the X tax could assume a variety of levels, depending on the desired degree of progressivity and the decisions made about various details of the tax design.

The 2005 Panel's Progressive Consumption Tax Plan. As we noted in chapter 2, the Progressive Consumption Tax Plan considered, but not adopted, by the President's Advisory Panel on Federal Tax Reform (2005, 182–90) called for the replacement of the income tax system by an X tax. We look to this proposal for guidance on possible rate structures and tax credits.

The proposal featured a 35 percent tax rate on business cash flow, which also applied to taxable wages in excess of $115,000 for married couples. A 15 percent rate applied to the first $80,000 of a couple's taxable wages and a 25 percent rate to taxable wages between $80,000 and $115,000. The corresponding bracket end points for unmarried taxpayers were half of those for married couples. The end points were specified for 2006, but were to be indexed for inflation, which would make the 2012 values about 15 percent higher. The proposal had no standard deduction, but included a Family Credit and a Work Credit. The proposal also featured limited deductions for charitable contributions and mortgage interest.

FIGURE 3-1

DISTRIBUTION OF THE FEDERAL INCOME TAX BURDEN UNDER 2015 LAW
AND UNDER THE 2005 TAX PANEL'S PROGRESSIVE CONSUMPTION
TAX PLAN, BY INCOME PERCENTILE

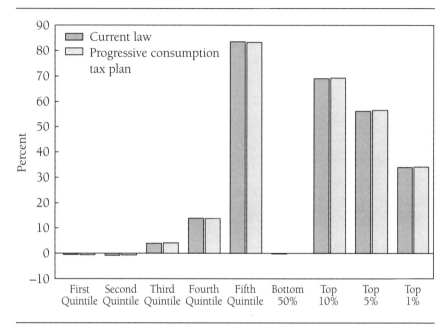

SOURCE: President's Advisory Panel on Federal Tax Reform (2005, 186).

As shown in figure 3-1, the proposal came remarkably close to replicating the distribution of the tax burden under the 2005 income tax system, as projected forward to 2015. The top quintile would have paid 83.3 percent of total federal consumption taxes under the plan, compared to 83.5 percent of total federal income taxes under the 2015 tax system. Similarly, the top 1 percent of taxpayers would have paid 34.1 percent of all federal consumption taxes under the plan, compared to 33.9 percent of all federal income taxes under the 2015 system.

Factors Affecting the Level of Tax Rates. Because consumption is smaller than income, particularly at the top of the income distribution, consumption taxes tend to require higher statutory tax rates than income taxes, holding fixed other factors. The panel's plan avoided an increase in the top statutory tax rate by including substantial base-broadening measures that were applied primarily to higher-income taxpayers.

We do not try to specify a precise rate structure in this book, because we do not wish to predetermine the numerous factors that may affect rates, including revenue requirements, distributional goals, and the scope of tax preferences. Policy makers must decide whether the level of revenue to be replaced is the revenue raised by the current system (with or without a partial or full extension of the 2001 and 2003 tax cuts and with or without continued relief from the alternative minimum tax) or a higher revenue level designed to address the long-term fiscal imbalance. Distributional goals may also change over time. The required level of tax rates will also depend on whether tax preferences for charitable giving, homeownership, employer-provided health insurance, and other activities are preserved under the X tax, topics on which (as we will discuss in subsequent chapters) we generally reserve judgment.

Low-income tax credits, similar to the current earned income tax credit and child credit, can also be provided under the household wage tax. As under the current system, such credits can be made partially or wholly refundable. We recommend that such credits be provided. We will discuss in chapter 4 administrative challenges posed by such credits, given the absence of information about capital income on household wage tax returns.

As noted above, the panel's plan set the top tax rate on wages, and therefore the flat tax rate on business cash flow, at 35 percent. Purely for illustrative purposes, we assume that the top X tax rate on wages will also be 35 percent. As we will discuss in chapter 4, the highest wage earners are also subject to a 3.8 percent Medicare payroll tax, as of 2013, which would remain in place after our proposed tax reform. The total marginal tax rate on the wages of the top earners will therefore be 38.8 percent.[4] As we will discuss in chapter 5, it is desirable for the flat tax rate on business cash flow to match the total tax rate, including Medicare tax, on the highest wage earners, so we assume a 38.8 percent flat tax rate on business cash flow.

We emphasize again, however, that these tax rates are merely illustrative. In view of the uncertainty about the factors described above, the actual rates could vary significantly in either direction.

Under the X tax, even tax rates significantly higher than those mentioned above would have relatively benign effects on economic incentives.

This is clearly true for incentives to save and invest; as we explained in chapters 1 and 2, the effective marginal tax rate on saving and investment is zero for any level of X tax rates. A similar point holds, although not to the same extent, for work incentives. As we noted in our discussion of the trade-off fallacy in chapter 1, the incentive to work does not depend solely on how taxes affect the trade-off between leisure and current consumption; it also depends on how taxes affect the trade-off between leisure and future consumption. Because much of the wages earned by high-wage households are saved to finance future consumption, the latter trade-off is particularly important for them. That trade-off is more work-friendly under an X tax with a high statutory tax rate on wages and no subsequent tax on the saving done with those wages than it is under an income tax with a lower statutory tax rate on wages followed by substantial taxes on saving.

Wage Averaging. Households are likely to face different marginal tax rates in different years under the household wage tax in an X tax system, as they do today under the income tax. Experience suggests that Congress is likely to periodically change the tax rate schedule for households; major changes in households' tax rates have occurred roughly every four years over the past three decades, and minor changes have been more common. Also, even with a fixed tax rate schedule, households will move into different brackets as their wages fluctuate from year to year.

Variations in a household's marginal tax rate under the household wage tax in an X tax system do not disrupt the neutrality of the X tax with respect to the choice between current and future consumption. As we discussed in chapter 2, the X tax, unlike the PET, provides its deduction for saving and investment at the firm level under the business cash-flow tax. So, although neutrality between current and future consumption requires a constant tax rate, the rate that must remain constant is the tax rate on business cash flow. Because the business cash-flow tax has a single flat rate, we need not worry about firms moving between tax brackets, although we cannot preclude the possibility that Congress will change the flat rate from time to time.

Variations in the household wage tax rates under the X tax system introduce essentially the same problems as rate variations under the income tax. Tax rate variations impose a penalty on human capital investments, in which workers forgo earnings in low-bracket years early in life to increase earnings in high-bracket years later in life. Tax rate variations also create incentives to shift labor income into low-bracket years, to shift deductions into high-bracket years, and to pursue occupations that involve smooth, rather than variable, labor earnings.

Allowing households with highly variable wages to average their wages across different years would offer a partial solution to these problems. Under such a provision, eligible households would be allowed to compute their tax liability under the assumption that their wages had been earned uniformly over a period of several years, disregarding their actual variation over time. The U.S. income tax system allowed income averaging until 1986, although the averaging provision was criticized for providing relief only to those who experienced income increases rather than income declines. In 1997, Congress restored income averaging for farmers and fishermen.

As we discussed in chapter 2, the progressivity achieved by the X tax is less finely calibrated than that achieved by the PET. Whereas household wage tax brackets under an X tax system are based on annual wages, PET brackets are based on annual consumption, which is likely to reflect a longer-term measure of well-being. Allowing households with variable wages to average their wages over several years would move the X tax toward a somewhat longer-term perspective.

Treatment of the Family. The proper tax treatment of the family is a long-standing issue in the literature on income taxation. It is well known that no tax system can satisfy progressive tax rates, equal taxation of married couples with equal incomes, and marriage neutrality. Because this issue arises under the household wage tax in an X tax system in essentially the same manner as under the income tax, the options for addressing it are similar under both systems. While the President's Advisory Panel on Federal Tax Reform set the bracket end points for joint filers at twice the level of those for single filers, an approach that avoids marriage penalties and offers extensive marriage bonuses, there is no reason why the household wage tax in an X tax system needs to follow this approach.

The options for addressing the thorny issue of classifying children as dependents of particular taxpayers are also the same under the household wage tax in an X tax system as under the income tax. The current-law tax relief for adoption expenses can also be maintained, if desired. Because there is no household tax on capital incomes, the X tax avoids the problems the current system faces in allocating capital income among family members, including the complexity of taxing property settlements in divorces.

We now discuss three factors that contribute to the progressivity of the X tax, some of which are not properly reflected in conventional distributional analysis.

Assessing the Distributional Effects of the X Tax

We discuss the true incidence of the corporate income tax, the taxation of above-normal returns under the X tax, and the implications of assessing distributional effects based on households' lifetime incomes rather than their incomes at a point in time.

Incidence of the Corporate Income Tax. Conventional distributional analysis assumes that owners of capital bear the full economic burden of the current corporate income tax. Traditionally, the U.S. Treasury and the Congressional Budget Office have distributed the corporate income tax to owners of corporate capital based on returns received as dividends and capital gains. Treasury changed its methodology in 2011, however, and now assigns a modest portion of the corporate tax burden to labor.[5]

The assumption that owners of capital bear the full burden of the corporate income tax has been challenged by recent research suggesting that labor bears part of the burden in an open economy. How is this important to the distributional effect of replacing the current income tax with an X tax? If a substantial portion of the burden of the corporate income tax is borne by labor in the form of lower real wages, then replacing the income tax system with a consumption tax is not as regressive as conventional analysis indicates.

Economic theory indicates that the burden of a tax is borne by the least mobile factor of production. In an increasingly global economy, where capital flows freely across borders but labor does not, labor is much more likely than owners of capital to bear the burden of the corporate income tax, which can generally be avoided by investing abroad. Under this scenario, higher corporate tax rates reduce capital accumulation, which lowers labor productivity and drives down real wages.

This emerging view of the incidence of the corporate income tax has been suggested in theoretical research, including Harberger (2008) and Randolph (2006), and supported by a series of empirical papers that have considered the relationship between corporate tax rates and wages among developed nations over the past two decades. Desai, Foley, and Hines (2007) find that between 45 percent and 75 percent of the corporate tax is likely borne by labor. Other studies show that the countries that have reduced corporate tax rates the most have tended to have the largest gains in real wages. A substantial share of business taxes therefore tends to show up as lower real wages rather than as lower after-tax returns to capital.

Although the precise extent to which corporate taxes affect real wages remains unclear, current research suggests that real wages are sensitive to corporate taxes. Distributional analyses that assume owners of capital bear the full burden of the corporate income tax overstate the regressivity of shifting to consumption taxation.

Above-Normal Returns. As emphasized by Gentry and Hubbard (1997), consumption taxes do not exempt from tax the entire return to saving and investment. Instead, as we discussed in chapter 2, the business cash-flow tax raises revenue from two sources, the return from existing capital in place on the reform date and above-normal investment returns. We now turn to the distributional effects of the latter component.

When there is no uncertainty, capital income can be decomposed into two components, the normal return earned on a marginal investment, which is sometimes referred to as the opportunity cost of funds or the return to waiting, and above-normal returns. Above-normal returns include economic profits from the exercise of market power or from innovation. Revenue collected on such returns may be significant in an economy with imperfectly competitive industries and a high rate of innovation and technological change.

As shown by the Patient-Impatient example in chapter 1, a consumption tax exempts the marginal return from tax whereas an income tax does not. But as we discussed in chapter 2, above-normal returns continue to be taxed under a consumption tax, just as they are under an income tax. The expensing of investment under the business cash-flow tax generates tax savings that exactly offset, in present value, the future cash flows generated by a *marginal* investment. We showed, however, that a net tax liability arises for investments that generate future cash flows whose present value exceeds the cost of the initial investment. In particular, future cash flows resulting from above-normal profits, such as those due to innovation or the exercise of monopoly power, are subject to tax. Compared to an income tax, a consumption tax exempts only the marginal investment return from tax.

Although this point may seem minor, it can have important implications for comparing the distributional effects of income and consumption taxes because it means that a significant portion of the return to saving and investment is taxed under both an income and a consumption tax. Whether this distinction is important depends on how large the opportunity cost of capital is in relation to total capital income and who receives this component of capital income. If this component is large and received primarily by higher-income taxpayers, then shifting to the X tax or any other consumption tax is significantly less beneficial to capital owners than it initially appears to be.

To be fair, some distributional analyses accurately account for this point. For example, the Treasury's analysis of the 2005 tax panel's consumption tax proposals appropriately allocated the burden of the business cash-flow tax to owners of capital, recognizing that this tax fell on existing capital and above-normal returns earned by owners of capital. In policy discussions, though, the myth that consumption taxes impose no burden on owners of capital is often still heard.

Estimates by Gentry and Hubbard (1997) shed light on the gap between this myth and reality. Gentry and Hubbard estimated the distribution of the tax burden associated with the current tax system and a revenue-equivalent consumption tax, first under the "traditional" assumption that a consumption tax imposes no tax on capital income and then under a "revised" assumption that the consumption tax applies to all returns except the marginal return, which they measured using the riskless interest rate. Their estimates, reproduced in table 3-1, suggest that, relative to the traditional methodology, the revised methodology, which accounts for the tax imposed on above-normal returns, shows a greater portion of the consumption tax being borne by higher income taxpayers.

As shown in the left-hand-side panel of the table, the share of the consumption tax burden paid by the top 5 percent of households ranked by income would be 30.9 percent under the revised methodology rather than 27.1 percent under the traditional methodology—a 14 percent increase.

TABLE 3-1

DISTRIBUTION OF THE TAX BURDEN BY HOUSEHOLD INCOME
AND HOUSEHOLD NET WORTH

| | Household Income | | | Household Net Worth | | | |
| | Consumption Tax Base | | | Consumption Tax Base | | | |
Income Decile	Current Tax Base	Traditional Methodology	Revised Methodology	Current Tax Base	Traditional Methodology	Revised Methodology	Net Worth Decile
1	0.3%	0.4%	0.3%	2.9%	3.8%	3.5%	1
2	1.5%	1.9%	1.7%	2.6%	3.4%	3.1%	2
3	2.6%	3.3%	3.0%	4.3%	5.6%	5.1%	3
4	3.7%	4.5%	4.2%	5.2%	6.9%	6.2%	4
5	5.1%	6.3%	5.8%	5.5%	7.3%	6.7%	5
6	6.5%	7.8%	7.3%	7.5%	10.0%	9.1%	6
7	8.2%	10.0%	9.4%	7.8%	10.0%	9.2%	7
8	10.0%	12.0%	11.4%	9.9%	12.2%	11.4%	8
9	14.0%	15.8%	15.2%	12.7%	13.5%	13.3%	9
10	48.1%	38.0%	41.8%	41.6%	27.3%	32.4%	10
Total	100.0%	100.0%	100.0%	100.0%	100.0%	100.0%	Total
Top 5%	37.5%	27.1%	30.9%	32.4%	18.6%	23.5%	Top 5%
Top 1%	21.3%	13.8%	16.3%	17.6%	8.0%	11.3%	Top 1%

SOURCE: Calculations from the 1989 Federal Reserve Survey of Consumer Finances by Gentry and Hubbard (1997).

For the top 1 percent of households, the difference is somewhat more striking, with 16.3 percent of the tax burden paid under the revised methodology rather than 13.8 percent under the traditional methodology—an 18 percent increase. Nevertheless, these are both less than under the current tax system, in which 37.5 percent of the tax burden is paid by the top 5 percent, and 21.3 percent is paid by the top 1 percent of households.

This analysis arguably overstates the point to some extent. In the presence of uncertainty, returns may be above or below the safe interest rate simply due to good or bad luck on risky investments. Because Gentry and Hubbard (1997) measure above-normal returns as the difference between the total return and the riskless return, they treat lucky returns on risky investments as part of above-normal returns (and treat unlucky returns as negative above-normal returns). As we now explain, the tax treatment of those returns generally does not affect the well-being of investors or the government.

We mentioned in chapter 2, deferring a full discussion until now, the fact that the business cash-flow tax collects taxes on lucky investments and rebates taxes on unlucky investments. As explained in the "Zero Revenue from Taxation of Risky Returns" box (pages 51–52), the tax on risky returns does not actually raise revenue for the government or impose a burden on investors, because the tax can be undone by simply trading in the underlying risky assets. In contrast, the tax on true above-normal returns raises revenue and burdens investors precisely because it cannot be undone through additional investment, which, by definition, yields only normal marginal returns. This zero-revenue property of risky returns will prove to be important for our analysis in chapters 6, 7, and 9.

Lifetime versus Annual Incomes. Another weakness of conventional distributional analyses of consumption taxes is their focus on annual incomes. Distributional analyses that focus on a snapshot of a taxpayer's income and characteristics fail to take into account fluidity in incomes and characteristics over time. Annual income may be a misleading indicator of ability to pay.

Economists studying the impact of the life cycle on taxpayer incomes generally find that annual incomes are a poor representation of their well-being over a longer time horizon. The lowest income group, for example, includes young taxpayers just entering the workforce, older taxpayers who just left the workforce, and some wealthy taxpayers who had a very bad year, as well as those taxpayers who are persistently poor. Younger taxpayers who just entered the workforce, for example, are likely to have relatively low incomes as they continue to acquire human capital through education and job experience, but as their human capital develops, their incomes tend to rise and peak shortly before retirement. Their savings and consumption patterns follow this cycle with a period of accumulation accelerating in midlife and peaking before retirement, when dissaving begins. Conversely, the top income group includes taxpayers who unexpectedly had a very good year or who sold a business or other assets, as well as those taxpayers with persistently high incomes.

These factors and others result in substantial movement of taxpayers through the income distribution over time, as documented by numerous studies. For example, Auten and Gee (2009) find that roughly 50 percent of taxpayers in the lowest quintile are in a higher quintile ten years later and roughly 50 percent of taxpayers in the highest quintile are in a lower quintile ten years later.

The right-hand-side panel of table 3-1 tabulates tax burden by household net worth. These computations at least partially abstract from year-to-year fluctuations in household incomes and provide a somewhat broader view of the distributional effects of shifting to a consumption tax. In general, the distribution of taxes paid is more uniform when tabulated by net worth. One reason for this more even distribution is that annual fluctuations in income can affect both a household's income and tax payments and its relative position in the income distribution, but such fluctuations are less important in distributional analyses based on net worth. Again, the decrease in the fraction of taxes paid by the top 5 percent of the net worth distribution accompanying a switch to a broad-based consumption tax falls by about one-third when the consumption tax base is appropriately defined to include some components of capital income.

Conclusion

The X tax can easily employ a rate schedule that roughly matches the progressivity of the current system, particularly when it is recognized that high statutory tax rates have significantly lower disincentive effects under an X tax than under an income tax.

Conventional distributional estimates of the impact of moving to a consumption tax are inaccurate because they assume that the burden of the current corporate income tax is borne by owners of business capital, despite recent evidence that workers bear a substantial part of the burden through lower wages. Policy discussions often overlook the fact that, under a consumption tax, affluent households continue to pay tax on their above-normal returns, as well as on their existing capital holdings at the time of enactment. Finally, lifetime measures that account for the considerable movement up and down the distributional ladder over a person's life suggest that a consumption tax is less regressive than it appears to be in analyses based on annual snapshots of a taxpayer's income.

Box
ZERO REVENUE FROM TAXATION OF RISKY RETURNS

Consider, for example, a $100 investment with a risky return. If the investment is successful, which happens with 50 percent probability, it earns a 10 percent return. If the investment is unsuccessful, which happens with 50 percent probability, it loses 5 percent. The expected return on this risky investment is therefore 2.5 percent. Furthermore, assume that the return on a safe investment is 1 percent, implying that the risky investment commands a 1.5 percent risk premium.

How is this investment treated under a 20 percent flat consumption tax? In the first period, the investor expenses the investment and receives a tax deduction that yields $20 tax saving. In the second period, if the investment is successful, the investor pays tax on $110, and the government receives revenue of $22. But if the investment is unsuccessful, the investor pays tax on $95 in the second period, and the government receives revenue of $19.

Under this 20 percent consumption tax, the government loses $20 of tax revenue in the first period and receives either $22 or $19 in the second period. Although a number of methods for computing the net revenue have been used, most of them lack a valid economic foundation. For example, using a discount rate of 1 percent (the safe interest rate) and looking at each possible outcome suggests that the government collects $1.78 in present value if the investment is successful and negative $1.19 in present value if the investment is unsuccessful. Another approach, which also uses the 1 percent discount rate, averages across the two possible outcomes and computes the expected value of the revenue as $0.30.

Unfortunately, these computations are meaningless because they use an economically invalid discount rate. The safe interest rate used in the computations does not measure the price at which the government or the taxpayers can undo the effects of the taxation on risk. In reality, the tax makes zero additional revenue available to the government, beyond what it can obtain from its own (or its citizens') financial transactions. The government can obtain exactly the same second-period funds—$22 under the successful outcome and $19 under the unsuccessful outcome—by simply buying one-fifth of the underlying investment, which would cost $20 in the first period. So, $20 is the true first-period present value of the uncertain second-period revenue. Because the government loses $20

(continued)

Box
ZERO REVENUE FROM TAXATION OF RISKY RETURNS
(*continued*)

---

in the first period from the expensing deduction, its net revenue on the whole transaction is exactly zero.

Notice the key difference between these risky returns and the above-normal returns arising from market power or innovation that are discussed in the text. When the government taxes the latter, it gleans returns greater than it can obtain on a marginal investment and thereby reaps a genuine revenue gain. In contrast, the taxation of risky returns gives the government nothing beyond what it can already obtain in asset markets.

The investor's burden in this example is the same as the government's revenue gain—zero. The investor can use his first-period $20 tax savings to buy an additional one-fifth of the risky investment, which will give him exactly the same after-tax payoff in the second period as if the tax did not exist.

There is again a sharp contrast between the risky-asset case and a case involving above-normal returns from market power or innovation. Investors cannot expand their above-normal-return investments, as they have already exploited those to their maximum extent; no investment with a return greater than the marginal return will ever be left undone. The fact that there is a limit on the volume of investments that yield such returns is precisely the reason that they offer a return greater than the *marginal* return on investment; if these superior investments could be made in unlimited amounts, no inferior investments would ever be made and the return on these investments would then be the marginal return.

Although consumption taxes appear to collect revenue on the returns to risky investments, these returns and the revenue raised by taxing them actually have zero value.

4

Fringe Benefits and Transfer Payments

In this chapter, we explore the X tax treatment of fringe benefits and work expenses, the implications of the X tax for the financing of Social Security and Medicare, and the X tax treatment of other public and private transfer payments.

Fringe Benefits

We first consider the treatment of nonretirement fringe benefits and then analyze the distinct issues posed by pensions and employer-sponsored retirement accounts.

Health Insurance and Other Nonretirement Benefits. Because the income tax and the X tax are fundamentally similar in their treatment of labor income, the same basic options for the treatment of nonretirement fringe benefits are available under both tax systems. In either case, neutral tax treatment calls for firms to deduct all labor compensation, including fringe benefit costs, as business expenses, and for workers to pay tax on all of their compensation, including fringe benefits.

The current income tax generally disregards this prescription, as health insurance and many other fringe benefits are deducted by employers but are not included in taxable income by workers. This approach is intended to encourage the provision of these benefits and avoid administrative difficulties. Fringe benefits that are exempt from income tax are generally also exempt from Social Security and Medicare payroll tax. The current income tax system also provides an itemized deduction for large out-of-pocket medical expenses and a deduction for health insurance costs of self-employed taxpayers.

The tax treatment of employer-provided health insurance raises a number of complicated issues, including whether such insurance should be encouraged as a good way to pool risks. Further complications arise from the changes slated to take effect under the health care reform law adopted in March 2010. Starting in 2014, refundable tax credits will be provided to workers who do *not* have access to affordable health insurance at work to help them buy health insurance on newly established exchanges. Penalty taxes will also be imposed on firms with fifty or more employees that do not provide affordable insurance and on certain individuals who do not have health insurance. Starting in 2018, a 40 percent excise tax will be imposed on employer-provided health insurance plans that exceed certain cost thresholds. The health care law also includes many other provisions, including temporary tax credits for some small firms that provide health insurance for their employees.

The appropriate treatment of employer-provided health insurance cannot be discussed in isolation from these provisions, which have important and complicated effects on health insurance obtained both inside and outside the workplace. We need not resolve the intense debate surrounding health care reform. Instead, we simply note that the decision to adopt the X tax leaves open all of the policy options in this area. The health insurance exclusion, the itemized deduction for medical expenses, the self-employed health insurance deduction, the refundable credits, and the penalty and excise taxes can be either maintained or eliminated, as desired, under the X tax, just as they can be under the income tax.

With respect to other fringe benefits, which do not pose some of these complications, we recommend that employees be taxed on the allocated value of their fringe benefits, with exceptions for small fringe benefits that would be administratively difficult to tax. We reiterate, though, that the X tax is also consistent with alternative approaches, such as continued exclusion of these benefits.

Service employees would also be subject to household wage tax on tips that they receive. Compliance would presumably be no better, and no worse, than under the current income tax system.

Work Expenses. Current law allows a tax credit for child care costs, a deduction for moving expenses, and a miscellaneous itemized deduction for large employee business expenses. Education costs, which may warrant tax relief as work-related costs or on other grounds, benefit from an assortment of tax credits and deductions.

These costs can be treated in fundamentally the same manner under the household wage tax as under today's income tax. The same trade-offs and complications arise, such as how to classify mixed business-personal expenses and how to verify employees' expenditures. In general, the appropriate treatment of these costs under the income tax, whatever that may be, is also appropriate under the X tax.

Pensions and Retirement Plans. Pensions raise issues distinct from those raised by employer-provided health insurance and other benefits and receive different tax treatment under current law. Unlike consumption benefits such as health insurance, pensions are a form of saving.

Under current law, firms deduct contributions to pension funds and to employees' tax-preferred savings accounts, and employees are not taxed. The capital income earned in the pension fund or tax-preferred account is exempt from tax. Recipients are taxed on their pension benefits or the amounts they withdraw from their accounts.

The initial deduction by the employer and the lack of employee tax make this treatment superficially similar to the treatment of employer-provided health insurance. Yet, the nature of the tax preference is fundamentally different. Here, the employee actually *is* taxed on the compensation, which was not true for health insurance. This occurs because the pension benefits or account withdrawals attributable to the employer contributions have the same expected market value as the employers' contributions. Although the tax payment is delayed until the money is withdrawn, tax is ultimately paid on the compensation, albeit at the tax rate applicable to the worker on the withdrawal date rather than the rate applicable when the compensation was earned.

Instead, the tax preference arises because the employee is allowed to save tax-free, as pensions and tax-preferred accounts effectively receive the same front-loaded treatment that the PET provides to all savings. Under a PET, the contributions and capital income would be excluded from the tax base because they are saved rather than consumed; tax would be imposed only when withdrawals are made from the saving vehicle. In this area, therefore, the current system follows the same consumption tax approach as the PET.

As we discussed in chapter 2, however, the PET's consumption tax approach follows different timing rules than the approach followed by the household wage tax in an X tax system. The household wage tax adheres to the back-loaded Roth approach, which features no deduction for saving and no tax on withdrawals from saving. Under normal X tax rules, therefore, the employee would be taxed on the employer contributions when they are made, with no subsequent taxes on withdrawals or pension benefits. As explained in chapter 2, the two approaches are equivalent in present discounted value when the tax rate remains constant, but the front-loaded approach is more generous if the worker's tax rate is lower when he or she receives the money. The "Zero Revenue from Taxation of Risky Returns" box in chapter 3 (pages 51–52) establishes that the presence of risky returns does not change this analysis.

To minimize disruptive changes from current law, promote simplicity, and preserve a role for employer-sponsored retirement plans, we propose that pension benefits and withdrawals from employer-sponsored retirement accounts continue to be taxed when workers receive the money, as recommended by Hall and Rabushka (1995, 55–59). The employer should deduct contributions into pension funds and accounts when they are made. To avoid the need to distinguish them from employer contributions, employee contributions into employer-sponsored plans should also be deductible.

Under the household wage tax in an X tax system, most households will be in lower brackets in their retirement years than during their working years, making this front-loaded treatment more generous than the back-loaded treatment given to other tax savings. This generosity will give workers some incentive to save through employer-provided savings vehicles and help to maintain these institutions, thereby promoting an environment conducive to saving.

Under the X tax, Roth IRAs and Roth 401(k) accounts are unnecessary because all saving enjoys Roth treatment at the household level. We propose that holders of existing Roth accounts be allowed to withdraw their balances tax-free, as they can under the current system, and that penalties for early withdrawals be abolished. We also propose that conventional front-loaded IRAs be abolished; we will discuss the treatment of existing accounts in chapter 8. We also propose to eliminate the savers credit provided by Internal Revenue Code section 25B; the credit has been ineffective under the current tax system and will be unnecessary under the X tax.

We now turn to public retirement programs.

Financing Social Security and Medicare

The federal government imposes a 12.4 percent payroll and self-employment tax, limited to the first $110,100 of wages and self-employment earnings in 2012, which is earmarked to finance Social Security old age, survivor, and disability benefits. The ceiling is adjusted each year, based on a two-year lagged measure of wage growth in the national economy. The federal government also imposes a separate payroll and self-employment tax earmarked to finance Medicare Part A, which has no ceiling on taxable earnings. As of 2013, this tax will be imposed at a 2.9 percent rate, with a 0.9 percent surtax on wages and self-employment earnings in excess of $200,000 ($250,000 for married couples). The highest earners will therefore face a zero marginal tax rate under the Social Security tax and a 3.8 percent marginal tax rate under the Medicare tax.[6]

Although half of the payroll tax is legally imposed on employers and half on employees, the economic effects are the same as those of a pure employee tax. The Social Security tax does not apply to the dwindling group of federal government employees hired before January 1984 or to employees of some state and local governments (those that opted out of Social Security when states and localities were still allowed to do so). Even these groups are subject to Medicare tax, however, except for the dwindling group of state and local government employees hired before 1986.

We recommend that the Social Security and Medicare payroll taxes be maintained when the X tax is adopted. Because a payroll tax is a wage tax, it, like the household wage tax in an X tax system, imposes no saving disincentive; the tax does not apply to interest, dividends, capital gains, or any other income from saving. So, the economic gains from replacing the payroll taxes with the X tax would be slight.

In contrast, the costs of replacing the Social Security payroll tax with the X tax would be substantial, for two reasons. First, such a replacement would eliminate the use of this tax as an earmarked financing source for Social Security, an arrangement that helps restrain the program's spending. Second, it would disrupt the current linkage between the benefits each worker receives from Social Security and the taxes he or she has paid into the program.

On the first point, Social Security is legally prohibited from paying benefits greater than the levels that can be financed from current and past earmarked taxes, as tracked by a trust-fund accounting mechanism. On the whole, this earmarking arrangement appears to promote fiscal responsibility and spending restraint. Legislation to restrain Social Security benefit growth was enacted in 1983 when earmarked taxes proved insufficient to support scheduled benefits, and the current discussion of Social Security reform is driven by the trustees' projections that earmarked taxes will again fall short around 2036. To maintain fiscal responsibility, therefore, Social Security should continue to be financed by an earmarked tax, rather than being given a blank check on general revenues.

On the second point, each worker's Social Security retirement or disability benefits are based on his or her Average Indexed Monthly Earnings (AIME), which is a measure of the worker's lifetime wages and self-employment earnings. AIME includes only earnings subject to Social Security tax and therefore excludes earnings that exceeded the taxable maximum or were earned in employment not covered by Social Security. A worker with higher AIME receives higher monthly benefits, although the increase is less than proportional; if Smith earns double the wages and pays double the taxes of Jones throughout their lives, Smith receives a higher monthly benefit than Jones, but less than double Jones's benefit. This benefit formula reflects a delicate compromise between competing objectives. Paying higher monthly benefits to those who have paid higher taxes (and awarding no benefits based on untaxed earnings) gives the program a contributory feature by linking benefits received to taxes paid. At the same time, paying benefits that rise less than proportionately with taxable earnings gives workers with lower lifetime earnings a higher rate of return on their tax payments, making the system redistributive. This delicate balance, and the associated tax-benefit linkage, would be upset if Social Security was financed by general revenue from the X tax rather than by the current payroll tax.

In view of these two points, we recommend that the Social Security payroll tax be retained when the X tax is adopted. The second point is largely inapplicable to the Medicare payroll tax, because there is almost no link between Medicare Part A taxes and benefits at the individual level.[7] The first point applies, however, because Medicare Part A spending is also limited to the amount that can be financed by its current and past earmarked tax revenue, as tracked by a trust fund mechanism. Accordingly, we recommend that the Medicare payroll tax also be retained. As we will discuss in chapter 5, we propose folding the self-employment tax into the payroll tax.

Another small payroll tax, legally imposed only on employers, is earmarked to finance the unemployment insurance (UI) program. The program's spending is limited to the revenue raised by this earmarked tax, so we recommend that this tax also be retained, for reasons similar to those discussed above.

As stated in chapter 1, we propose to replace the Unearned Income Medicare Contribution tax, which is slated to take effect in 2013, with the X tax. Despite the name of this tax, all of its revenue is paid into the general treasury, and none of it is earmarked for Medicare. Accordingly, the repeal of this tax has no implications for Medicare financing.

We now turn to broader issues that affect transfer payments.

Public and Private Transfer Payments

The first issue is whether transfer payments should be taxed.

Current Tax Treatment. Most public transfer payments are excluded from taxable income. Long-standing Internal Revenue Service (IRS) rulings stipulate that government social welfare benefits are excluded from taxable income, unless they are specifically *included* by a provision in the tax code. Specific code provisions require the inclusion of UI benefits and a portion of Social Security benefits, but most other public transfer payments are excluded. Exclusion is the rule for all means-tested transfer payments and also for many non-means-tested payments, such as veterans' benefits.

The current income tax system generally disregards private transfer payments, providing no deduction to the payer and imposing no tax on the recipient. This treatment applies to gifts and bequests to individuals and organizations (other than gifts to charities, for which the payer receives a deduction) and to child support payments. The major exception is that alimony payments are taxable to the recipient and deductible to the payer. Due to the difference in tax treatment, litigation sometimes ensues over whether payments between ex-spouses should be classified as child support or as alimony.

X Tax Treatment. Of the potential tax treatments of transfer payments, exclusion is simplest and most compatible with the philosophy of the X tax. Recall from chapter 2 that the X tax is generally imposed on real production activity; unlike the PET, it disregards financial transactions and eschews tracking cash flows to their ultimate recipients. This philosophy suggests that transfer payments should be similarly disregarded.

Accordingly, those public and private transfer payments that are currently excluded should continue to be excluded under the X tax. Exclusion should also be extended to alimony, UI benefits, and Social Security.

The exclusion for alimony received should be accompanied by nondeductibility for alimony paid, which would avert litigation by bringing its treatment into line with that of child support. This policy also frees family courts from the need to consider taxes in setting payment amounts. Current-law treatment (deduction by payer and inclusion by recipient) should continue to apply to payments under existing alimony decrees, however, until and unless a court modifies the alimony amount for any reason.

As discussed in the "Taxation of Gambling" box (pages 66–67), gambling winnings and losses can also be viewed as private transfer payments. In keeping with the above principles, we propose that the X tax ignore those amounts, imposing no tax on winnings and allowing no deduction for losses.

Charitable Contributions. As mentioned above, current law treats charitable contributions to 501(c)(3) organizations more favorably than other private transfer payments, allowing the donor to claim an itemized deduction while imposing no tax on the recipient. The corporate income tax also allows a deduction for charitable contributions. Tax relief for charitable giving has wide support, although controversy sometimes occurs over the appropriate magnitude of such relief. The Congressional Budget Office (2011a) discusses recent proposals to limit the deduction. For the most part, the decision of whether to provide tax relief for charitable contributions and the generosity of any such relief can be resolved separately from the decision of whether to adopt the X tax.

The X tax design may have some impact, though, on the manner in which such relief is provided. A deduction for contributions under the household wage tax would not only be of no value to households too poor to pay tax (who also receive no benefit from the current itemized deduction), but would also be of no value to households with only investment income. Screening out the latter group could significantly diminish the effectiveness of an incentive for charitable giving. It may therefore be best to provide a refundable credit, offering a uniform subsidy to giving by all households. Firms' contributions could be given similar treatment under the business cash flow tax. Batchelder, Goldberg, and Orszag (2006) and Jenn (2008) note that a uniform refundable credit is the best way to subsidize a socially beneficial activity, if the social benefits do not depend on which household performs the activity. Seidman (2011) further argues that tax credits are more transparent and flexibile than deductions.[8]

Social Security. As stated above, we recommend exemption of Social Security benefits, in line with our treatment of other transfer payments. But the tax treatment of these benefits raises distinctive issues that merit separate discussion.

Social Security benefits were originally excluded from taxable income, but a 1983 law required the inclusion of up to 50 percent of benefits, and a 1993 law increased the maximum includable fraction to 85 percent. The includable fraction rises with the recipient's income, with benefits remaining fully excludable for recipients with incomes below $25,000 ($32,000 for couples). Because earning additional income can cause additional benefits to become taxable, the provision increases effective marginal tax rates on some recipients' labor and capital incomes.

The income tax revenue due to the 1983 law is earmarked to the Social Security trust fund, and the incremental revenue from the 1993 law is earmarked to the Medicare Part A trust fund. In 2010, $38 billion of income tax was paid on $702 billion of benefits, with $24 billion going to Social Security and $14 billion to Medicare. Because the income thresholds are not indexed for inflation, a larger portion of benefits is slated to become taxable in upcoming decades.

Excluding Social Security benefits from the X tax base promotes simplicity and reduces effective marginal tax rates. Moreover, the current income-based inclusion regime cannot be easily administered under the X tax in any event, because household wage tax returns do not provide information on any income other than wages.

Repealing the taxation of benefits will reduce the resources available to the Social Security and Medicare Part A trust funds. If this result is considered undesirable, it can be offset through general revenue transfers.[9]

Design and Administration of Means-Tested Transfers. Another issue concerns the administration of means-tested spending programs and tax credits in a world without the income tax. Steuerle (2005a, 239), who offers important insights on this matter, complains with some justice that consumption tax advocates "never deal" with this issue. In the discussion below, we seek to correct this oversight of our fellow consumption tax advocates.

Means tests are employed by many programs, including Medicaid, Temporary Assistance to Needy Families (TANF), food stamps, Supplemental Security Income (SSI) for the elderly and disabled poor, subsidized Medicare Parts B and D premiums, the earned income tax credit, the refundable tax credits for private health insurance slated to take effect in 2014, and housing assistance. These means tests generally rely on a mixture of labor income, capital income, and assets to determine eligibility and benefit amounts. The income information is sometimes obtained, or at least verified, from income tax returns. As Steuerle (2005a) notes, replacement of the income tax therefore poses complications for these means tests. Yin (1995) discusses this issue in the context of a PET.

We recommend changing the means tests for Medicare Part B and Part D premium subsidies to base them on lifetime labor earnings, as measured by AIME. We recommend that the other programs' means tests remain largely unchanged, while recognizing that the loss of capital income information from income tax returns may create some administrative difficulties.

One might expect us to recommend means tests based on recipients' current consumption. Because a means test is effectively a form of taxation, our argument in chapter 1 for why consumption taxes are more neutral than income taxes may suggest that consumption-based means tests are more neutral than income-based or asset-based means tests. Indeed, Hubbard, Skinner, and Zeldes (1995) emphasize the savings disincentives created by asset-based means tests. Moreover, consumption may best measure the recipient's standard of living and need for assistance. But, as Steuerle (2005a) notes, consumption-based means tests are not administratively practical, because household consumption cannot be accurately measured.

Interestingly, consumption-based means tests would not actually be neutral with respect to the saving decision. As we explained in chapter 1, the neutrality of the consumption tax relies on the tax rate remaining constant over time. Means-tested transfer programs apply steep marginal tax rates to households in years in which they receive benefits and zero marginal rates in other years. A consumption-based means test would therefore discourage saving during good times in preparation for possible bad times; the means test would offer no reward for reducing consumption during good times, when the individual is not on the means-tested program, but would penalize the resulting additional consumption during bad times, when the individual is on the program. As Steuerle (2005a) observes, households could receive transfer payments simply by reducing their consumption. As discussed below, however, such savings disincentives are unavoidable in this context. We do not reject consumption-based means tests because of such disincentives; we reject them because they are administratively impractical.

Basing means tests on lifetime labor earnings is another option. This method faces two potential problems, though, and we recommend its use only in contexts in which both problems can be avoided. First, a satisfactory measure of lifetime earnings cannot be obtained for young and middle-aged workers, because their expected future earnings cannot be observed. A means test based on lifetime labor earnings is therefore appropriate only for programs for the elderly or the disabled, who have little or no future labor earnings. Second, we consider it morally and socially unacceptable to deny minimum safety-net benefits to a person with high lifetime labor income who, for whatever reason, failed to save. Of course, our unwillingness to condemn such a person to total destitution precludes the complete removal of saving disincentives from transfer programs. A means test that reduces transfer payments based on lifetime labor earnings is therefore appropriate only if a back-up mechanism guarantees minimum benefits to those individuals with high lifetime earnings who failed to save.

Under these principles, means tests based on lifetime labor earnings can be used in a few contexts. As discussed above, the current Social Security benefit formula provides higher rates of return to workers with lower lifetime earnings, as measured by AIME. SSI, which has a means test based on current income, provides the necessary safety net for high lifetime earners who failed to save.

Also, under current law, higher Medicare Part B and Part D premiums are charged to recipients with high adjusted gross incomes. We recommend linking the premiums to AIME rather than adjusted gross income. Steuerle (1997) proposed this approach to avoid saving disincentives, even with the income tax system in place. Biggs (2011) also notes the advantages of using lifetime earnings rather than the retiree's current income in means tests. With the X tax replacing the income tax, the proposal is even more useful because adjusted gross income, except for wages, is no longer available from household tax returns. Although high lifetime earners who failed to save will pay higher Medicare Part B premiums under this proposal, they will escape destitution by receiving benefits from Medicaid and SSI, which will continue to have means tests based on current income.[10]

Under the X tax, means tests for other programs should remain largely unchanged, continuing to rely on income and assets. Steuerle (2005a) comments that consumption tax proponents seem to implicitly and indirectly propose the continuation of income-based means tests in transfer programs; we now explicitly advance that proposal, subject to the exceptions noted above. The lack of capital income information on household tax returns may make it somewhat more difficult for administrators to check recipients' reported capital income and assets, possibly requiring additional enforcement resources. Although these means tests create saving disincentives, that outcome is unavoidable, given our commitment to protect from destitution those who fail to save. The disincentive should be minor for most households, who have a low probability of receiving means-tested transfers.

Means Tests within the Tax System. As we noted in chapter 3, the X tax can provide either refundable or nonrefundable credits to low-income households, much as the income tax system does today. But the lack of capital income information on household returns will pose administrative challenges for these credits, just as it does for the transfer programs discussed above. Under the current tax system, for example, low-wage workers lose part or all of the earned income tax credit to which they would otherwise be entitled if they have too much capital income, as shown on the tax return itself. If something like the earned income tax credit is maintained under the X tax system, as we recommend, recipients will be required to certify that they do not have large amounts of capital income as a condition of eligibility. We recognize that the IRS will have to rely on outside information to check the accuracy of the certifications.

In addition to low-income credits, the current tax system includes dozens of income phase-out provisions that reduce or eliminate the benefit of credits or deductions as taxpayers' incomes rise, as detailed by Brill and Viard (2008). Most of these provisions are unwarranted within the context of the current tax system, as progressivity is better promoted through the rate schedule rather than by phasing out specific tax breaks. Such phase-outs will be even harder to administer under the X tax, as household tax returns do not provide a complete picture of income. Accordingly, income phase-outs, other than those related to low-income credits, should be removed from the tax system when the X tax is adopted.

Conclusion

The X tax offers essentially the same options as the income tax with respect to the treatment of nonretirement fringe benefits and work expenses. Employer-sponsored retirement plans should be taxed in line with current law, which already adheres to consumption tax principles, although with timing rules that differ from the basic design of the household wage tax in the X tax system. The Social Security and Medicare payroll taxes should be maintained. Public and private transfer payments should be excluded from the household X tax. Most means tests should remain largely unchanged, but those for Medicare premium subsidies should be based on lifetime labor earnings rather than current income.

Box
TAXATION OF GAMBLING

Although it may not be immediately obvious, the taxation of gambling raises similar issues as the taxation of financial transactions and transfer payments. Gamblers as a group enter into wagers with gaming firms, in which they expect, or should expect, to lose money. Their expected losses, which presumably equal their actual losses *in the aggregate,* are payments for the services that they receive from the gaming firms. To tax these services, the X tax requires gaming firms to pay business cash-flow tax on their net winnings, which are the gamblers' aggregate net losses.

But some gamblers lose more than the expected amounts, and others lose less than expected or even win. In effect, all gamblers pay the firms for services, while unlucky gamblers make transfer payments to lucky gamblers. The question is how to treat those implicit transfers; the appropriate answer is to ignore them.

For example, suppose that "the house" has a 10 percent edge on each bet. A large number of gamblers each places $100 bets, and each receives $10 of services from the gaming firm in exchange for his or her expected losses. But in the actual event, half of the gamblers lose $25 apiece, and the other half win $5 apiece. Conceptually, each gambler pays $10 to the firm for services and each losing gambler makes a $15 implicit transfer payment to a winning gambler. Taxing the gaming firm on its winnings yields the correct aggregate tax base, $10 per gambler, and accurately measures the services provided to the gamblers.

It is possible, though, to take the further step of taxing each winner on $15 and allowing each losing gambler a $15 deduction. Note that these amounts are equal to the amount won or loss *plus the $10 expected loss;* this expected-loss adjustment is necessary to prevent gamblers from deducting the cost of the services that they received from the gaming firm. As with financial transactions and explicit transfer payments, this further step does not change the aggregate tax base but merely allows each individual's final consumption to be accurately measured. As with financial transactions and explicit transfers, the X tax should omit this step because this tax system generally eschews attempts to measure each individual's final consumption. Accordingly, we propose that there be no tax on gambling winnings and no deduction for gambling losses.

Although it may seem desirable for the tax system to spread risk by taxing the winners and providing relief to the losers, it is unclear why the tax system should spread risks that gamblers voluntarily undertook or why gamblers would not undo such risk spreading by simply placing larger wagers. In any case, attempting such a task is a fool's errand. The tax system cannot accurately track each individual's winnings and losses, let alone apply the appropriate expected-loss adjustments. The current income tax adopts a complex and compliance-proof approach to gambling; in principle, taxpayers pay tax on each winning wager and deduct losses on losing wagers, with losses claimed only as itemized deductions and with each year's loss deductions limited to that year's winnings. The expected-loss adjustment needed to measure the implicit transfers correctly is not even attempted. In practice, of course, gamblers pay tax only on the large winnings that gaming firms are required to report to the IRS and deduct as many losses, up to the amount of reported winnings, as they can document or fabricate. Pollack (1997) and Raby and Raby (2001) discuss the problems posed by the current income tax treatment of gambling. The X tax offers a better approach.

5

Business Firms

This chapter discusses the taxation of business firms under the X tax. The key issues are the need to distinguish between wages and business cash flow for closely held firms, and the treatment of firms with negative cash flows.

General Issues

Current Tax Treatment of Firms. Under current law, profits earned by C corporations are first taxed under the corporate income tax and then taxed again under the individual income tax when paid out as dividends to shareholders or retained and eventually realized as capital gains when investors sell their stock holdings. The double taxation is currently offset to some extent not only by the deferral of capital gains tax until realization but also by the preferential individual income tax rates for dividends and capital gains, which face a top rate of 15 percent. Without further congressional action, though, starting in 2013, dividends will become taxable as ordinary income, and the top capital gains rate will rise to 20 percent.

The flow-through organizational forms allow firms to avoid the double tax imposed on C corporations. Profits earned by flow-through firms are taxed only once; when profits are earned, they are allocated to individual owners and subjected to individual income tax.

Most business firms operate in flow-through form, as sole proprietorships, general and limited partnerships, or S corporations. Sole proprietorships are unincorporated business entities owned by a single individual. Partnerships are unincorporated business entities owned by two or more entities or individuals. There is no limitation on the size of a partnership or the types of partners. All partners in a general partnership have unlimited liability for the partnership's debts; limited partnerships require a general partner that has unlimited liability, but that partner can itself be an entity, such as a corporation, whose owners have limited liability. S corporations are domestic corporations that meet certain conditions and that elect not to be subject to the corporate income tax. Notably, S corporations may have no more than one hundred shareholders, who generally must be individuals, and may have only one class of stock. A key restriction is that publicly traded firms must be taxed as C corporations and cannot enjoy flow-through status.

Although income, expenses, and tax credits are largely measured in the same way for flow-through firms as for C corporations, flow-through firms are generally not treated as taxable entities. Instead, income, expenses, and credits are flowed through to the firm's owners. An owner's flow-through income is combined with any income from other sources and subjected to individual income taxes. Losses, rather than accumulating at the firm level, are passed through to the owners, who may use them to offset income from other sources, subject to limits imposed by the at-risk and passive-loss rules.

Beginning in the late 1980s, the limited liability corporation (LLC), a business entity formed under state law that is described as noncorporate but shares the limited liability feature of the corporate form, gained considerable traction. Once the IRS determined in 1988 that LLCs would generally be classified as partnerships and taxed as flow-through businesses, many states adopted statutes to allow firms to organize as LLCs, and the use of this organizational form grew rapidly. Beginning in 1997, the IRS simplified the process by allowing LLCs to simply "check the box" on Form 1065-B indicating their election to be treated as a corporation or partnership (or sole proprietorship) for tax purposes. IRS data show that, from 1995 to 2008, the number of LLCs in the United States grew from 119,000 to 1.9 million.

The United States differs from many of its counterparts in the Organisation for Economic Co-operation and Development (OECD) by allowing firms, other than those that are publicly traded, to organize in ways that receive limited liability protection without having to face the corporate income tax. S corporations, limited partnerships, and LLCs offer flow-through tax treatment along with limited liability for some or all of their owners. Of seventeen countries responding to an OECD questionnaire, seven reported having no form of business organization that provides limited liability without an obligation to pay corporate income tax. The business forms available in other countries push firms toward the corporate form in pursuit of limited liability, while such limited liability is attainable in the United States through other organizational forms.

The noncorporate sector is a vital part of the U.S. economy, providing a source of innovation and risk taking, and its importance has grown steadily over the past several decades. IRS data show that the share of businesses choosing the flow-through form (primarily sole proprietorships) rose from 83 percent in 1980 to 94 percent in 2008. The economic activity generated by these businesses has also grown steadily, with the flow-through share of total receipts rising from 13 percent in 1980 to 36 percent by 2008. In 2008, flow-through businesses employed 54 percent of the private sector workforce and paid 44 percent of all business taxes.

The noncorporate sector is markedly larger in the United States than in most other developed nations. Of the fifteen nations reporting in a recent survey conducted by the Organisation for Economic Co-operation and Development, Center for Tax Policy and Administration (2007, tables 1–3), only in Mexico did the unincorporated sector represent a larger share, 88 percent, of the total number of businesses than the 82 percent share observed in the United States. (Although S corporations are taxed as flow-through businesses, they are included with other corporations in these data.) The influence of noncorporate businesses on general economic activity is further magnified in the United States by the fact that such businesses are more heavily represented among large businesses than in other countries. Sixty-six percent of the U.S. businesses reporting profits of $1 million or more were not incorporated, compared to 27 percent in Mexico, 26 percent in the United Kingdom, and 17 percent in New Zealand.

Although the current tax system has the favorable effect of allowing many firms to escape double taxation, it has complex tax rules that apply separately to three different kinds of business entities—C corporations, S corporations, and partnerships. Moreover, all these firms still face one level of tax on their marginal investments, and some firms, particularly those that are publicly traded firms, face double taxation.

Fortunately, the X tax allows all firms to escape tax on their marginal investments, without the need to distinguish between the different organizational forms.

X Tax Treatment of Firms. The basic structure of the X tax does not require, or envision, a flow-through sector at all. Rather, under the X tax, all firms' business cash flows are taxed at a flat rate at the entity level. Because it is imposed at the firm level, the business cash-flow tax is administratively similar to the corporate income tax imposed on C corporations today. There is a key economic difference, though, because the business cash-flow tax allows firms to immediately deduct, or expense, their investments, rather than depreciating them over time. As we explained in chapter 2, the use of expensing causes the business cash-flow tax to impose a zero effective marginal tax rate on new investment. Another difference is that the business cash-flow tax ignores financial transactions, including interest payments.

The current tax system includes numerous provisions that are often viewed as preferences for particular industries and types of investment. Although these provisions are often criticized, it is hard to condemn all of them unreservedly within the context of the current income tax system. In general, these provisions are intended to reduce the effective marginal tax rate on the targeted investments toward zero. For the reasons discussed in chapter 1, we believe that zero is the desirable level of the effective marginal tax rate on all investments.

Of course, some of these current-law provisions can be criticized for lowering effective tax rates in a selective manner that artificially favors some investments over others and for adding complexity. As Viard (2009c) notes, however, efforts to curtail these provisions and to broaden the corporate tax base are not always beneficial. Some widely criticized provisions actually narrow the disparity in effective tax rates and thereby promote neutrality because they provide relief to investments that would otherwise be taxed particularly heavily. Moreover, curtailment of these provisions sometimes increases, rather than reduces, complexity. Also, because economic rates of depreciation cannot be measured precisely, it is sometimes hard to know the true impact of these provisions on effective marginal tax rates.

Fortunately, the X tax sweeps away all of these concerns. Because the X tax lowers the effective marginal tax rate on all new investment to zero, no special provisions are necessary except subsidies for investments that have spillover benefits to society, as may be true for some forms of research spending.

The current tax system includes firm-level provisions that reduce the tax burden on certain forms of labor income, such as the work opportunity credit and the Indian employment credit, and provisions that increase the tax burden on other forms of labor income, such as restrictions on the deductibility of corporate executives' salaries. These provisions can be either maintained or eliminated, as desired, under the X tax, because they do not affect the tax burden on investment.

Ironically, the move to the X tax may appear to increase the tax burden on flow-through firms, because their business cash flow is taxed at a high flat rate rather than under the graduated rate schedule of the individual income tax. Again, though, expensing ensures that the marginal effective tax rate on new investment is zero under the X tax. Because any increase in taxes applies only to above-normal returns, only firms with large above-normal returns are likely to systematically pay more under the X tax than under the current income tax.

The treatment of business firms under the X tax does raise two serious issues, which we discuss below.

Distinguishing Wages from Business Cash Flow

Because owners of small businesses often contribute both labor and capital to their enterprises, it can be difficult to distinguish the return to labor from the return to capital. To appreciate the issues involved, we first describe how the current income tax handles this issue and then consider how it would be treated under the X tax.

Current Tax Treatment. Under the current income tax, owners of flow-through firms pay tax at the individual rates on the firm's net income. The distinction between labor and capital generally does not matter for income tax purposes because the owners are taxed at individual rates on both types of income. For partnerships, the tax neutrality carries over to the payroll and self-employment taxes as well, which apply to both types of income for general partners. However, S corporation shareholders who work for the firm are subject to payroll tax on their labor income but not on their capital income, creating an incentive to understate wages. To prevent the avoidance of payroll taxes, IRS rules require that owners of S corporations pay themselves a reasonable level of wages.[11] Opposite incentives generally arise for C corporations. As noted above, the capital income generated by such firms is subject to double income taxation. In contrast, wages are taxed only once under the income tax, although they are also subject to payroll tax. In C corporations, the incentive is to overpay compensation to avoid the corporate income tax. Bull and Burnham (2008) discuss the impact of the current tax rules on different types of firms.

Another problem posed by the current system is that the self-employment tax applies to the full income of sole proprietors and general partners, including the income generated by their capital investments. Accordingly, the self-employment tax imposes a penalty on saving.

X Tax Treatment. Under the X tax, the firm is subject to an entity-level tax on its business cash flow, with a deduction for wage payments. Households are not taxed on dividends or capital gains, and wages are taxed at graduated rates with a top bracket assumed to be equal to 35 percent. When combined with the 3.8 percent Medicare payroll tax, this rate equals our assumed 38.8 percent flat tax rate on business cash flow.

A key feature of the X tax is that the highest-wage earners should face the same marginal tax rate on their wages as firms face on business cash flow. This equality of tax rates offers significant simplification by eliminating the need to worry about the correct division between business cash flow and wages for high-bracket owners. For example, there would be no need to worry about the correct treatment of the carried interest received by fund managers, all of whom would surely be in the top bracket. In general, high-bracket individuals are likely to receive a large portion of total business cash flow; Urban-Brookings Tax Policy Center (2010) projected that 44 percent of flow-through business income would go to individuals in the top two income tax brackets in 2011.

Although we need not worry about the distinction between wages and business cash flows for workers in the highest bracket, things are more difficult elsewhere. Owners in lower household tax brackets may have an incentive to report wages, which are taxed at the owner's household tax bracket, rather than business cash flow, which is taxed at the 38.8 percent flat rate. The incentive is mitigated, but generally not eliminated, by the fact that wages, unlike business cash flow, are subject to Social Security and Medicare payroll taxes.

To address this problem, we recommend that all firms other than sole proprietorships be required to pay owners actively engaged in the operation of a business a reasonable level of compensation, similar to the rules that currently apply to S corporations. Payroll tax would apply only to that compensation; there would be no separate self-employment tax. The distinction between C corporations, S corporations, and partnerships would be abolished under both the X tax and the payroll tax.

As a simplification measure, we recommend that sole proprietors be given an election to treat an unlimited amount of their cash flows as wages. As with other owners, the amount treated as wages would be subject to the household wage tax and payroll taxes, and any amount not treated as wages would be subject to the 38.8 percent cash-flow tax.

International experience suggests that enforcing a distinction between labor and capital can be challenging. As Sorensen (2009) explains, several Nordic countries have dual income tax systems that tax labor income at progressive rates and subject capital income to a lower flat tax rate, usually set at the lowest tax bracket applicable to labor income. (In contrast, the X tax sets the cash-flow tax rate equal to the *highest* labor-income bracket.) To prevent understatement of capital income, these countries generally impute a return to capital and then treat the difference between the total return and the imputed return to capital as labor income. Complex income-splitting rules are required under these systems. There has been some evidence of significant behavioral responses to take advantage of the resulting asymmetries in tax treatment; for example, Sorensen (2009) cites a large reduction in the number of corporations subject to income splitting as owners changed their status from active to passive.

We therefore recognize that there may be some difficulties in applying the above rules. Under the X tax, though, the net incentives to misstate wages are smaller than under the Nordic systems; indeed, such incentives are nonexistent for owners in the top household tax bracket. Enforcement efforts should also be aided by the simplicity resulting from having a single set of rules for all firms with more than one owner.

Firms with Negative Business Cash Flows

Another issue confronting the X tax concerns the treatment of firms with negative business cash flows. Negative business cash flows arise whenever a firm's investment exceeds the net receipts generated by its existing investments. One option, at least in theory, is to treat positive and negative business cash flows symmetrically, which can be achieved with full refundability or some other, equally generous, treatment. Full refundability requires that if a firm must make a tax payment to the government equal to 38.8 percent of any positive business cash flows, then the firm receives a payment from the government equal to 38.8 percent of any negative business cash flows. As explained below, however, this may not be the best policy.

To explore this issue, we begin by looking at how the income tax handles similar problems.

Losses under the Income Tax. Income tax principles suggest that income and losses be treated symmetrically, with full refundability for losses, because such treatment is neutral with respect to the riskiness of investments. Limiting tax relief for losses increases the cost of capital for risky investments, because the government shares in the gains from profitable investments to a greater extent than it shares in the losses from failed investments.

Despite the preceding analysis, actual income tax systems offer tax relief for losses that is considerably more limited than full refundability. The limitations are intended to help prevent abuse by deterring taxpayers from overstating losses, either by committing fraud or by exploiting tax shelters or rules that allow artificial losses to be reported for tax purposes. With full refundability, there would be no upper bound on the savings that could be obtained by claiming spurious losses. Although the case for symmetric treatment outlined above is compelling for genuine losses, the picture changes when spurious losses are possible. Of course, it is best to directly identify and disallow spurious losses. Because that can be difficult, though, a useful backup is to simply limit the amount of tax savings that can be derived from reported losses.

Another source of political opposition to full refundability is the perception that direct cash payments to firms with losses constitute unwarranted "corporate welfare." This objection was forcefully raised in 1981 against the practice of safe-harbor leasing, which effectively enabled firms to sell their loss deductions to other firms. For genuine losses, the corporate-welfare objection is unfounded; as discussed above, making payments to a firm with a risky investment that failed is required for neutrality, given that the firm would have been taxed had the investment succeeded. Of course, refund payments based on spurious losses are indeed unwarranted corporate welfare.

The most common income tax treatment of losses is a combination of carryback and carryforward. Carryback allows losses to be carried back to offset previous years' income and most closely resembles refundability. Under carryback, taxpayers recompute their tax liability for previous years by claiming a deduction against the past income for the current year's loss and then receive a refund based on the lower computed liability. Most developed countries allow carryback of losses for several years or less; the United States generally allows only two years of carryback. Under U.S. rules, then, a taxpayer with current losses may receive an immediate cash payment from the government, but never greater than the taxes paid on income in the two preceding years.

Two-year carryback replicates the effects of full refundability for taxpayers with occasional minor losses, but falls short of refundability for taxpayers with large losses or those with three or more consecutive years of losses. Denying relief to taxpayers with repeated losses presumably helps screen out those with spurious losses, as genuine losses resulting from bad luck are likely to be transitory. Moreover, cash payments resulting from carryback may escape the corporate welfare stigma because they are viewed as refunds of the taxpayer's recent tax payments rather than as outright grants from the federal treasury.

Carryforward, sometimes called carryover, allows taxpayers to deduct current losses against income reported on future tax returns and thereby reduce future tax liability. Carryforward does not provide a taxpayer with full relief for losses, because no interest is paid on the amounts carried forward, causing the future tax savings to have a lower present discounted value than current tax relief would have had. U.S. taxpayers are currently allowed to carry losses forward for twenty years.

For C corporations, these limits on loss deductibility are applied at the firm level. As a result, the losses of one C corporation generally cannot be offset against income generated by another C corporation, but must instead be carried back or forward to offset the corporation's own income in the two preceding years or twenty upcoming years, in accord with the rules discussed above. The exception is that a group of C corporations that are under at least 80 percent common ownership may generally file a consolidated tax return, which allows the losses of one group member to be offset against the contemporaneous incomes of other group members.

The treatment of flow-through businesses is more generous in this regard because the loss limits are applied at the owner level, rather than at the firm level. A flow-through business's loss is flowed through to its owners without restriction. Each owner may then offset his share of the loss against any income he may have from other flow-through firms or against any wage income. If a net loss remains after this netting is done, the owner must carry the net loss back or forward to offset the owner's income in the two preceding or twenty upcoming years. In contrast to the rule for C corporations, therefore, a loss from one flow-through firm can be offset (by each owner) against income from other flow-through firms.

For industries with diffuse ownership structures, this ability to offset losses is particularly important. For example, commercial real estate is predominantly held by flow-through businesses, allowing ownership of a single building to be spread over dozens or more business entities. An individual may own a small stake in many different buildings, facilitating diversification across location and type of holding. Some of the individual's investments might produce income while others produce losses, which are netted against each other on an investor's individual tax return. Businesses can also benefit from this feature. Two firms can enter a joint venture by forming a partnership, and any losses from the joint venture then flow through to the two parent firms, each of which can net them against its other income.

Congress often lengthens the carryback period during economic downturns. In 2002 and again in 2009, for example, Congress lengthened the period to five years. Two factors made it appropriate to loosen the restrictions during these periods. First, during hard economic times, firms are more likely to have large genuine losses, for which relief should be provided. Second, during each of these episodes, at or shortly before its enactment of the longer carryback period, Congress also enacted a stimulus provision allowing part of equipment investment to be expensed. Firms were likely to have large tax losses due to their use of this stimulus provision, and Congress wished to provide relief for such losses to make the stimulus effective. In short, losses reported during these episodes were less likely to be spurious and more likely to be losses that Congress wished to recognize, either real economic losses from the downturn or losses arising from firms' intended use of a stimulus provision.

On a related note, Congress has provided longer carryback periods for selected categories of losses. For example, certain product liability losses can be carried back ten years, and certain farming losses can be carried back five years. In these contexts, too, Congress has reasonably concluded that large losses are more likely to be genuine, reflecting the possibility of large product liability claims and the riskiness of farming, and to therefore merit relief.

Negative Business Cash Flows under the X Tax. X tax principles similarly call for symmetrical treatment of positive and negative business cash flows. Indeed, the issue is even more important than under the income tax. As we explained above and in chapter 2, expensing yields a zero effective marginal tax rate because the tax savings from deducting the initial investment cost are equal, in present value, to the taxes on the marginal investment's future payoffs. If a firm cannot receive full tax savings for the investment costs due to limitations on refundability, but expects to be taxable when the future payoffs are received, this present-value equality is destroyed, and the effective tax rate on the investment becomes positive.

As in the income tax context, the case for symmetrical treatment applies only to genuine negative business cash flows. If firms can spuriously report negative business cash flows, that case is weakened. Even so, the case for symmetrical treatment is stronger in the X tax context than in the income tax context. Because business cash flow is much easier to measure than income, spurious negative values should be less common under the X tax than under an income tax, although they can arise if firms fail to report sales receipts, deduct personal expenses, or fabricate costs, or if the firm's "business" is actually an owner's hobby rather a genuine effort to make money. Conversely, genuine negative business cash flows are likely to be more common under the X tax than genuine losses are under an income tax. Whereas a firm has negative income only if it makes risky investments that fail, a firm can have negative business cash flow simply because its new investments are larger than the payoff from its existing investments. That condition may hold true for many years during a firm's growth phase. Accordingly, limitations on refundability are more likely to impede genuine deductions under the X tax than under the income tax.[12]

Given the importance of providing relief for negative business cash flows, it is unfortunate that one of the X tax's design features makes such relief harder to provide. As we noted above, the basic X tax design does not feature a flow-through sector; all firms are taxed at the entity level, as C corporations are now taxed. Accordingly, one firm's negative business cash flows cannot be offset against other firms' positive business cash flows, except when the firms are allowed to file consolidated tax returns. For example, in the joint venture discussed above, any negative business cash flows would be trapped within the joint venture because they would no longer be flowed through to the parent firms.

To be sure, large businesses might be able to combine activities with positive and negative business cash flows through mergers and acquisitions. But such self-help solutions would often be more difficult or less desirable for smaller businesses. Also, tax-driven merger and acquisition activity is itself distortionary and unproductive.

We propose two modest steps to allow a small amount of netting. First, firms, whether corporate or noncorporate, should be allowed to file consolidated returns, and the threshold for such filing should be lowered to require only greater-than-50-percent common ownership. Second, as discussed above, sole proprietors should be allowed to report their business cash flows on their household tax returns, where negative business cash flows can be netted against wages.

Broader steps to permit netting across firms do not appear to be practical within the X tax framework. One potential remedy would allow individuals to choose to file a separate schedule with their individual tax return, on which their business cash flows would be reported and subjected to a flat 38.8 percent rate rather than collecting the 38.8 percent tax at the entity level. This would allow owners to mix and net positive and negative business cash flows across their various business entities. Unfortunately, there would be no easy way to coordinate which business cash flows would be taxed at the firm level and which would be taxed at the owner level.

Given the difficulty of allowing negative business cash flows to be netted against positive business cash flows at the owner level, it is necessary to ensure that firms with negative business cash flows can receive adequate tax relief at the entity level. We do not reject out of hand the straightforward option of full refundability, accompanied by stringent enforcement against spurious claims. Nevertheless, we are reluctant to recommend this untested experiment, particularly given the political obstacles. We instead recommend a system that is almost as generous as full refundability for most firms.

To begin, we propose a carryback period of five to ten years. As discussed above, under the income tax system, Congress has provided carryback periods of this length in situations in which losses are more likely to be genuine, such as economic downturns and farming and product liability losses. For many firms, a carryback period of this length will replicate the effects of refundability. To provide appropriate incentives in the early years of the new tax system, we propose that firms be allowed to carry losses back to pre-reform years and offset them against their past income tax liabilities.

As we explained above, carryforward fails to provide full relief under the current tax system because interest is not paid on the amounts carried forward. We therefore recommend unlimited carryfoward with interest as suggested by the Growth and Investment Tax Plan recommended by President's Advisory Panel on Federal Tax Reform (2005, 162) and Hall and Rabushka (1995, 144–45). This treatment would be largely equivalent to refundability, because the future tax savings would have the same present value as current tax savings. To be sure, this treatment would fall short of refundability for those firms that go out of business and forfeit their unclaimed deductions or those that have consistent negative business cash flows. To mitigate this problem, we recommend repeal of the section 382 limits on the use of carryforwards after an ownership change. For simplicity, interest could be computed using the rate on short-term Treasury debt.[13]

Conclusion

We recommend that firm-level taxation under the X tax be combined with a requirement that firms pay reasonable wages to owners who work for the firm. These wages would be deducted by firms under the cash-flow tax and would be subjected to the household wage tax and the payroll tax. The self-employment tax would be abolished, as the labor earnings of business owners would be taxed under the payroll tax. A unified set of rules would apply across the X tax and the payroll tax system and would apply to all kinds of firms, except that sole proprietors would be allowed the benefits of some simplification provisions. To avoid the positive effective tax rates on investment that would result if negative cash flows cannot be deducted, we recommend at least a five-year carryback period and an unlimited carryforward period with interest.

6

Financial Services

Although the treatment of financial institutions and services is often said to pose a difficult issue for consumption taxes, that statement is misleading. As discussed below, this issue poses challenges for both income and consumption taxes. The problems are more visible, but no more severe, under consumption taxation.

The financial sector is a significant part of the economy. The national income and product accounts data reported by Harris et al. (2011) show that the finance and insurance industry had value added of $1,172 billion, or 8.3 percent of gross domestic product (GDP), in 2009. Of this amount, $568 billion was employee compensation, $45 billion was taxes net of subsidies, and $558 billion was gross operating surplus (business cash flow). The industry had 5.8 million employees, 4.2 percent of employment for all industries. The sector includes a diverse set of institutions. Of the total 2009 value added, $514 billion was in "Federal Reserve Banks, credit intermediation, and related activities," $175 billion was in "securities, commodity contracts, and investments," $424 billion was in "insurance carriers and related activities," and $58 billion was in "funds, trusts, and other financial vehicles."

Neutral Tax Treatment

There is little dispute about the treatment of financial services that are provided to firms for use in the production of real output. Any tax imposed on such services should be offset by a deduction for the purchasing firm. So long as such purchases contribute (on the margin) to the production of real business output, the tax imposed on that output is sufficient; the imposition of a second tax would give rise to inefficient production. A tax deduction for business purchases of financial services has the same economic justification as a tax deduction for business purchases of office supplies, machinery, or raw materials.

This justification vanishes for consumer purchases of financial services. Just as consumer purchases of consumer goods are not exempted, neither should consumer purchases of financial services.[14]

It is easy to see this in a simple example. Consider an economy in which Smith produces ten apples today, and Jones produces ten apples tomorrow. Because both workers wish to eat some apples today and some tomorrow, it is beneficial for Jones to borrow some apples produced by Smith today and to repay Smith from the apples that he will produce tomorrow. Suppose, though, that the two cannot make this transaction happen unless a third person, Thompson, puts in an hour of labor to make the arrangements. A sales tax, VAT, or X tax must separately include the financial services in the tax base. The tax on the apple production taxes Smith's and Jones's work, but not Thompson's work.

The X tax must therefore distinguish between personal and business use of financial services, just as it must distinguish between personal and business use of cars, computers, and meals. But it is worth mentioning what personal and business use means. The relevant question is whether the financial service pays for itself on the margin in terms of additional real business output on which the X tax is imposed. This may not always be the same question as whether the services are provided to households or to firms. If financial services purchased by a firm facilitate its transactions with its owners without affecting the production of real output, then the services are personal in nature. If financial services purchased by a household lead to improved resource allocation that increases real output, then the services are business in nature. For administrative reasons, though, the dividing line will probably have to be drawn on the basis of whether the purchaser is a household or a firm.

The Problem of Mislabeled Transactions

The tax challenge posed by financial intermediation is the need to look behind the labeling of transactions to determine whether they are actually real or financial in nature.

Different Ways to Charge for Financial Services. Financial transactions would pose no special problem, for either income or consumption taxes, if financial institutions charged explicit fees for all of their services. In that case, the costs of financial services would be readily identifiable, allowing them to be taxed in the same manner as other services, with the only challenge being the need to distinguish between business and personal services. In practice, however, financial institutions often recover the costs of providing services by paying below-market, or charging above-market, interest rates rather than by charging explicit fees. This arrangement makes it difficult to identify the costs of financial services and properly tax them, because the costs look like variations in interest income or expense, which warrant different tax treatment.

Suppose that a 5 percent interest rate is offered on safe assets that provide no financial services, such as Treasury bills. A checking account depositor with a $1,000 balance will not receive a $50 net annual return, even though she would have done so if she had held Treasury bills. The reason is that the depositor receives, and must pay for, costly services provided by the bank, such as check processing and record keeping. If the services cost $30 per year, the bank must charge the depositor these costs in some form, allowing her to clear only $20 per year on the account. The question is the form in which the charge is made.

The bank could pay a 5 percent interest rate on the account but then charge a $30 explicit fee. Alternatively, the bank could pay a 2 percent interest rate and charge no explicit fee. Or the bank could use a mixture of the two approaches, such as a 3 percent interest rate and a $10 explicit fee. In a no-tax world, the choice between these methods might turn on a variety of considerations. Economic efficiency might be promoted by charging fees closely tied to marginal costs; for example, it may be efficient for check-processing costs to be recovered through a fee based on the number of checks written, rather than through an interest income reduction linked to the account balance. On the other hand, administrative savings might be achieved by simply reducing the interest rate rather than administering a whole set of fees.

A similar process occurs on the other side of the ledger. Suppose the bank lends the $1,000 to a borrower. For the time being, assume that there is no default risk on the loan. If the bank performs $10 of services for the

TABLE 6-1

TAXATION OF BANK TRANSACTION UNDER ALTERNATIVE TAX SYSTEMS

	Correct Income Tax	Naïve Income Tax	*Correct VAT*	Naïve VAT	*Correct X Tax*	Naïve X Tax
Bank workers	*20*	20	*0*	0	*20*	20
Supply workers	*20*	20	*0*	0	*20*	20
Bank	*0*	0	*20*	−20	*0*	−40
Supply firm	*0*	0	*20*	20	*0*	0
Saver	*50*	20	*0*	0	*0*	0
Borrower	*−50*	−60	*0*	0	*0*	0
Total	***40***	**0**	***40***	**0**	***40***	**0**

SOURCE: Example constructed by authors.

borrower, there is again a choice of ways to charge for these services, including the option of charging a 5 percent interest rate and a $10 fee and the option of charging a 6 percent interest rate and no fee.

In a world with income or consumption taxes, proper tax policy requires that true interest income and expense be treated differently from the costs of check processing and record keeping. In this example, the true interest rate on both the deposit and the loan is 5 percent, regardless of what "interest rate" the bank may quote, because 5 percent is the compensation for the use of money. Similarly, the true costs of the financial services are $30 for the depositor and $10 for the borrower, regardless of the fees that the bank charges.

Assume that the bank's $40 costs of providing services to the depositor and borrower consist of $20 wage payments to bank workers and the purchase of $20 of supplies from another firm. Also assume that the supply firm pays its $20 of receipts to its workers in wages. For simplicity, the bank and the supply firm are assumed to use no capital and to have no business cash flow.

The treatment of this transaction under a conceptually correct income tax, VAT, and X tax is shown (in italics) in the first, third, and fifth columns of table 6-1, under the assumption that the depositor and the borrower are both households rather than firms. In each case, the $40 of financial services is taxed, and there is no net tax on the borrower's payment of true interest to the depositor.

Under a conceptually correct income tax, savers are taxed on interest income, and borrowers deduct interest expense, so taxable income is $50 for the depositor and negative $50 for the borrower. The workers are taxed on their wages. The firms have no tax liability because their sales receipts are offset by wage payments to their workers.

Under a VAT, the true interest income and true interest expense are disregarded because the VAT is a real-based tax system. The bank and the supply firm are taxed on their value added. The X tax is similar to the VAT, except that the wage component of each firm's value added, which is the only component in this example, is taxed to the workers.

All three tax systems readily achieve the correct treatment if the bank applies the 5 percent market interest rate to both the checking account and the loan and charges explicit fees for its services.

Taxing Mislabeled Transactions. But what happens if the bank charges no explicit fees, instead paying a 2 percent interest rate to the depositor and charging the borrower 6 percent? If the tax system naïvely accepts the bank's labeling of the transaction, incorrect taxation occurs, as shown in the second, fourth, and sixth columns of the table.

Under the naïve income tax, the bank and supply workers continue to be taxed on their wages, and the supply firm continues to have no net tax liability. The same is true for the bank; it reports $60 interest income and deducts $20 interest expense, $20 wage costs, and $20 supply purchases. The depositor reports $20 interest income, while the borrower reports negative $60 interest income. The combined tax base is now zero; the financial services have vanished from the tax base. The problem is that the financial services have been disguised as a reduction in interest income and an increase in interest expense, each of which lowers taxable income.

The naïve VAT encounters fundamentally similar problems. As under the correct VAT, there is no tax on workers or on the depositor and the borrower. The supply firm's treatment is also the same as under the correct VAT, as it reports $20 value added from its sale of supplies to the bank. The bank, though, has a value added of negative $20, reflecting the fact that it spent $20 on supplies while appearing to earn nothing from its real business activity. (We assume, for the moment, that the bank can obtain refunds for its negative tax base.) The naïve VAT ignores the bank's $40 net margin on deposits and lending because this spread looks like net interest income. Once again, the net tax base is zero and the $40 of financial services escape tax, thanks to their interest disguise.

The naïve X tax is identical to the naïve VAT, except for the treatment of wages. The tax on the supply firm's activity is imposed on its workers rather than on the firm. The bank's tax base moves even further into negative territory, to negative $40, as it deducts its $20 wage payment on which its workers are taxed. The net tax base is still zero, and the financial services still escape tax.

Comparison of the Taxes. There is no net tax on the financial services under any of the naïve taxes because none of them recognizes that some of the "interest" flows are actually real transactions in disguise. Under the income tax, the flows are excluded from the tax base through offsetting interest income tax and interest expense deduction; under the VAT and X tax, the flows are simply ignored. To be sure, these tax systems yield the correct outcome if both the depositor and the borrower are businesses, as there should then be no net tax.

The fact that the same fundamental outcome occurs under each of the three tax systems demonstrates that the problem of improper taxation of financial services is not unique to the X tax or to consumption taxes. As Bradford (1996a) notes, the only difference is that the problem is more visible under the VAT, where it is reflected in the bank's negative tax base, than it is under the income tax, where it is reflected in incorrect measures of the depositor's interest income and the borrower's interest expense. As shown in the table, the problem is even more visible under the X tax than under the VAT, because the wage deduction makes the bank's tax base even more negative.[15]

This problem of improper taxation of financial services is not confined to banks, as many other financial institutions also provide services for which explicit fees are not charged. For example, insurance companies often cover the costs of such services by charging premiums in excess of benefit payments, and brokers often recover the costs of their services from the bid-ask spread. As we discuss below, any solution to the problem must apply to a wide range of financial institutions.

The Search for a Solution

A number of solutions have been proposed, some of which are more promising than others.

Criteria. Any solution to the problem should have the following properties:

- Consumer financial services, as defined above, should be inside the tax base, and business financial services, as defined above, should be outside the tax base.

- A unified tax system should apply to all *financial* institutions, avoiding the need to draw lines between them.

- *Nonfinancial* firms should not be subject to a counterintuitive or profoundly unfamiliar tax system.

- The correct tax, *in present value*, should be collected on both safe and risky transactions.

- There should be no arbitrary transition effects.

As highlighted by the italicized terms in the above bullet points, we omit three potential criteria from our list. First, we do not insist on a unified tax system for financial institutions and other firms; that goal cannot be achieved because the economics of the problem require distinctive treatment of financial institutions.

Second, we allow financial institutions to be subject to an unfamiliar or counterintuitive tax system, an outcome that occurs under the method we ultimately propose. As explained below, we view that as an acceptable price for satisfying the other criteria. But we shield ordinary nonfinancial firms from such problems.

Third, we do not require that the tax imposed on risky transactions always equal the value of the financial services, ex post. By merely demanding equality in present value, which is sufficient to provide the correct incentives, we gain enormous flexibility, as discussed below.

We now discuss two proposed solutions that we have opted not to embrace. We can quickly dismiss one approach, which simply exempts banks and other financial institutions from tax. At first glance, that method may seem appealing. In table 6-1, setting the bank's tax liability to zero moves halfway to the correct outcome under the VAT and actually yields the correct outcome under the X tax. (In both cases, exemption is a tax increase, as the bank's tax liability would otherwise be negative.) Moreover, the method spares the bank from complicated tax computations, indeed from any tax computations at all. But this approach fails to distinguish between the provision of financial services to households and the provision of such services to firms, as it would bring both sets of services into the tax base. That outcome would be improper when the services are provided to firms, given that there would be no easy way to provide the firms with an offsetting deduction under this method.[16]

The other method that we have rejected requires much more elaborate discussion.

Basic Interest-Spread Method. The interest-spread method can be used under an income tax, X tax (or flat tax), or VAT (or retail sales tax). Hall and Rabushka (1995, 73–75) and the FairTax plan embrace this method. As explained below, the national income accounts also use the spread method to measure the aggregate provision of financial services.

As we will see, the method has some appeal, along with some limitations. When it can be implemented successfully, the method directly solves the problem by correcting the mislabeling of the costs of financial services.

The method imputes an interest rate on each financial transaction and uses it to distinguish true interest income and expense from the cost of financial services. In the above example, the conceptually correct 5 percent interest rate is imputed to both the checking account and the loan, deeming the borrower to pay, and the depositor to receive, $50 of true interest. The spread method recognizes the difference between the stated interest and the imputed true interest as the cost of providing financial services and taxes it as such. The bank is deemed to charge the depositor $30 and the borrower $10 for financial services and is required to treat these amounts as receipts from the sale of real services, even though it has labeled them as interest.

Adjusting the Spread Method for Risk. Unfortunately, this method has great difficulty specifying the proper interest rate whenever risk is present.

In the above example, the checking account can be treated as riskless, because the bank has a definite obligation to furnish the depositor the account balance on demand, and it is virtually certain that the bank (or a deposit insurer) will fulfill this obligation. In our description above, we also treated the loan as riskless by assuming that it was fixed-rate and that default could not occur. In practice, however, the loan would surely be risky. If it is an adjustable-rate loan or if there is a prepayment option, the amount and timing of the borrower's repayment are uncertain. Of course, there is also the risk that the borrower will default. It would be particularly misguided to overlook default risk in the wake of the 2008 financial crisis. Surprisingly, however, much of the literature on the spread method does ignore default risk.

A simple example suffices to illustrate the challenges facing the spread method; the challenges become more severe in more complicated examples. Suppose that the loan lasts one year, that the probability that the borrower will completely default by making no payments is one in twenty-one (and the probability that the borrower pays in full is twenty in twenty-one), and that the bank and borrower are risk neutral. Then, the interest rate on the loan, in the absence of any financial services, would be 10.25 percent, rather than the safe rate of 5 percent, to account for the default risk. (The twenty in twenty-one probability of receiving an extra 5.25 percent above the safe rate compensates for the one in twenty-one probability of losing everything, which is 105 percent worse than receiving the safe rate.) If we continue to assume that the borrower receives $10 of financial services and that the bank does not charge any explicit fees, the interest rate on the $1,000 loan is 11.3 percent. Note that the interest rate must be increased by 1.05, rather than 1, percentage points to cover the cost of the financial services, because there is one chance in twenty-one that the interest will not be received.

What happens if the spread method ignores default risk and treats the 5 percent safe interest rate as the true interest rate applicable to this loan? Then, the bank is taxed as if it had supplied $63 of financial services to the borrower, when it actually provided only $10. The entire 6.3-percentage-point excess of the loan's interest rate above the safe rate is treated as covering the cost of providing services, when 5.25 percentage points actually compensate for default risk. To work, the spread method must be modified to account for risk.

In principle, an ex ante adjustment could be made by replacing the safe interest rate with the interest rate that would apply to a loan *with the same default risk* that was not accompanied by any financial services. In this example, the spread method would use the 10.25 percent risk-adjusted interest rate instead of the 5 percent safe rate and would tax only the excess above that rate, correctly measuring the financial services.

Although such an approach is theoretically possible,[17] it is not practical because risk cannot be accurately measured, as Bradford (1996a, 447) emphasizes. The probability of default is difficult to determine; moreover, if the bank and the borrower are risk averse, a further adjustment must be made to determine the appropriate interest rate.

As Fixler, Reinsdorf, and Smith (2003) explain, the U.S. national income accounts employ the spread method, using a safe interest rate linked to the average rates banks earn on Treasury and federal agency securities. They allude to the possibility of using a risk-adjusted rate as the reference rate, but note that the use of a safe rate accords with international practice, as set forth in the System of National Accounts. If the national income accounts have not yet identified a risk-adjusted rate to apply, purely for statistical purposes, to the financial sector as a whole, it is unlikely that a tax system can identify risk-adjusted rates for each of the millions of financial transactions in the economy, particularly rates sufficiently reliable to use in tax computation.

A more workable version of the spread method adjusts for risk, ex post. This version still uses the safe interest rate, but in a different way. The bank is not taxed on the difference between the stated interest rate and the safe rate, but instead on the difference between the actual payments it receives and those it would have received if it had earned the safe rate. In this example, if the borrower repays the loan with its 11.3 percent interest rate, which has a twenty in twenty-one probability of occurring, the bank is taxed on $63 because it has earned a surplus of that amount over the safe rate. So far, this is the same as the basic spread method, with no risk adjustment. But if the borrower defaults, which has a one in twenty-one probability of occurring, the bank is taxed on negative $1,050 because it receives nothing, which is $1,050 less than it would have received if it had earned a 5 percent return on the $1,000 loan.

At first glance, this ex post spread method appears to completely fail at measuring the financial services provided to the borrower. The borrower receives $10 of services in all cases, yet the method never taxes the bank on $10. There is a twenty in twenty-one probability that the bank will be taxed on $63, which is much higher than the value of the services actually provided, and a one in twenty-one probability that it will be taxed on negative $1,050, which is utterly removed from the correct value.

In reality, though, the method does work because the expected present value of the taxable amount equals the value of the financial services. (Note that $[20/21]*[63] + [1/21]*[-1,050] = 10$.) The method adjusts for the risk of default, not in advance but rather by making an allowance for it if and when default occurs. This has the tremendous advantage that the tax system need not know anything about the probability of default, as it would have had to do in order to make the ex ante adjustment rejected above. Because the ex post method makes the adjustment if and when default occurs, the probability of the adjustment automatically equals the probability of default, whatever that may be.

Although we have assumed risk neutrality in the above discussion, the ex post spread method also works under risk aversion. With risk aversion, the compensation that the bank demands for default depends not only on the probability of default but also on how averse the bank's stockholders are to the potential losses. For example, if the outcome in which default occurs is one in which stockholders are already doing poorly, making them particularly reluctant to bear further loss, the compensation they demand for default risk will be greater than the expected value of the loss. Although an ex ante adjustment would have to estimate this effect to compute the proper interest rate, the ex post spread method labors under no such difficulty. Because the ex post method provides a deduction for default loss if and when the loss occurs, the deduction has the same greater value to stockholders as the loss, whatever that value might be. This illustrates yet again the point discussed in the "Zero Revenue from Taxation of Risky Returns" box in chapter 3 (pages 51–52), namely, that the taxation of risky returns has zero effect on the government and on investors.

In all of these cases, then, the present value of what is taxed under the ex post spread method equals the value of the financial services. This equivalence of present value is sufficient for tax purposes, as it ensures that all parties face the correct incentives when they make their decisions. Of course, equivalence in present value would not be suitable for national income accounting, which seeks to measure the financial services actually provided in each year.

Assessing the Ex Post Spread Method. Although the ex post spread method is a viable approach, it becomes more complex when it is applied to financial transactions other than simple loans. In many transactions, there are numerous cash flows in each direction, and it is necessary to track what each party receives, relative to a safe return on all of the past cash flows.

The risk adjustment represents a departure from the real-based nature of the X tax. The bank is taxed on the $10 of services it provides to the borrower, plus a random term that has a twenty in twenty-one probability of equaling $53 and a one in twenty-one probability of equaling negative $1,060. The second term has zero expected present value, but its ex post value depends on whether the borrower pays or defaults, which reflects a financial transaction that a fully real-based tax would ignore.

This departure from the real-based system is not, however, a weakness of the method. Indeed, simplicity can be promoted by taking a further step in this direction, as is done by the real-plus-financial (R+F) cash-flow method.

The R+F Cash-Flow Method

We first discuss a pure R+F cash-flow method and then consider an important revision required to make the method practical. This method has also been discussed by Hoffman, Poddar, and Whalley (1987), Merrill and Edwards (1996), Merrill (1997), and Poddar and English (1997).

Pure R+F Cash-Flow Method. As we emphasized in chapter 2, the X tax is relatively simple because it is a real-based tax that ignores financial flows. Unlike the PET, the X tax does not attempt to track cash flows to their ultimate destination among households. In the context of financial services, however, the real-based nature of the tax creates problems.

The R+F cash-flow method that we now consider departs from the X tax's real basis by taxing financial intermediaries' transactions on a real-plus-financial basis. As we discussed in chapter 2, financial transactions have zero expected present value, so taxing both real and financial cash flows results in the same expected-present-value tax liability as taxing the real alone, assuming that tax rates remain constant. Given that the expected-present-value tax liability ends up being the same, it is ordinarily simpler to tax only the real flows and to ignore the financial transactions. But in the present context, where the challenge is to distinguish real and financial flows, it is simpler to tax all the flows, thereby avoiding the need to disentangle the two categories.

In the above example, under the R+F cash-flow method, the bank initially deducts the $1,000 that it lends to the borrower and is then taxed on any payments received. Under the above assumptions about default risk, there is a twenty in twenty-one probability that the bank is taxed on a $1,113 repayment and a one in twenty-one probability that it is taxed on nothing. The expected value of this taxable amount, minus the initial $1,000 deduction (compounded forward with 5 percent interest), is equal to the $10 cost of the financial services provided to the borrower.

The R+F cash-flow method is similar in many respects to the ex post spread method. Under each method, the ex post tax payment ultimately made by the bank depends on whether default ends up occurring, which has nothing to do with the cost of the financial services. In each case, though, the expected present value of the uncertain tax payment equals the cost of the services. By making the tax payment depend on the outcome of a financial transaction, each method departs from the real-based nature of the X tax.

The R+F cash-flow method is simpler to administer than the ex post spread method because there is no need to track past flows and apply the safe interest rate to them. In the example, the ex post spread method requires that the bank's initial outlay of $1,000 to the borrower be tracked, so when the bank subsequently receives payments, it is taxed only on the difference between its receipts and a safe return, computed from the time of the outlay to the time of the subsequent payment, on the $1,000. The R+F cash-flow method is simpler. The $1,000 payment is deducted when it is made and thereafter ignored, as the bank is taxed in full on subsequent receipts from the borrower. The simplicity advantage is magnified in situations involving multiple payments in both directions. Bradford (1996a, 460) aptly states that "cash-flow approaches promise relatively simple solutions."

One trade-off for this simplicity is a loss of intuitive appeal. (Another, discussed below, is the need for transition arrangements). The R+F cash-flow method is highly counterintuitive in many contexts, including this one. The bank deducts the $1,000 it lends to the borrower, even though such lending is in no sense an expense or loss, and is then taxed on the borrower's subsequent payment, including the repayment of principal. The method also applies to the checking account, with the bank paying tax on deposits into the account and deducting withdrawals, including interest, from the account. The inclusions and deductions not only have no visible relation to the cost of financial services (as was also true under the ex post spread method) but also have little visible relation to income and loss. Discussing R+F cash-flow methods, Shoven (1996, 462) notes that "their appearance can be quite different from their actual economic incidence, and this can make them less politically viable."

Nevertheless, we recommend the use of the R+F cash-flow method. However counterintuitive the bank's calculations may be, they are simple to perform, and they correctly measure the expected present value of the financial services.

But one challenge yet remains. Under the normal working of an X tax, firms are taxed on sales to both households and firms, and firms deduct their purchases from other firms. If the R+F cash-flow method is applied in accord with that principle, then, if the bank's customer is a business firm, it must perform the mirror image of the bank's computations in order to deduct (in expected present value) its purchase of financial services. For example, the firm must deduct each bank deposit it makes and pay tax on each withdrawal, including each check written.

Such a policy is obviously unacceptable. The owner of a local hardware store would surely not comprehend the logic of paying tax on each check the store writes and would not be mollified by the assertion that doing so helps tax the expected present value of financial services received on the checking account. As we noted earlier in this chapter, an acceptable method cannot require ordinary businesses to engage in counterintuitive tax computations. Moreover, the transition arrangements, discussed below, would be impossible to implement if they had to apply to all firms, rather than merely to financial institutions.

Some proposals that apply the R+F cash-flow method, including Poddar and English (1997), address this issue by requiring the bank to allocate its tax liability among its customers and to inform each business customer of the amount it can deduct. As Merrill (1997, 35–36) notes, such allocations would be complex.

Limiting the Method to Transactions with Households. Fortunately, this problem can be solved by modifying the R+F cash-flow method to have the tax system ignore transactions between financial institutions and business firms, an option discussed by Bradford (1996a, 448) and Merrill (1997, 36). Under this approach, financial institutions are not taxed on their sales of financial services to firms, and firms do not deduct their purchase of such services. Financial institutions are taxed, using the R+F cash-flow method, only on their transactions with households, which do not claim offsetting deductions. Under this modification, only the financial institutions need to use the counterintuitive R+F cash-flow method. (In chapter 7, we will also recommend the application of the R+F method to transactions between U.S. firms and their foreign affiliates, on the premise that it is acceptable to require counterintuitive tax computations by multinational firms.)

Recall that the X tax, like the VAT, imposes no net tax on transactions between firms, as the taxation of the seller is offset by a deduction for the buyer. The retail sales tax reaches the same net result by simply ignoring both ends of the transaction and taxing only sales to consumers. Our proposal effectively applies the sales-tax approach to this set of transactions. Although enforcement for a high-rate tax is normally improved by having an offsetting inclusion and deduction for sales between firms, it is preferable to ignore the transaction if doing so allows ordinary businesses to escape counterintuitive tax computations. This proposal illustrates the principle we mentioned in chapter 2, that the X tax can mix and match different methods in different contexts to achieve the best administrative results.

Bradford (1996a) and Merrill (1997) each note that there would be some complexities associated with requiring financial institutions to distinguish between transactions with firms and those with households. (Retail sales taxes face this same challenge with respect to a wide range of transactions.) But the complications are surely manageable. Customers should be presumed to be households unless they demonstrate business status and file business tax returns of their own.

The success of this proposal relies on financial institutions charging different prices, either in terms of interest rates or fees, to business and household customers. On two otherwise identical loans, the bank must charge a tax-inclusive price to a household borrower and a tax-free price to a business borrower. Recall that the X tax or VAT normally does not require such differential pricing; households and business firms buying computers pay the same tax-inclusive price, with the firms, but not the households, claiming offsetting deductions on their own tax returns. In contrast, the retail sales tax, which we are imitating in this context, requires such differential pricing, as firms charge tax to their household customers, but not their business customers. If financial institutions are constrained to charge uniform prices, then the method will not work. Any regulatory barriers to differential pricing should therefore be removed as part of the tax reform.

Unified Treatment for Financial Firms. One advantage of the R+F cash-flow method is that it applies uniformly to almost all financial institutions. There is no need for separate rules for banks, insurance companies, and other institutions. Although it is necessary to distinguish financial institutions from nonfinancial firms, it is generally not necessary to distinguish among financial institutions. Almost all financial institutions are subject to the same rules, paying tax on cash inflows and deducting cash outflows. As discussed above, banks and thrifts pay tax on deposits received, and loan proceeds collected, from households and deduct deposit withdrawals by, and loans made to, households. Similarly, property and casualty insurance companies pay tax on premiums paid by households and deduct benefit payments made to households; there are no loss reserves. The R+F cash-flow method's application to insurance companies is more intuitive, and more similar to current law, than its application to most other financial firms.

As discussed below, however, there may be some special cases in which the method cannot be applied, such as to some transactions of securities dealers. Special rules will be required for those cases.

Coverage. With respect to the coverage of the R+F cash-flow method, two dimensions must be addressed. First, it is necessary to determine which firms are financial institutions and therefore subject to the method on some or all of their transactions. Second, for those institutions, it is necessary to determine which of their transactions are subject to the method.

The first question is relatively easy to address. A simple rule is that the R+F cash-flow method should apply to any firm that is regulated as a financial institution by any federal or state agency under any statute. If a firm is not regulated as a financial institution, it is unlikely that it provides a significant amount of financial services.

The second question is more difficult, as it may often not be possible to precisely identify the transactions that include financial services for which explicit fees are not charged. It is probably better, when in doubt, to err on the side of subjecting transactions to the R+F cash-flow method. If the transactions actually include financial services, the failure to apply the R+F method allows financial services to escape tax. On the other hand, if the transactions actually do not include financial services, the application of the R+F method does not lead to any mismeasurement of the tax base, because the R+F method imposes zero tax in expected present value on transactions that do not include financial services. At worst, the unnecessary application of the method could cause additional complexity, but even that need not occur. Given that some of a firm's transactions are subject to the R+F method, complexity has no necessary relationship to the volume of the transactions subject to the method. Instead, complexity depends on how readily the firm can determine which transactions are subject to the method.

Accordingly, if an institution is subject to the R+F cash-flow method, the method should apply to all of its transactions, except those that are specifically removed by regulation. Transactions should be removed only if they clearly involve no significant provision of financial services, such as the issuance of securities in organized markets, or if any services are clearly financed in full through explicit fees. Bright lines should be drawn to minimize complexity. If one set of transactions includes real services disguised as financial flows while another set of transactions does not, and no simple rule can be written to distinguish between them, then both sets of transactions should be subject to the R+F cash-flow method.

Transition. As discussed above, the R+F cash-flow method relies on the expected present value of the cash flows being equivalent to the cost of the financial services. Because this equivalence holds only over the entire life of the transaction, the method faces significant transition issues, as Bradford (1996a, 443) notes.

In the above example, suppose that the $1,000 loan was made before the X tax's effective date, but the borrower's repayment occurs after that date. Then, the bank is taxed on the borrower's potential repayment, which has an ex ante market value of $1,010, far more than the $10 cost of the financial services. The problem is the missing $1,000 deduction for the initial loan. For a checking account, the opposite problem arises. If an account is withdrawn after the reform, the bank deducts the withdrawn amount, although it was never taxed on the initial deposit.

The problem would be solved if the bank could include the market value of its outstanding deposits and deduct the market value of its outstanding loans on the effective date. Although market value is difficult to measure, a ready proxy is provided by the tax basis that banks have in their accounts and loans. If subsequent rate changes are large, they should be handled in a similar manner.

Accounting Methods

Many transactions in the nonfinancial sector, such as sales on credit, involve a bundling of real and financial transactions. Suppose, for example, that a firm sells apples to a consumer at a stated price of $100 and gives the consumer one year to pay the $100 without any stated interest. Also assume that the consumer makes the $100 payment on schedule. To tax consumer purchases, the X tax system should ideally impose tax at the sale date on the value of the apples. Unfortunately, that value is not readily determinable, although it is clear that it must be less than $100. In economic terms, the $100 payment includes an interest payment to compensate for the deferral of payment, even though the firm has chosen not to label any of the payment as interest. If tax is to be imposed at the sale date, the tax should not apply to the interest component of the $100 payment, as the X tax ignores interest income and expense. The tax should apply only to the underlying value of the apples.

As Bradford (1996a) notes, however, a simple solution is available. It once again involves the R+F cash-flow method, which, in this context, simply means using a cash method of tax accounting. The cash method taxes all of the cash flows arising from the sale of the apples when the cash flows occur; in this example, that involves imposing no tax on the sale date and instead taxing the firm on the $100 payment when it is received. The cash method works because the present value of the deferred $100 payment must be equal to the value of the apples on the sale date. The cash method continues to work in the presence of default risk, just as it did for the bank loan discussed above, because the expected present value of the uncertain future payment equals the value of the apples on the sale date. If there is a risk of default, the firm increases the stated price to compensate for the possibility that no payment will be received. The cash method then taxes the increased payment if the increased payment is received and taxes nothing if nothing is received; the expected present value of what is taxed then necessarily equals the value of the apples on the sale date.

So, the cash method imposes no tax and offers no deduction when goods are exchanged for a receivable or payable. Instead, inclusions or deductions are made with respect to all future cash generated by the receivable or payable. Under the cash method, it is not necessary to specify a time at which the sale is deemed to have occurred; only the dates of receipts and payments need be determined.

For example, a firm that sells on credit is not taxed at the time of sale. Instead, it is taxed when it collects on the resulting account receivable, regardless of whether the collection is labeled as principal or interest. If it does not collect, due to the buyer's default, no tax is paid. It is also taxed if it sells the receivable.

Conversely, a firm that buys on credit claims no deduction at the time of sale. Instead, it deducts any payment on the resulting account payable, regardless of whether the payment is labeled as principal or interest. A buying firm also deducts the cost of paying cash to a third party to assume an account payable.

Strictly speaking, the expected present values of the tax payments are correct only if tax is paid at the same instant that the payment is made or received. Weisbach (2000, 637–39) observes that the cash method works less well if firms' accounting periods are long relative to the durations of the financial items, because tax payments then do not coincide with the recognition of the cash flow. Under current law, C corporations are required to pay estimated tax on a quarterly basis; the X tax should also require quarterly tax payment by firms.

The cash method also provides proper treatment, in expected present value, for contingent payments, deposits, defaults, and returns. The method also easily handles leases, including leases with options to purchase. The method simply includes the cash that changes hands, all of which is payment for either the use of the leased item or the possibility of purchase. Note that the latter payments are treated correctly in expected present value, regardless of whether any purchase ultimately occurs.

The cash method is similar in some respects, and different in others, from the methods typically used in VAT systems. As Weisbach (2000, 628, 640) and Tait (1988, 373–90) discuss, European VATs typically tax the purchase price of the good or service at the time that the good or service is deemed to be supplied. Tait notes that the time of supply can be defined as the time when the invoice is issued, when the goods are made available or the services rendered, or the time of payment, if earlier. The measurement of the purchase price can also be difficult. Tait explains that this price is normally net of discounts, that contingent payments are generally taxed only when they are determined, that customer deposits are usually not taxed until the purchase is finalized, and that tax is rebated if items are returned for credit. For an installment sale, the stated principal may be taxed at the time of sale, with no tax on the stated interest. The cash method offers a simple unified approach that can handle all these situations.

Special Cases

In some circumstances, application of the R+F cash-flow method is difficult, potentially warranting the use of alternative methods. Problems would occur, for example, if the cash flows arising from a sale stretch out over an extended period.

In the tax accounting context, suppose that the firm is paid for the apples with a share of stock. The mechanical application of the cash method would require that the firm pay tax on all dividends received while it holds the share and on the gross proceeds from any subsequent sale of the share. In principle, the cash method still works in this context; because the firm accepted the share as payment for the apples, the expected present value of the dividends and sale proceeds must be equal to the value of the apples on the sale date. If the firm were to hold the share for an extended period, though, the cash method would prove cumbersome, as it would require the imposition of tax on dividends received years after the sale of the apples. It would be preferable to instead tax the receipt of the share by treating it as a "cash" receipt in the amount of the share's market value. Of course, few consumers make payments of this kind.

Problems of this kind could also arise in the context of financial institutions. Consider, for example, a dealer who buys and sells securities and receives compensation for his financial services through the bid-ask spread rather than through explicit fees. If the dealer purchases securities from a household, the mechanical application of the R+F cash-flow method calls for the dealer to deduct the purchase price and to pay tax on the subsequent cash flows from the sale of the security. If the security is sold to a business, though, the cash flows are improperly measured, because the sale proceeds would include the implicit value of services provided to the business purchaser, services on which the dealer is not supposed to be taxed. Here, too, it may be necessary to impute a market value to the security at the time it is purchased from the household or to adopt some other special rule.

Weisbach (2008, 85–86) also observes that the R+F cash-flow method does not work for barter transactions, in which goods are exchanged for goods or assets. Here, too, it may be necessary to impute the market value of the goods.

Conclusion

The advantage of the real-based approach that underlies the X tax is that it allows the tax system to ignore financial flows. Its disadvantage is that it requires the tax system to distinguish between real and financial flows. The best approach is to use the real-based approach when it is easy to distinguish the two and to use a real-plus-financial cash-flow method when it is difficult to distinguish between them. In that spirit, we recommend that a real-plus-financial cash-flow method apply to those transactions between financial institutions and households in which real services may be disguised as financial flows.

7

International Transactions

The tax treatment of international trade is often viewed as a challenge for the X tax. The primary issue is whether the X tax should be an origin-based tax on domestic production or whether a border adjustment should be adopted to transform it into a destination-based tax on domestic consumption. We conclude that the X tax should be origin based to avoid a large transfer of wealth from Americans to foreigners.

The Border Adjustment Question

The current income tax system is origin based, meaning that business and personal income taxes are imposed on production inside the United States, including production of goods that are exported to other countries. Conversely, business and personal income taxes are generally not imposed on production outside the United States, even when the resulting goods are imported into the United States.

Early proposals for the flat tax, which, as we discussed in chapter 2, led to the development of the X tax, assumed that the tax would be imposed on an origin basis. The use of the origin basis would promote continuity with the current income tax system.

Because the X tax is a modified VAT, though, one could argue that it, like all of the world's VATs, should be destination based. A destination-based X tax would apply to consumption inside the United States. To place the tax on a destination basis would require a border adjustment, consisting of a tax on imports and a tax rebate for exports. The adjustment would tax imported consumer goods at the 38.8 percent business cash-flow tax rate, deny firms a deduction for imported business purchases against the 38.8 percent cash flow tax, and provide a full 38.8 percent tax rebate on exports. Exporting firms would still deduct all their (domestic) business purchases and their wage payments, even though they would pay no tax on their overseas sales.[18]

Auerbach (2010) proposes a "modern corporate tax" that is almost a destination-based cash-flow tax. This proposal is similar to the X tax in that the corporate income tax is transformed into a business cash-flow tax where businesses can deduct all purchases from other businesses and employee compensation. Because the plan leaves the individual income tax unchanged, employee wages plus investor returns continue to be taxed at the household level. In his proposal, all cross-border transactions would be ignored by excluding sales abroad from the tax base and not allowing a deduction for purchases or investment abroad. The proposal appears to deviate from a destination-based tax in one respect: foreign consumer purchases are excluded from the tax base, rather than taxed when entering the United States, an approach apparently adopted to preserve the simplicity of ignoring all cross-border transactions.

Many discussions of the X tax argue, or simply assume, that it would be preferable for it to be border adjusted and destination based. Starting from this premise, some analysts see international trade rules as a problem for the X tax. Although the rules allow "direct" taxes to be border adjusted, they prohibit border adjustments for "indirect" taxes. The credit-invoice VATs that prevail in most other countries clearly qualify as direct taxes, but the weight of authority indicates that a flat tax or X tax is likely to be classified as an indirect tax that cannot be border adjusted. Hufbauer (1996, 47–61, 69–70) provides a thorough discussion of these rules.

If desired, it might be possible to overcome this perceived problem. As Weisbach (2000, 623) points out, other nations would probably find it difficult to maintain the current rules if the United States forcefully pressed for modification, particularly because the direct/indirect distinction lacks economic foundation. We conclude, however, that it would be preferable not to border adjust the X tax, which removes the trade rules as a problem.

To begin, we reject an argument that seeks to impose the destination basis as a matter of vocabulary. The argument observes that a destination basis is a true consumption tax, whereas an origin tax is a tax on consumption plus net exports. A destination basis may therefore seem more faithful to this book's call for a "consumption tax." But vocabulary should not control policy. As we explained in chapter 1, the economic advantage of a tax on consumption is that it eliminates the marginal tax burden on new investment. Because an origin-based X tax would retain this advantage, as shown below, it is also a "consumption tax" in the economic sense. The border adjustment question should be decided on the basis of economic consequences, not terminology.

The most common argument for border adjustment is that it would make U.S. producers more "competitive," thereby permanently boosting exports and reducing imports and "improving" the trade balance.[19] As we explain below, this argument is invalid because the competitiveness effect would be offset by movements in the real exchange rate. Moreover, a permanent reduction in the trade deficit, even if it could be achieved, would not be an economic improvement.

To be clear, we argue below that border adjustments have no competitiveness effect—positive or negative. If competitiveness were the only relevant factor, we would be neutral or agnostic with respect to the desirability of a border adjustment. But we also explain below that border adjustments would involve a significant transfer of wealth from Americans to foreigners, which, in our view, decisively tips the balance against a border adjustment.

The "Competitiveness" Illusion

In analyzing border adjustments, economists often emphasize a simple model that makes a number of restrictive assumptions. The model assumes that the border adjustment applies uniformly to all goods and services; the prime example is the addition of a border adjustment to a comprehensive uniform-rate VAT that previously lacked such an adjustment. The model also assumes that the border adjustment is perfectly implemented, with no enforcement problems. It is also simplest to begin with a single-period model in which there is no passage of time. This discussion draws on Viard (2004a, 2008, 2009a).

Irrelevance in Single-Period Model. In this simple model, as set forth below, a border adjustment does not make domestic producers more competitive. Indeed, the model actually yields the more dramatic conclusion that the border adjustment has no real economic effects at all; origin and destination taxes are equivalent. (As will be seen, more realistic models reveal that border adjustment has some real effects, but not the commonly imagined competitiveness effects.) The equivalence of origin-based and destination-based tax systems was first noted by the Tinbergen Report (European Coal and Steel Community, High Authority, 1953). Numerous economists have reiterated this point over the last six decades.[20]

Because taxing an activity tends to discourage it and subsidizing an activity tends to encourage it, it seems plausible to argue that an import tax reduces imports and that an export subsidy increases exports. The argument is invalid, however, because it ignores the budget constraint linking imports and exports. In the single-period model now being considered, the budget constraint simply requires that imports equal exports.

The terms of trade at which a country buys and sells with respect to the world adjust to keep exports equal to imports in the single-period model. For countries with flexible exchange rates, changes in the terms of trade generally occur through exchange-rate fluctuations. (The "Border Adjustment with Fixed Exchange Rates" box (pages 116–17) examines the case of fixed exchange rates.) The adoption of a border adjustment by the United States triggers an exchange-rate movement that offsets the perceived change in competitiveness.

Suppose that the United States initially has a 38.8 percent X tax with no border adjustment and that it exports 100 goods to Europe at a price of $10 apiece and imports 100 goods from Europe at a price of $10 each. Trade is in balance, with exports and imports both equal to $1,000. Suppose that the initial exchange rate is 1 euro per dollar.

What happens if the United States border-adjusts, imposing a 38.8 percent tax on imports and paying a 38.8 percent rebate on exports? At first glance, the change appears to increase exports and reduce imports. Before the adjustment, American producers charged $10 for each good that they exported to Europe, but cleared only $6.12 after tax. Because exports are now tax free, American exporters need charge only $6.12 to clear $6.12. If the exchange rate remained unchanged, goods from the United States would sell in Europe for $6.12 rather than 10 euros, giving American sellers a competitive edge. Conversely, European imports are now subject to a 38.8 percent U.S. tax, so European sellers must charge 16.34 euros to clear 10 euros (they pay tax of 6.34 euros, 38.8 percent of 16.34 euros). If the exchange rate remained unchanged, goods from Europe would sell in the United States for $16.34 rather than $10, putting European sellers at a disadvantage. In equilibrium, though, these outcomes cannot occur because they violate the budget constraint requiring that imports remain equal to exports.

Instead, the dollar appreciates to 1.634 euros; in other words, the euro declines to 0.612 dollars. Although American producers can now sell goods in Europe for $6.12, that translates into an unchanged price of 10 euros at the new exchange rate. Although foreign producers must now charge 16.34 euros for goods sold in America, that price translates into an unchanged price of $10 at the new exchange rate. Trade flows are unaffected.

The border adjustment also leaves after-tax real wages and other producer incomes unchanged. The border adjustment raises the prices paid by American consumers, as expressed in euros, by 63.4 percent, but also increases the after-tax incomes received by American producers, as expressed in euros, by 63.4 percent. As measured in foreign currency, destination-based taxes raise consumer prices, while origin-based taxes lower disposable income, but both taxes cause the same reduction in real disposable income.

Irrelevance in Simple Multiperiod Model. The fact that the economy lasts for many periods does not, by itself, make border adjustment relevant. The equality between exports and imports continues to hold, although in a slightly different form. For any household or nation, purchases must equal sales in present discounted value over their lives. Purchases are financed by the proceeds of sales, and sales are made to finance desired purchases. For any nation, the present discounted value of exports equals the present discounted value of imports over its entire history. Any policy that permanently reduces imports also reduces exports; any policy that permanently increases exports also increases imports. The quest to permanently increase exports and reduce imports is futile, whether pursued through border adjustment or otherwise. As in the single-period model, the adoption of a border adjustment that applies to the country's entire history causes an exchange-rate appreciation that leaves exports and imports unchanged in each year.

So, a border adjustment would not permanently increase exports and reduce imports. This is a good thing, too, because such an outcome would permanently reduce American living standards, as Viard (2008) emphasizes. We would forever send more goods and services, produced by our toil and natural resources, to foreign consumers while forever receiving fewer goods and services for our own enjoyment in return. Imports are the gain from trade, and exports are the cost of trade; we give up exports to obtain imports. The desire to increase exports and reduce imports reflects the mercantilist fallacy that Adam Smith (1976, book IV, chapter 1) condemned in 1776.

The simple form of the present-value equality rests on the assumption that no cross-border investments have above-normal returns. Moreover, the assumption that the border adjustment applies to the country's entire history implies that no cross-border investments are in place when the adjustment is adopted. As discussed below, the two most dramatic effects of border adjustment concern the treatment of above-normal returns (which is intertwined with the transfer pricing issue) and the transitional impact on existing cross-border investments.

For now, we note that the border adjustment has no impact on the choice of where to locate a new investment that yields only the marginal rate of return. To be sure, a destination-based tax applies to investments made abroad by Americans but not to investments made in the United States by foreigners, while an origin-based tax applies to the latter but not the former. But these distinctions make no difference for new investments earning the marginal rate of return because, as we explained in chapters 1 and 2, the X tax imposes a zero effective tax rate on such investments. Being subject to the X tax therefore poses no disincentives for such investments.

Still another way to explain why border adjustments have no effect is to analogize them to traditional and Roth IRAs. From a national perspective, border adjustment resembles a traditional IRA, as the deduction for exports is similar to the upfront deduction for contributions, while the tax on imports is similar to the tax paid on distributions. In contrast, an origin-based tax resembles a Roth IRA, in which individuals receive no deduction for contributions and pay no tax on distributions; an origin-based tax offers no deduction for exports and imposes no tax on imports. As we explained in chapter 2, the value of the upfront tax deduction exactly offsets the tax on the distribution in present value, provided that the tax rate remains constant over time.

Some Cases in Which Border Adjustment Is Relevant. Before discussing the critical issues of transitional impact and above-normal returns, we briefly examine some other, generally less significant, factors that can cause border adjustment to have real effects.

A border adjustment has real effects if the tax that is being border adjusted does not apply uniformly to all value added. Consider, for example, a value-added tax that exempts food and assume that food is readily tradable across international borders. Border adjusting such a tax does improve the competitiveness of the producers who are subject to the tax (those outside the food industry) and does increase their net exports. But the border adjustment reduces the competitiveness of food producers, who receive no direct benefit from the border adjustment of a tax from which they are exempt while facing competitive pressures from the resulting appreciation of the exchange rate. Although it is impossible to simultaneously make all industries more competitive, it is possible to make some more competitive while making others less competitive, and one way to do that is to border adjust a tax that applies to only some industries.

When tax rates differ across goods and services that are readily tradable across international frontiers, the differentials are primarily reflected in consumer prices under destination-based taxes and are primarily reflected in producer prices under origin-based taxes. In general, tax rate differentials tend to produce more sensible results under destination-based taxes. For example, preferential rates for food are intended to aid consumers, not producers, of food, and a tobacco excise tax is intended to reduce the country's consumption, not its production, of tobacco. To obtain the desired results, such policies should be adopted on a destination basis.

Despite initial appearances, however, this consideration actually supports putting the X tax on an origin basis. The fact that tax rate differentials will not accomplish their intended goals under an origin-based tax is likely to be clear to policy makers, which should dissuade them from adopting such preferences. That outcome is desirable because it allows the business cash flow tax to remain uniform across different types of goods. If a tax preference for medical services is desired, for example, it can and should be provided to consumers of such services through a deduction or credit on the household wage tax returns, where it can be calibrated to the household's circumstances; it should not be provided through a tax reduction for the firms producing medical services. If a tax on tobacco consumption is desired, it can be imposed as a separate destination-based excise tax (which is how today's tobacco tax is imposed) rather than being made part of the X tax system.

The present-value equality between import taxes and export rebates breaks down if the border adjustment faces compliance problems, either the evasion of tax on imports or the filing of refund claims for nonexistent exports. Import tax evasion is likely to become a greater challenge as Internet transactions become more numerous. Fraudulent export refund claims have been a significant problem with European border adjustments, as discussed by Ernst and Young (2010, 2011), Tait (1988, 313–14), and Keen and Smith (2006, 870–72). Also, because the equality of import taxes and export rebates arises from residents' budget constraints, it breaks down if residents are able to avoid the tax by consuming abroad, either as tourists or as retirees in foreign jurisdictions.[21] On the whole, these compliance issues appear to offer support for the origin basis.

But two significant differences remain to be considered: transitional wealth effects and the treatment of transfer pricing and above-normal returns. As shown below, the former consideration provides a powerful argument for origin-based taxes, and the latter consideration supports destination-based taxes. We conclude with a recommendation for the origin basis and a proposal to address the potential problems posed by transfer pricing and above-normal returns.

Giving Wealth Away without Really Trying

A border adjustment has important effects on revenue and domestic and foreign wealth, due to cross-border asset holdings at the time the adjustment is introduced. The present-value equality between exports and imports must be modified, as follows, at any point in the midstream of a nation's history: The present discounted value of future exports equals the present discounted value of future imports plus the country's net foreign debt (or minus its net foreign assets).

The revenue effects of border adjustment depend on *net* cross-border asset holdings at the time of reform. According to Bureau of Economic Analysis (BEA) data reported by Nguyen (2011), the United States had a net external debt of $2.5 trillion at the end of 2010. As a result, the present discounted value of future U.S. exports exceeds the present discounted value of future U.S. imports by $2.5 trillion. In other words, today's trade deficits must eventually be followed by trade surpluses, with a $2.5 trillion larger present value, to service the external debt. Under simple assumptions, a 38.8 percent X tax with a border adjustment, relative to a 38.8 percent X tax without a border adjustment, lowers revenue by $0.97 trillion, in present discounted value. This is true even though the border adjustment raises revenue in the short run, due to current trade deficits.

But the revenue impact is the least of the story. A border adjustment also has profound transitional effects on asset values, effects that have drawn surprisingly little attention. The border adjustment brings into the tax base the consumption of Americans financed by their existing foreign assets and removes from the tax base the consumption of foreigners financed by their existing American assets. As a result, Americans' holdings of foreign assets decline in real value, while foreigners' holdings of American assets rise in real value. The appreciation of the dollar reduces the dollar-value of Americans' foreign assets and increases the foreign-currency value of foreigners' American assets.

For two reasons, these wealth effects have more far-reaching policy implications than the revenue impact. First, the revenue impact is merely a transfer among Americans. If the border adjustment causes the tax to raise $0.97 trillion less than it otherwise would, the Treasury suffers a $0.97 trillion loss, but American taxpayers enjoy a $0.97 trillion gain. Changing the tax rate can undo these effects. In contrast, the wealth transfer to foreigners is a net loss for the American people. Second, the wealth effects are vastly larger than the revenue impact. The reason is that, as Viard (2004b; 2008) and Auerbach (2007; 2008) note, the wealth effects depend on the *gross* holdings of American assets by foreigners and foreign assets by Americans, while the revenue effect depends on the much smaller net difference of those holdings.

The BEA data reveal that Americans held $20.3 trillion of foreign assets at the end of 2010, and foreigners held $22.8 trillion of American assets (the difference is the $2.5 trillion U.S. net external debt, mentioned above). A stylized calculation suggests that a 38.8 percent X tax with a border adjustment, relative to an identical tax without a border adjustment, imposes a $7.88 trillion heavier tax burden on American consumers and an $8.85

trillion lighter tax burden on foreign consumers, in present discounted value. (The difference is the $0.97 trillion net revenue loss, mentioned above.) A wealth transfer to foreigners of $8.85 trillion, roughly seven months of GDP, is a staggering burden on Americans. Viard (2009a) and Auerbach (2007, 45–46; 2008, 19–20) provide similar calculations with older data and different tax rates.

Transition relief is likely to reduce the wealth transfer to some extent. If the tax is not border adjusted, transition relief is likely to be provided at the firm level, as we will recommend in chapter 8, easing the burden on firms' foreign stockholders. In contrast, transition relief for a border-adjusted tax would presumably be provided to Americans at the household level, as we will discuss in chapter 10 for a destination-based VAT, with no benefit to foreigners. Even so, the wealth shift would still be several trillion dollars. Because this transfer would dwarf the efficiency gain from tax reform, the move to a border-adjusted consumption tax would actually be a gift to the world, rather than a gain for the United States.

This discussion reveals that other nations' VATs are gifts to the United States, reflecting the fact that these nations have gone astray in the pursuit of mercantilism. It is ironic that international trade rules thwart the adoption of a border adjustment that would actually benefit the world at Americans' expense. This issue highlights the insidious effects of the competitiveness fallacy. Proponents of the fallacy imagine that a U.S. border adjustment would tax the foreigners who sell goods to us, when it would actually tax the American consumers who buy these products.

Although transition effects provide a strong argument against border adjustment, we must now consider the countervailing implications of above-normal returns and transfer pricing.

Above-Normal Returns and Transfer Pricing

The equivalence of origin and destination taxes breaks down in the presence of above-normal returns, just as the equivalence of conventional and Roth IRAs breaks down in the presence of such returns.

The Problem Facing Origin-Based Taxes. As we emphasized in chapters 2 and 3, consumption taxes, including the X tax, impose tax on above-normal returns, such as returns from innovation or the exercise of market power, even though they do not tax marginal returns to investment. The presence or absence of a border adjustment can affect which above-normal returns are taxed and thereby alter incentives for generating above-normal returns in different places, as Avi-Yonah (2010) and others have noted.

Suppose, for example, that an American has an idea that will give rise to $1 million of profits. A destination-based tax is neutral with respect to the location at which the idea is developed, because it taxes consumption done by Americans. No matter where the American develops the idea, his consumption will be taxed under a destination-based tax. In contrast, an origin-based tax appears to have the potential to deter the development of the idea inside the United States, because the tax applies to investment inside the United States but not investment abroad. Moreover, the disincentive may be more severe than under the current tax system under our assumed 38.8 percent cash-flow tax rate, which is higher than the current corporate income tax rate.

As Bradford (2004, 19–20) and Grubert and Newlon (1997, 18–20) explain, the origin-based tax need not always have these dire effects. To begin, there is no disincentive if the American sells or leases his idea to an unrelated foreign firm for $1 million. The American's $1 million receipt is from the export of an intangible asset and is therefore subject to the origin-based tax. After making this payment to the American, the unrelated foreign firm earns only normal returns on its investment. Because the above-normal return is generated by the American's idea, not by the development of the idea overseas, it is subject to the origin-based U.S. tax.

In principle, nothing changes if the American instead develops the idea through a wholly owned foreign firm. The wholly owned firm should make the same $1 million payment to the American, and this amount should still be taxed as an export receipt.

But the transfer pricing problem, the distinctive bane of origin-based taxes, comes to the fore in this situation. Because the American owns the firm, the price he "charges" it is merely an accounting entry rather than a real payment, leaving him free to choose a value that minimizes tax liability. Suppose, for example, that the American charges his wholly owned firm a mere $700,000 for the idea, even though it is actually worth

$1 million. Then, the firm appears to generate a $300,000 above-normal return, which escapes tax due to its location abroad. The American ultimately receives this return in dividends or other profit distributions, but these payments are financial flows that are not taxed by the real-based X tax. In cases in which the correct market value cannot be objectively determined, as will often be true in cases involving above-normal returns, the origin-based tax offers an incentive to relocate investment abroad and to misstate prices to prevent the proper amount of tax from being collected in the United States.

In contrast, border adjustment eliminates transfer-pricing problems between firms. Under a destination-based tax, only sales to domestic consumers, whether by domestic or foreign firms, are ultimately taxed. Transactions between firms wash out, with the selling firm's inclusion offset by the buying firm's deduction. In principle, a destination-based tax need not even distinguish domestic and foreign firms, because the net tax liability depends only on the consumer's identity.[22]

Transfer pricing problems are not unique to an origin-based X tax; they arise today under the origin-based income tax. As Weisbach (2000, 642) notes, the transfer pricing regime of an X tax need not be much more strictly enforced than that employed under the current income tax system. In either case, though, the presence of above-normal returns suggests that an origin-based tax can have undesirable effects on the location of innovation.

It is desirable that the X tax avoid the complexity and administrative costs associated with transfer pricing enforcement under the income tax system. Fortunately, Bradford (2003; 2004, 34–45) proposed a solution to this problem.

Bradford's Solution. As we explained in chapter 2, the basic design of the X tax is real based. By ignoring financial transactions, the X tax generally achieves greater simplicity than the PET, which uses a real-plus-financial approach. As we also noted in chapter 2, though, it is possible, and sometimes desirable, to depart from the basic X tax design in particular areas. Bradford's transfer-pricing solution applies an R+F cash-flow method to cross-border transactions between related parties, the same approach that we recommended in chapter 6 for transactions involving financial intermediation.

The Bradford proposal calls for U.S. firms and households dealing with foreign related parties to include all inflows, both real and financial, from the related parties and to deduct all outflows, both real and financial. This procedure accurately captures the effect of the transactions with the related parties on the consumption of the U.S. firm or household. In the example given above, if the American sets a $700,000 price on the $1 million idea and therefore avoids tax on $300,000 of export receipt, he will be taxed on an additional $300,000 (in expected present discounted value) of dividend inflows from his wholly owned firm.

Ex post, the R+F cash-flow method may not correctly measure the net gain from the taxpayer's real transactions with the foreign related parties. Suppose, for example, that the wholly owned firm invests its $300,000 profit in a risky option that, one year later, has a 50 percent chance of paying nothing and a 50 percent chance of paying $600,000 and that the firm then paid a dividend to the American equal to the proceeds. The ex post dividend payment, either zero or $600,000, has no relationship to the $300,000 net payoff from the idea (above and beyond the $700,000 already booked by the American).

From the relevant ex ante perspective, though, there is no problem. If a security offering this pattern of payoffs sells for $300,000, the market value of these uncertain payoffs must be $300,000. (With risk aversion, the market value may differ from the expected value; the method continues to work, as we explained in chapter 6.) In other words, the deviation of the ex post payoff from the purchase price must have a market value of zero. So, the Bradford solution actually taxes the $300,000 real payoff plus an uncertain component (which ultimately turns out to be either negative $300,000 or positive $300,000) that has zero market value. This approach gives the American the correct ex ante incentives at the time he decides where to develop his idea. This example illustrates, yet again, the principle we discussed in the "Zero Revenue from Taxation of Risky Returns" box in chapter 3 (pages 51–52), namely, that the taxation of risky returns has no real effects on the government or on taxpayers.

The R+F cash-flow method faces the same challenges in this context that we discussed in chapter 6. In particular, it would be necessary to adopt transition arrangements similar to those we recommended in that chapter.

Other Cross-Border Issues

The United States currently maintains withholding taxes on dividends and some forms of interest paid to foreign persons, which are typically reduced as part of the bilateral treaties that the United States has with more than fifty nations. The United States should maintain its withholding taxes as a bargaining chip while seeking their bilateral elimination in treaty negotiations.

Today, the five overseas U.S. possessions (Puerto Rico, Northern Marianas, Guam, the U.S. Virgin Islands, and American Samoa) are largely, though not completely, exempt from U.S. corporate and individual income taxes. Because exempting these areas from the X tax minimizes disruption and maximizes simplicity, the geographical scope of the X tax should be limited to the fifty states and the District of Columbia. Of course, the tax treatment of the possessions may change if and when their political status changes.

Conclusion

Despite broad political support for the destination basis, the origin basis represents better policy because it avoids a massive transfer of wealth from Americans to foreigners with no loss of "competitiveness." Transfer pricing problems can be addressed by applying a real-plus-financial cash-flow method to transactions between U.S. and foreign related parties.

BOX

BORDER ADJUSTMENT WITH FIXED EXCHANGE RATES

Graetz (2008, 81) and others argue that the analysis in the text breaks down when a foreign country pegs its currency against the U.S. dollar. The argument holds that the exchange rate adjustment relied on in the text cannot occur when the foreign currency is pegged. In reality, though, the analysis in the text holds with little change when the exchange rate is pegged, as Viard (2009a) emphasizes.

A pegged exchange rate remains fixed only until the pegging country changes it. If a foreign government that pegs its currency at ten units to the dollar observes a 38.8 percent border adjustment by the United States, it can immediately repeg its currency at 13.88 units to the dollar. That simple step maintains an unaltered real equilibrium with no change in exports or imports, thereby preserving the real advantages that the government perceives from its decision to peg. Unless the foreign government is metaphysically attached to the number ten, it has no apparent reason not to repeg. In short, a border adjustment is an unpromising strategy to alter trade patterns between the United States and a pegging country because it can be defeated by the pegging government's choice of a number.

Consider the impact on traffic speeds if the United States switched from the English to the metric system of measurement. If a state "pegs" its highway speed limit at 65, would a switch to the metric system impose a crippling slowdown on the highways by reducing the allowable pace of travel within the state from 65 miles per hour to 65 kilometers (40.39 miles) per hour? Surely not. The state's choice of a 65-mile-per-hour speed limit reflects a desired balance between traffic safety and transportation efficiency, not a metaphysical attachment to the number 65. After the switch to kilometers, the state would "repeg" its speed limit, now expressed in kilometers per hour, to a number around 104.61, thereby maintaining the desired balance and avoiding any change in traffic speeds.

The only jurisdictions that cannot repeg are those that use the U.S. dollar as their own currency, for whom the exchange rate cannot deviate from one-to-one. Aside from the five overseas U.S. possessions, the British Virgin Islands, East Timor, Ecuador, the Marshall Islands, Palau, Panama, and Turks and Caicos Islands currently use the U.S. dollar. If the foreign government cannot repeg, economic balance is restored through a decline in the pegging country's price level. A 38.8 percent border adjustment would cause prices and nominal wages in these jurisdictions to fall 38.8 percent, thereby eliminating any competitive advantage for American producers.

To be sure, prices and nominal wages do not move as quickly as exchange rates. Before the price decline is complete, the border adjustment does indeed increase U.S. exports and reduce U.S. imports. But the border adjustment thereafter reduces U.S. exports and increases U.S. imports to maintain the present-value equality between exports and imports. The border adjustment therefore delivers only a temporary "improvement," followed by a long-run "deterioration," of the U.S. trade balance, and it does so only for U.S. trade with a small number of tiny dollarized jurisdictions. In the process, it inflicts a wrenching price decline on those jurisdictions, which are either our own overseas possessions, home to four million U.S. citizens and nationals, or friendly foreign jurisdictions whose use of the U.S. dollar brings in revenue for our Federal Reserve.

8

The Transition

Transition issues have received considerable attention in discussions of fundamental tax reform. Indeed, the impact of a move to consumption taxation on the value of existing capital has become a prototypical example in general discussions of transition policy.

Transition Burden on Existing Capital

Transition issues arise because movement from one tax system to another can involve significant changes in asset values. The largest single transition issue concerns the impact of tax reform on existing business capital.

We divide the impact into two components: the gains that existing capital reaps from income tax repeal, and the burdens imposed on existing capital from the introduction of the X tax. To simplify the analysis, we initially assume that the economy is closed, that the tax reform is completely unexpected, and that no transition relief is provided.

Income Tax Repeal. Intuition suggests that income tax repeal increases the value of existing capital because its returns are no longer taxed. Although this turns out to be correct for most real-world income taxes, the path to that result is not as straightforward as one might expect.

The Johansson-Samuelson theorem of Johansson (1969) and Samuelson (1964) establishes that income tax repeal actually leaves the values of existing capital unchanged when two conditions hold. The first condition is that an unlimited amount of new capital (which substitutes perfectly for existing capital in the production process) can be produced as quickly as desired at a constant replacement cost, so that there are no costs of adjusting the quantity of capital. Under this assumption, changes in the demand for capital translate fully and immediately into changes in the quantity of capital while the price remains fixed and equal to the constant replacement cost. The second condition is that the income tax on capital is collected concurrently, so that the ratio of tax payments to income is constant throughout the lifetime of each capital asset.

When the no-adjustment-cost and concurrent-tax assumptions hold, the value of each unit of existing capital is equal to the constant replacement cost of a new unit of capital, at any value of the income tax rate. For further discussion of this result, see Bradford (1998), Lyon (1990), Sandmo (1979), and Viard (2000).

Suppose, for example, that a machine can be produced at a constant cost of $100. Assume that, with a 20 percent income tax in place, the machine produces $5 before-tax output per year and therefore has after-tax output of $4 per year. (For simplicity, the machine is assumed to last forever, with no depreciation.) And assume that savers demand a return of 4 percent per year on funds provided to the firm. The machine's after-tax output has a present discounted value of $100, matching its production cost. What happens if the 20 percent income tax is repealed?

At first glance, it may seem that repeal of the 20 percent income tax would raise the value of each existing machine to $125. The after-tax output of the machine appears to rise to $5 per year, which has a $125 present value when discounted at a 4 percent interest rate. If the no-adjustment-cost and concurrent-tax assumptions hold, though, the existing machine cannot be worth more than $100, because an identical new machine can always be produced at that fixed replacement cost. Under those assumptions, the present value of the machine's after-tax output must still be $100, despite the above computations.

The paradox is resolved by realizing that income tax repeal changes the machine's before-tax output and the interest rate. Income tax repeal increases the volume of investment and saving. With more machines competing against it, each machine's marginal before-tax output is lower. Also, with more saving, the after-tax interest rate demanded by savers is higher. The volume of saving and investment rises until these changes bring the present value of the machine's after-tax output back down to $100. There are many possibilities for how this comes about; for example, the machine's before-tax output may fall to $4.50, while the after-tax interest rate rises to 4.5 percent. Without knowing more about the economy, we do not know exactly what changes occur, but some combination of changes that keeps the machine's value constant at $100 must occur. Under the no-adjustment-costs and concurrent-tax assumptions, income tax repeal does not increase the value of existing wealth, a conclusion that continues to hold when depreciation is introduced into the model.

The unchanged value of capital means that income tax repeal does nothing to help an owner of capital who consumes her entire wealth in the instant after repeal. Many owners, though, are likely to consume the proceeds of their investments over a period of time. Even with no increase in the value of the existing machines, these investors gain because income tax repeal increases their after-tax rate of return, thereby increasing their consumption, as Bradford (1996b, 146) and Diamond and Zodrow (2008, 231–32) note. The gain can be particularly large if the owner or her heirs consume over a period of decades. So, income tax repeal is generally beneficial to owners of capital, even when the value of capital does not rise.

In the actual economy, the effects of income tax repeal are likely to be even more favorable, because the no-adjustment-costs and concurrent-tax assumptions generally do not hold. Income tax repeal then changes the value of existing capital through demand changes and deferred-tax-liability effects. For most types of business capital, both of these forces push up the value of existing capital.

First, contrary to the no-adjustment-costs assumption, the replacement cost of capital typically rises as more is produced. If income tax repeal causes more machines to be produced, the production costs of new machines rise, and the values of existing machines rise accordingly. Moreover, firms that use machines are likely to incur adjustment costs as they install the new machines. In these cases, a change in the demand for machines does not instantly increase the quantity of machines with no price change; instead, the quantity responds sluggishly, and price also responds. Actual experience shows, of course, that the capital stock does not fully and instantly adjust in response to tax changes and other economic events that alter the demand for capital.

If increased machine production pushes the replacement cost of machines up to $105, then the value of an existing machine must also rise to $105. Relative to a world governed by the no-adjustment-costs assumption, the after-tax interest rate rises by less, and the before-tax marginal output of machines falls by less. If income tax repeal increases the demand for capital, the value of existing capital rises. While income tax repeal will increase the demand for most types of capital, it may reduce demand for a few types. Because types of capital that have been tax favored relative to other types under the income tax system will lose their artificial tax advantage, their production will decline relative to the production of other capital and may even decline in absolute terms. The decline in demand for these types of capital will reduce the value of existing units of these types of capital.

Second, contrary to the concurrent-tax assumption, the U.S. income tax on business capital is usually collected in a deferred manner, meaning that taxes are a lower fraction of net income early in the asset's life. Accelerated depreciation has this effect, as do the up-front tax credits that are provided for some types of investment. When capital is taxed in a deferred manner, existing capital has a lower value than replacement cost because existing capital, having already passed through part or all of its low-tax early years, faces a heavier future tax burden than newly produced replacement capital. In economic terms, existing capital carries a deferred tax liability. Income tax repeal effectively forgives this liability, thereby raising the value of existing capital back into equality with replacement cost.

The impact on different types of capital depends on the degree of deferral in its current tax treatment. The timing, not the size, of the tax burden is what matters. Capital that is assigned a uniformly low tax rate throughout its life carries no deferred tax liability, but capital that carries an up-front credit of equal generosity has a deferred tax liability. Repealing the income tax in midstream boosts the value of the latter capital, which banked its tax breaks prior to repeal; it does not boost the value of the former capital, which was waiting to receive future tax breaks that vanish when the income tax is repealed. Auerbach (1996, 36) estimates that business capital as a whole carries a deferred tax liability equal to 8 percent of asset value.[23]

In summary, income tax repeal will boost the value of most types of existing capital. The increase in demand for most types of capital will push up replacement costs and the value of existing capital. And the widespread deferred tax treatment of business capital means that existing capital will further rise in value due to the forgiveness of deferred tax liabilities. As previously noted, aside from the increase in the value of their capital, income tax repeal also allows the owners to enjoy higher after-tax rates of return.

But the gains from income tax repeal must be weighed against the transition burden imposed by the introduction of the X tax.

Introduction of the X Tax. The introduction of the X tax, or any other consumption tax, reduces the value of existing capital. The loss of value arises because existing capital is treated less generously than newly produced capital. Under the X tax, new investment is expensed at the 38.8 percent business cash-flow tax rate. Existing capital is then worth 61.2 percent of the replacement cost of new capital. A new unit of capital has an after-tax cost of only 61.2 percent of the before-tax replacement cost, due to the immediate tax savings from expensing, and existing capital has a value equal to that after-tax cost.

Using the above terminology, we note that expensing gives rise to a deferred tax liability. Under the X tax, a new $100 investment with no above-normal returns receives a $38.80 tax savings up front and faces $38.80 of future taxes (in expected present value) on its future cash flows, yielding a zero net tax burden. An instant after the investment has occurred, though, the capital is worth only $61.20, as its $38.80 tax savings is in the past and the $38.80 of cash-flow taxes are still in its future. Similarly, the value of capital in existence when the X tax is introduced immediately moves to 61.2 percent of replacement cost because it faces a 38.8 percent tax on future cash flows but does not receive the expensing deduction, which applies only to investments made after the reform is adopted.

The existence of a market in used capital does not change this outcome. Although the market-clearing price for used capital is still $100, the selling firm nets only $61.20 from the sale because the full sale proceeds are subject to the 38.8 percent cash-flow tax, and the purchasing firm incurs a net cost of only $61.20 because it can expense the purchase under the cash-flow tax.

So, at the same time that income tax repeal forgives deferred income tax liabilities, the X tax introduces a new 38.8 percent deferred tax liability. Note that the deferred tax liability depends on the business cash-flow tax rate rather than the household wage tax rates. This fact implies that the transition burden on existing capital, per dollar of revenue raised, is higher under the X tax than under a sales tax or VAT, assuming that each tax completely replaces the income tax and provides no transition relief. Whereas a sales tax or a VAT taxes business cash flow at the same rate as wages, the X tax applies a higher tax rate to business cash flow than to wages.

Net Impact on Existing Capital. If the no-adjustment-costs and concurrent-tax assumptions were valid, the replacement of the income tax by the X tax would reduce the value of existing capital by 38.8 percent. Existing capital that was worth 100 percent of replacement cost under the income tax would fall in value to 61.2 percent of that unchanged cost under the X tax. The above analysis reveals, though, that the actual decline is likely to be well below 38.8 percent in most cases. Most existing capital is currently worth less than 100 percent of replacement cost due to deferred tax liabilities, so the decline in value, relative to replacement cost, is smaller than 38.8 percent. Moreover, tax reform generally increases the demand for capital, driving up the replacement cost and the value of existing capital. Even so, it is clear that most existing capital falls in value to some extent.

We next consider which households bear the transition burden.

Incidence of Transition Effects. Consider a simple economy with two individuals, Smith and Jones, and a single firm. The firm holds $100 of capital and has issued $30 of bonds, so its equity is worth $70. Jones holds the $30 of bonds issued by the firm and has also loaned $20 to Smith; his net worth is therefore $50. Smith holds the $70 equity issued by the firm but owes $20 to Smith; his net worth is therefore $50. Aggregate wealth—Smith's net worth plus Jones's net worth—is $100, which equals the value of the capital stock. Note that the issuance of debt does not change aggregate wealth because debt is an asset for the holder and an offsetting liability for the issuer, with debt issued by the firm being a liability of the firm's equity holders.

Suppose that the replacement of the income tax by the X tax causes the value of the firm's capital to fall from $100 to $80, as an $18.80 gain from income tax repeal partly offsets the $38.80 transition burden inflicted by the X tax. To a first approximation, the $20 burden is borne solely by Smith as the equity holder. Jones, who owns the firm's bonds, escapes unscathed, because he still has a $30 claim against the firm. Because the firm still has $30 of debt outstanding, the devaluation of its capital from $100 to $80 reduces the value of its equity from $70 to $50.

We assume in this example that the real value of the firm's bonds is roughly unchanged, as is the real value of the loan between Smith and Jones. In reality, the value of existing bonds could be altered by changes in equilibrium interest rates and (depending on the transition rules applicable to existing bonds) the repeal of interest income taxes and interest expense deductions. The net effects are unlikely to be large, though, unless the remaining time to maturity is long. Our analysis also assumes that reform does not cause any changes in the consumer price level that would alter the real value of interest and principal payments. As we will explain in chapter 10, the Federal Reserve would probably increase the consumer price level in response to a VAT, but the forces prompting such a response are absent for the X tax.

Because the business cash-flow component of the X tax is imposed at the firm level, its burden falls on equity holders as the firms' residual claimants, as does any other unexpected shock to the firm's finances. The equity holders similarly enjoy the gains from income tax repeal, which are also manifested at the firm level.

The size of the burden on equity holders is difficult to estimate. With moderate adjustment costs, Diamond and Zodrow (2008, 243) estimate a 10.4 percent decline in the value of business equity from switching to a 21 percent Hall-Rabushka flat tax. The decline would be larger, though, for a 38.8 percent X tax.

Normative Issues

Simulation studies such as Altig et al. (2001) consistently find that the long-run output gains from reform are greater when there is a heavier transition burden on existing capital. We consider the source and policy implications of these gains.

Two sources of long-run output gains must be distinguished. First, the transition burden has a redistributive effect, harming older generations alive at the time of reform and benefiting subsequent generations. Second, the transition burden is, at least in principle, a progressive lump-sum tax that can promote economic efficiency.

Intergenerational Redistribution. The redistributive effect directly transfers resources between generations. The decline in the value of capital is borne by the living generations who own the capital at the time of reform. As Summers (1981) and Auerbach and Kotlikoff (1987) demonstrated in simulation models, this transfer triggers an increase in saving, as older generations cut back on their consumption. The increased saving expands the capital stock and boosts output, driving up wages and driving down the before-tax rate of return on investment. The net effect of the changes in wages and rates of return is also beneficial to future generations and harmful to older current generations.

Because these long-run output gains reflect redistribution between generations, they improve social welfare only under the value judgment that current policy assigns too few resources to future generations, relative to current generations. It is also important to realize that this redistribution could be achieved through other means. Lowering Social Security and Medicare benefits or reducing budget deficits would have this effect, as would a revenue-neutral tax change that raises taxes on the old and lowers them on the young. By the same token, the intergenerational redistribution from tax reform could be undone by changes in those other policies.

The other source of long-run output gains from the transition burden raises deeper philosophical issues.

Efficiency Gains from Progressive Lump-Sum Taxation. At least at first glance, an unexpected tax on existing wealth is an efficient way to raise revenue because such a tax creates no incentives for people to change their behavior to avoid the tax. Auerbach and Kotlikoff (1987) emphasized this point. Of course, there are other efficient ways to raise revenue, such as imposing a poll tax or lowering the standard deduction, but these measures are regressive. Because it is imposed on holders of equity, who are generally affluent, the transition burden uniquely combines progressivity with efficiency.

Leaving the transition burden in place would raise revenue, which would allow the government to meet its budget constraint with lower wage tax rates than would be feasible if transition relief removed the burden.[24] This reduction in wage tax rates narrows economic distortions.

To be sure, the X tax already eliminates the worst distortions of the current tax system, including the penalty on saving, the preference for noncorporate over corporate investment, and the preference for corporate debt over corporate equity. Nevertheless, the X tax still embodies a work disincentive, an incentive to evade taxes, and some other distortions, all of which become larger as tax rates rise. Raising revenue from the efficient unexpected tax on existing wealth would allow tax rates to be lowered, mitigating these distortions.

This unique combination of progressivity and efficiency is possible only because the tax is unexpected. An anticipated tax on capital has adverse effects on savings incentives; indeed, as we explained in chapter 1, the whole point of moving to a consumption tax is to remove anticipated taxes on capital. Economists refer to such a tax—one that would be undesirable if anticipated, but is desirable if unanticipated—as a capital levy. Another example arises in the context of patent policy; unexpectedly eliminating patent protection for past inventions allows greater diffusion of the benefits of those inventions, but an anticipated elimination of patent protection impairs incentives for future innovation.

In this context, the transition burden becomes inefficient if, contrary to the above assumptions, taxpayers anticipate it during the lead-up to reform. If firms know that they can expense investments made next year but must depreciate investments made this year, they will delay investment until next year and expense it then. If a significant amount of investment ends up being expensed anyway, it is better to allow expensing for this year's investment and avert the inefficient delay. In general, explicit transition relief is more efficient than self-help transition relief. This point has long been recognized in tax legislation; depreciation changes typically apply retroactively to capital placed in service between the date on which the House Ways and Means Committee formally begins to consider a bill and the date it becomes law.

Although transition relief clearly should be provided for investments made while reform is being considered, the more interesting question is how to treat capital in place before consideration of reform begins.

Ethics of the Capital Levy. Auerbach and Kotlikoff (1987) and others argue that the transition burden is beneficial because it can substitute for distortionary taxes, as discussed above. But another school of thought, represented by Kaplow (2008a) and Viard (2009b), holds that deliberate attempts to impose such unexpected taxes are inappropriate. They view the quest for capital levies as antithetical to the rule of law, which Barro

(1997) and others find empirically to be an important contributor to economic growth. It seems hard to deny that economic welfare is higher under a government that steadfastly honors patents as a matter of principle and abhors suggestions to deviate "just this once" than under a government that continually searches for excuses to invalidate prior patents while persuading today's innovators that their patents will be honored. A policy of imposing a levy on past productive activity whenever the nature of the levy can be concealed seems pernicious, particularly because this policy must itself be concealed. Viard (2009b) notes that the capital levy is truly the policy that dares not speak its name. As Shaviro (2000) and Steuerle (2005b) emphasize, it also seems doubtful that such a policy can be concealed.

Moreover, because capital levies can be imposed at any time, the switch to consumption taxation does not offer a unique opportunity to impose a levy. Given that Congress can unexpectedly tax existing wealth at any time while promising never to do so again, why should it wait for the introduction of a consumption tax? To be sure, the promise not to repeat the levy appears to be more credible if the levy is imposed during a switch to consumption taxation, because nobody expects such a switch to happen again. That advantage disappears, though, if it becomes publicly known that the tax on existing capital is an opportunistic measure intended to unexpectedly tax capital that has already been accumulated, revealing that the government is likely to behave in a similar manner in other policy contexts. And it is hard to see how that intention can remain hidden.

The relevant issue is the proper treatment of existing capital under a reform that lowers the marginal tax rate on new investment to zero. It is hard to see any reason why the entire value of existing capital should be taxed at the same rate that applies to above-normal returns on new investment. But there is also no compelling reason why existing capital should be completely protected, particularly when it benefits from income tax repeal, through higher asset values and higher after-tax returns.

It is hard to identify a single correct treatment of existing policy. But it is desirable that the transition policy be based on announced principles that apply to all policy changes, including those that lower after-tax rates of return, ensuring that reform is not used as an excuse to opportunistically tax existing capital.

Outline of a Transition Policy

In this section, we sketch the outlines of a transition policy based on the above principles. We do not attempt to lay out all the details, which will need to be hammered out in Congress. Two principles guide our thinking on transition. First, transition relief should not distort decisions made by firms and households under the new tax system. Second, the movement from the existing to the new tax system should occur as quickly and simply as reasonably possible.

We discuss some broad issues shaping transition policy, including the use of grandfathering and the timing of relief. We also offer proposals for key aspects of the transition, including business capital, debt, and future rate changes.

Broad Issues. In many contexts, transition relief takes the form of "grandfathering," broadly defined as allowing an existing arrangement to be treated under the old rules *so long as that arrangement continues unchanged.* For example, environmental regulations often exempt existing factories that are not remodeled from new rules, and zoning changes generally exempt existing nonconforming uses of property as long as those uses continue unchanged. In the current context, firms could be allowed to claim current-law depreciation allowances on existing capital, unless and until they sell the capital to another firm.

As noted by Brys (2010, 120) and others, however, grandfathering gives firms and households inefficient incentives to avoid behavior that would cause the loss of transition relief. For example, firms refrain from remodeling or replacing factories or from selling capital. A better approach provides taxpayers with fixed amounts of relief (dependent on their behavior prior to the implementation date) that do not depend on future behavior.

A few other guidelines also seem reasonable. Because exact justice is hard to achieve, or even define, a spurious quest for precision should not be allowed to induce needless complexity. When possible, relief should also accord with popular views of fairness.

Business Capital. Business capital poses a large transition issue. As indicated in table 8-1, Treasury Department estimates indicate that there will

TABLE 8-1
STOCKS OF CREDITS, NET OPERATING LOSSES,
AND REMAINING BASIS CARRIED INTO TAX YEAR 2013
($ BILLIONS)

	Total Business	C Corporations	Flow-through Businesses[a]
Losses and Credits			
Net operating losses	1,995	1,850	145
Foreign tax credits	75	75	0
General business credits	37	33	4
Alternative Minimum Tax credits	26	26	0
Undepreciated Basis			
Equipment:			
3-year property	110	70	40
5-year property	625	320	305
7-year property	600	260	340
10-year property	130	60	70
15-year property	730	270	460
20-year property	445	200	245
Total	2,640	1,180	1,460
Structures:			
Residential structures (27.5-year depreciation)	2,495	50	2,445
Nonresidential structures (39.5-year depreciation)	3,825	950	2,875
Inventories	2,015	1,200	815

[a]Includes partnerships, S corporations, and sole proprietorships.
SOURCE: U.S. Department of the Treasury, Office of Tax Analysis, unpublished data.

be approximately $2 trillion in unused net operating losses and nearly $9 trillion in undepreciated basis of existing equipment and structures at the end of 2012 under the current income tax.

As discussed above, expensing would be allowed for investments made during the period after serious consideration of reform began. Conversely, sellers of used capital during this period would be taxed on the full sales proceeds, without recovery of cost basis.

For new investment, we take the preservation of current-law depreciation schedules for existing business capital (including current-law cost-of-goods-sold deduction for inventories) as our benchmark for the appropriate generosity and allocation of transition relief. As discussed below, however, we modify the form of this relief to promote simplicity and efficiency.

It has been past U.S. practice to apply depreciation schedule changes only to new capital while maintaining previous depreciation schedules for existing capital. Adhering to that practice is thus consistent with the principle of avoiding opportunistic taxation and accords with popular intuitions of fairness.

For the same reason, this policy should satisfy the political demand for transition relief; indeed, calls for transition relief gravitate toward the preservation of depreciation allowances. Hall and Rabushka (1995, 78–79) suggest maintenance of current-law allowances. The President's Advisory Panel on Federal Tax Reform (2005, 173–74) proposed a less generous policy, under which firms deduct 80 percent of current-law allowances in the first year, declining by 20 percent in each subsequent year, with unspecified relief for inventories.

For the most part, the preservation of current-law depreciation also allocates transition relief appropriately. To begin, this firm-level relief is captured by equity holders rather than debt holders, so the incidence of the relief matches the incidence of the transition burden. The allocation of relief among different kinds of capital is also generally appropriate. Types of capital with low tax basis relative to market value receive less relief, but their low basis indicates that they have received more accelerated depreciation. Because they have been taxed on the most heavily deferred basis, they benefit the most from the forgiveness of deferred tax liabilities.[25]

Although the preservation of current-law depreciation schedules generally provides an appropriate amount and allocation of relief, two factors make it an undesirable form in which to provide relief. First, it adds complexity by prolonging the use of depreciation schedules; for example, a nonresidential structure placed in service the year before reform must be depreciated over the following thirty-eight years. Second, as a form of grandfathering, it impedes the efficient treatment of asset sales. Efficiency requires that all sales made after reforms be subject to X tax treatment, with immediate full inclusion of gross sale proceeds by the selling firm and immediate deduction by the purchasing firm, without any impact on past depreciation allowances.

Fortunately, these problems can be avoided while roughly matching the generosity and allocation of relief provided by preservation of current-law depreciation schedules. On the implementation date, each firm groups its capital holdings into several broad categories based on the number of years remaining in the asset's tax life. For each category, the firm is assigned a transition allowance equal to a percentage of its tax basis in the assets in that category, and the resulting transition allowances are claimed over a speci-fied time interval. The percentages are set to roughly match the generosity, in present value, of adhering to the current-law depreciation schedule. The allowances belong to the firm that held the assets on the effective date, so subsequent asset sales do not affect the amount or the ownership of transi-tion allowances.

What should be the length of the specified interval over which these transition allowances would be claimed? Several conflicting factors are rel-evant. A shorter period promotes simplicity. Given that the federal budget records tax revenues on a cash basis and transition relief is therefore booked in the fiscal years in which it is disbursed, providing transition relief over an interval longer than the ten-year budget window may be perceived as an attempt to camouflage its full cost. On the other hand, providing transition relief over a year or two artificially increases the perceived up-front cost of reform. Stretching firm-level transition relief over a longer period also makes it less likely that firms will have negative tax bases; as we discussed in chapter 5, the efficiency advantages of the X tax are diminished when firms have negative cash flows that (even under our generous carryback and carryforward proposals) may go unused. While any choice of interval must be somewhat arbitrary, permitting the allowances to be claimed over a ten-year period seems reasonable.

Debt. Another major issue concerns the treatment of existing debt securities and loans. The approach suggested by Hall and Rabushka (1995, 79–80) seems attractive. Under this approach, holders of existing debt continue to include interest income to the extent includable under current law. Bor-rowers continue to deduct interest expense to the extent deductible under current law, but with a 20 percent haircut. For individuals, inclusion and deduction would occur at their household tax rates. If the debt instrument is renegotiated, as many would be, the normal X tax rules of ignoring interest income and expense become applicable.

The incentives for rapid renegotiation would be strong in many cases. Renegotiation would allow the lender to escape further tax while having no adverse effects on the borrower, assuming that the debt is of a type for which interest expense is currently nondeductible. Even for debt that currently carries an interest deduction, the lender's tax saving is likely to exceed the additional tax on the borrower. In all such cases, the parties should renegotiate, setting a new interest rate that allows them to share in the net tax savings. Provided that renegotiation is not too costly, most debt instruments should quickly move into the X tax rules.

Another possible approach is that proposed by the President's Advisory Panel (2005, 173), which recommended that inclusion by the lender and deduction by the borrower decline over a four-year period under the 80-60-40-20 schedule. This approach may phase out the old rules less rapidly in some cases because it does not encourage renegotiation, but it provides an absolute guarantee that the old rules are completely gone after four years and avoids the transaction costs of renegotiation.

Other Special Issues. Some tax provisions resemble, or are related to, contractual or treaty commitments and would need to be preserved. The low-income housing tax credit, for example, provides credits with a present value of up to 90 percent of the project's cost while requiring the project to rent largely to low-income tenants at very low rental rates for thirty years. It would be appropriate to continue the credits, and the corresponding requirements, for existing projects. The exclusion for income derived from the exercise of fishing rights granted by Indian treaties should also be maintained, and the tax preferences for empowerment zones and other favored geographical areas should be preserved for a reasonable period of time.

On the effective date of tax reform, existing conventional IRAs, 401(k)s, and other tax-preferred accounts with front-loaded tax preferences should be closed to new contributions. Withdrawals from such accounts should be taxed upon withdrawal, but there should be no penalties on early withdrawals, and the mandatory distribution rules that apply to older account holders should be abolished. No transition rules are required for pensions and employment-based savings accounts, because, as we explained in chapter 4, we recommend a continuation of current-law treatment.

There are undoubtedly many other special issues for which transition policy must be worked out when the reform is adopted.

Future Tax Rate Changes. Transition issues arise whenever the tax rate on business cash flow is changed. Just as tax rates have changed under the corporate income tax, it is likely that the cash-flow tax rate will sometimes change under the X tax. Given the U.S. fiscal outlook, increases are presumably more likely than reductions, but neither can be precluded. Corporate tax rates have been changed only twice over the past three decades, although numerous special provisions influence marginal tax rates. For example, the deduction for production activities enacted in 2004 lowered the effective corporate tax rate from 35 percent to 32 percent on many industries.

Bradford (2004, 28–30) proposes that, instead of expensing investment, firms compute and claim depreciation allowances in the same manner as current law, but with interest accruing on the tax basis each year. This approach is equivalent in present discounted value to expensing, so long as the tax rate remains constant, but exempts the market value of existing capital from tax rate changes if the depreciation allowances are correct. Unfortunately, this approach continuously maintains the complexity of depreciation and adds the complexity of interest adjustments solely to accommodate rate changes that we hope would rarely occur.

We advise against any policy that requires ongoing computations to prepare for possible future tax rate changes. Indeed, we believe that most rate changes are likely to be sufficiently small that no special adjustment is required. A change of a few percentage points certainly does not raise the same concerns as the initial introduction of the 38.8 percent tax. In the absence of any adjustment, the rate changes will apply to all subsequent cash flows, including those from existing capital. Although this approach alters the value of existing capital, the effects do not seem large enough to warrant policy action.

If a large rate change occurs, some type of transition policy may be warranted. Kaplow (2008a, 130, 142n9) proposes that firms receive a credit equal to the tax rate increase (or pay a surtax equal to the tax rate decrease) multiplied by the firm's market value, but this approach has the formidable complication of measuring market value. A simpler approach would be to apply a transition policy similar to what we recommended here for the initial adoption of the tax.

Macroeconomic Policy During the Transition

The replacement of income taxation by consumption taxation may cause a shortfall in aggregate demand as consumer spending declines. Business cycle stabilization may therefore require offsetting monetary policy actions by the Federal Reserve. It may also be desirable to avoid implementing the tax reform during an economic downturn. In no case, however, should short-run business cycle considerations prevent the enactment of a permanent tax reform that is designed to promote long-term economic growth.

Conclusion

Transition issues do not pose an insurmountable obstacle to an X tax. Transition policy should strive to avoid opportunistic exploitation of existing capital while also limiting windfall gains to such capital. Transition relief should be provided in a manner that does not distort behavioral incentives after the tax is in place and that does not create undue complexity.

9

The Nonbusiness Sector

A substantial amount of production occurs outside of the business sector, including the services provided by owner-occupied housing, consumer durables, governments, nonprofit institutions, and household employees. In this chapter, we explore the treatment of these sectors under the X tax.

Owner-Occupied Housing and Consumer Durables

Although Mintz (1996, 471), the Tax Executives Institute (1992, 24), Conrad (2010, 471), and others argue that owner-occupied housing poses a difficulty for VATs and other consumption taxes, the reality is almost exactly the opposite. The proper income tax treatment of owner-occupied housing is very difficult to achieve, and no actual income tax system even approximates the correct treatment. In contrast, the correct treatment, in expected present value, can be easily achieved under consumption taxation.

Ironically, the current U.S. tax treatment of owner-occupied housing is thoroughly incompatible with the principles of income taxation, but is relatively similar to the treatment prescribed by the principles of consumption taxation. The move to correct consumption tax treatment under the X tax, therefore, involves making only minor changes to the current tax treatment.

As explained below, the appropriate treatment of owner-occupied housing can be achieved by taxing the sale of new homes and ignoring all resales. The sale of a new home is treated as the sale of a consumer good, and all the basic X tax rules are then applied without modification. As explained below, these rules should also apply to owner-used consumer durables.

An owner-occupied home is an investment asset that produces output in the form of housing services. The value of these services is equal to the imputed rental value of the home. Nevertheless, as explained below, treating the home as a consumer good yields the correct result in expected present value.

We first consider the treatment of housing under the income tax and then examine its treatment under the X tax.

Owner-Occupied Housing under Income Taxation. Under a textbook income tax, purchases of investment assets are not deducted, and the net-of-depreciation return is taxed. Accordingly, an ideal income tax allows no deduction for home purchases, taxes imputed rent net of maintenance costs and economic depreciation, and taxes accrued real capital gains net of losses. Mortgage interest payments, like other interest payments, are deducted.

Implementation of the correct income tax treatment of owner-occupied housing is impractical. The taxation of imputed rent and accrued capital gains would involve formidable measurement problems each year for each homeowner in the United States. Distinguishing maintenance expenditures, which should be currently deducted against imputed rent, from improvement expenditures, which should be capitalized and amortized, involves the standard complexities that income taxes face in distinguishing between current and capital expenditures, as we discussed in chapter 1.

Unsurprisingly, the current tax treatment of owner-occupied housing deviates sharply from the income tax principles outlined above. Notably, imputed rent is excluded from taxable income. Repair and maintenance expenditures are nondeductible because they constitute costs of earning tax-exempt imputed rental income. Most, but not all, capital gains are also excluded from taxable income; a taxpayer who has used a home as a principal residence for at least two of the previous five years may exclude up to $250,000 ($500,000 for a couple) of gain on the home's sale, with smaller maximum exclusions if the home was used as a principal residence for less than two years. Any gains that do not qualify for this exclusion are taxed, in nominal rather than real terms, at the time of sale, not as the gains accrue. Capital losses on owner-occupied homes are nondeductible, except that an itemized deduction is allowed for casualty losses that exceed 10 percent of adjusted gross income. Improvement expenditures are capitalized, but, rather than being amortized, are added to the taxpayer's cost basis and deducted from any future capital gains that do not qualify for the exclusion described above. An itemized deduction is allowed for interest payments on up to $1.1 million of mortgage debt on up to two homes. The Joint Committee on Taxation (2011) provides a thorough description of the current tax treatment of owner-occupied housing.

Under the current tax system, owner-occupied housing faces an effective tax rate of approximately zero, because imputed rent and most capital gains are not taxed. In contrast, business capital is generally taxed at significantly positive effective rates. This nonneutral tax treatment drives investment away from business capital and toward owner-occupied housing. Altering the allocation of capital in this manner is economically inefficient unless investment in owner-occupied housing provides spillover benefits to society that cannot be captured by the homeowner.

Some people argue that homeownership provides such spillover benefits by promoting social stability and neighborhood cohesion. Economists and others continue to debate the validity of this argument. But even assuming that the argument is correct and that some tax preference for homeownership is therefore desirable, today's tax treatment is still improperly designed. Although society may benefit from a person owning a home rather than renting, it is hard to see how society receives significant additional benefits from a person owning an expensive home rather than one of modest value. While current tax policy may prompt some taxpayers to become homeowners, it also prompts many others who would own homes anyway to buy more expensive homes. Indeed, the highest-income taxpayers, who would generally own quite expensive homes in any event, are in the highest tax brackets and therefore receive the largest percentage subsidy from the exclusion of imputed rent, giving them the strongest incentive to buy even more expensive residences.

Political difficulties aside, neutral treatment of owner-occupied housing is unlikely to be achieved under the income tax. To begin, neutrality requires the taxation of imputed rent. Although such taxation is not impossible (the Joint Committee on Taxation [2011, 30] reports that nine of the thirty-three OECD countries tax imputed rent to some extent), it is clearly administratively difficult. Economists sometimes propose that mortgage interest be made fully or partly nondeductible as a rough-and-ready offset to the exemption of imputed rent. Although such a policy probably would be beneficial, it would be imperfect because it would impose positive tax only on debt-financed home purchases while maintaining a zero effective tax rate on equity-financed purchases. It would therefore only partly correct the current system's bias in favor of home purchases and would actually introduce a new distortion by favoring equity-financed purchases over debt-financed purchases.

Owner-Occupied Housing under the X Tax. Fortunately, things are much more straightforward under the X tax, as there are two ways to provide appropriate treatment to owner-occupied housing: an ex post method and a prepayment method. In keeping with the real-based nature of the X tax, both approaches ignore financial transactions, so there are no tax implications of mortgage interest or principal payments for either the homeowner or the lender. Although the ex post method would be difficult to administer, the prepayment method is largely similar to, but slightly simpler than, the approach adopted by the current income tax system.

Under the ex post method, taxpayers deduct home purchases and repair, maintenance, and improvement expenditures. Imputed rent is taxed, as are the full proceeds from home sales. Homeowners are effectively subject to the cash-flow tax, with imputed rent treated as "cash" flow, so homes are treated in the same manner as business capital is treated under the X tax. Although this method is slightly simpler than the treatment prescribed by income tax principles because it need not measure accrued capital gains and losses or distinguish repair and maintenance costs from improvements, it retains the formidable difficulties of taxing imputed rent.

Fortunately, the prepayment method allows dramatic simplification while remaining faithful to consumption tax principles. This approach provides no deduction for home purchases or repair, maintenance, and improvement costs and imposes no tax on imputed rent or home sales. This method exempts homeowners from the cash-flow tax that applies to business firms. The only tax on homes is the tax on original construction that arises because the wages and business cash flow associated with the construction are taxed; a zero effective marginal tax rate applies to the imputed rental returns that the house subsequently generates.

This zero effective tax rate is essentially equal to that imposed by the current tax system. This equality is no coincidence; the prepayment method is identical to current tax policy, if we set aside the fact that the current system taxes a few capital gains from home sales. (The other apparent difference from the current tax system—the inability of the homeowner to deduct mortgage interest payments—is offset by the absence of tax on the mortgage lender, as further discussed below.)

But if it is undesirable for the current income tax system to apply a zero effective tax to owner-occupied homes, how can it be beneficial for the X tax to do the very same thing? The difference is that the X tax is designed to apply a zero marginal effective tax rate to *all* investment returns. The prepayment method delivers exactly the right result under the X tax, giving owner-occupied homes the same zero effective tax rate that the X tax applies to business capital, and thereby maintaining neutrality between the two types of investment. And, as we discussed in chapter 1, the zero effective tax rate also maintains neutrality between investment and current consumption.

In contrast, an income tax is supposed to impose a positive effective tax rate on all investment returns, and the current tax system generally does so for business capital. By using the prepayment method and applying a zero effective tax rate to owner-occupied homes, the current system improperly favors them over business capital. To achieve neutrality, the income tax would need to extend the positive tax rate on business capital to owner-occupied homes by taxing imputed rent. The X tax achieves neutrality by moving in the opposite direction, extending the zero effective tax rate that now applies to owner-occupied homes to business capital.

Because it avoids the taxation of imputed rent, the X tax prepayment method is as simple as the current tax system. Actually, it is slightly simpler, because it sweeps away the current system's vestiges of capital gains taxation and the associated capitalization of improvement costs and, as discussed below, eliminates the casualty loss deduction. But unlike the current tax system, the X tax achieves this simplicity without favoring owner-occupied housing over business capital.

Owner-Occupied Housing and the Business Cash-Flow Tax. Although the prepayment method results in owner-occupied homes facing the same zero effective tax rate as business capital, the two types of investment are not treated the same; business capital is subject to the cash-flow tax, and owner-occupied homes are exempt from it. A steel manufacturer that builds a factory claims an up-front deduction for its cost, whereas a homebuyer receives no up-front deduction for his purchase. On the other hand, the steel manufacturer is taxed on the output generated by the factory, whereas the homeowner pays no tax on the imputed rent produced by the home. This differential treatment causes no divergence in effective tax rates, however, because, as we have emphasized from chapter 2 onward, the business cash-flow tax imposes a zero effective marginal tax rate on new investments. On a new marginal factory investment, the tax savings from the manufacturer's up-front deduction offset, in expected present value, the subsequent taxes on its output, and the business cash-flow tax therefore imposes no net burden.

Exempting owner-occupied homes from the business cash-flow tax promotes simplicity because the "cash" flow consists of imputed rent, which is difficult to measure. What are the other implications of this exemption? As we explained in chapters 2 and 3, the business cash-flow tax has three effects. First, it taxes capital in existence when the reform is adopted, subject to transition relief. Second, it taxes above-normal returns. Third, under uncertainty, it gives the government a proportional share in the risks associated with the future cash flows. Exempting owner-occupied homes from the business cash-flow tax therefore means that the value of existing homes escapes tax, as do above-normal imputed rental returns, and that the government does not share in the riskiness of future imputed rental returns on homes. We defer the existing-homes issue to the discussion of transition below, but we now assess the other two effects.

The failure to tax above-normal returns on owner-occupied homes is largely unavoidable, given that such returns manifest themselves as high imputed rents. If such rents cannot be accurately measured, then above-normal returns cannot be detected and taxed. Moreover, such returns are surely of limited significance. Whereas many business firms exploit innovative ideas and market power to earn large above-normal returns, few homeowners are likely to be able to generate above-normal housing services.

The risk issue may appear to be more important. Suppose that two equally costly houses are constructed. Because the prepayment method taxes only the original construction, it imposes the same tax on each house, which is ex ante reasonable because the future imputed rents on the two houses have the same expected market value. But subsequent events may cause their actual imputed rents to sharply diverge. The neighborhood around one home may unexpectedly improve while that around the other home may unexpectedly deteriorate. Or one home may burn to the ground shortly after construction. The prepayment method leaves the full risk of such events on individual homeowners, whereas the ex post method applies the cash-flow tax to homes and thereby spreads part of these risks. The latter method both gives homeowners an up-front deduction for the house purchase and then taxes them on the actual imputed rents they later receive; homeowners lucky enough to earn high imputed rents pay extra tax, whereas unlucky homeowners who earn low imputed rents pay little future tax, leaving them with a net tax saving from their up-front deduction.

Although the risk spreading done by the ex post method may seem desirable, it has no real effect so long as homeowners can achieve the same risk spreading in private markets, as discussed in the "Zero Revenue from Taxation of Risky Returns" box in chapter 3 (pages 51–52). There is no reason to think that the government can observe and insure against the relevant risks more cheaply than the private sector. Nearly all homeowners privately insure against casualty losses such as their home burning down; although there is almost no private insurance against general economic developments, the same problems that preclude private insurance in this area, such as the difficulty of measuring imputed rents, are likely to make public insurance impractical or undesirable.

In view of the availability of private insurance, we recommend that there be no deduction for casualty losses. Of course, because the X tax is real based, insurance recoveries for such losses are tax exempt.

At first glance, it may seem that the government could achieve some risk spreading without having to measure imputed rents simply by taxing gains and allowing loss deductions on home resales. For reasons explained in the "Taxation of Home Resales" box (pages 154–55), however, we advise against such a policy.

Transition. By exempting owner-occupied homes from the business cash-flow tax, the prepayment method spares from tax the future housing services provided by homes in existence when the reform is adopted. In other words, these homes escape the X tax transition burden that we discussed at length in chapter 8, a fact noted by the Congressional Research Service (1996), Bradford (1996b, 140), Diamond and Zodrow (1998, 25; 2008, 231), and Viard (2000). On balance, sparing homeowners from the transition burden seems appropriate.

We concluded in chapter 8 that the government should not opportunistically target existing capital for taxation, because doing so would create harmful expectations about future policy. We also concluded, though, that existing capital should not be fully spared the transition burden of the X tax. Instead, we recommended that firms be allowed to recover the value of their unclaimed depreciation deductions, which would offset part, but far from all, of the transition burden.

Given this treatment of business capital, completely sparing homeowners from the transition burden may seem unduly lenient. Poddar (2010, 450) and Mintz (1996, 471), among others, condemn this outcome. But we believe that this disparate treatment can be justified on four grounds.

First, properly imposing the transition burden would require measuring and taxing the homes' imputed rents in each future year or, alternatively, appraising and taxing the market value of all homes on the reform date. These administrative costs should not be incurred unless there is a very strong case for imposing the transition burden.

Poddar (2010, 455) outlines a rough-and-ready way to impose a transition burden on existing homes. His proposal would tax gains on home resales, with the proviso that, on the first resale after reform of a home purchased prior to reform, the entire sales proceeds would be treated as gain. Of course, no transition burden would be imposed unless and until the home was resold. The tax policy would penalize sales, as discussed in the "Taxation of Home Resales" box. If a transition burden is to be imposed, it is not clear that this is a better way to do it than taxing imputed rents. In any case, the remaining reasons persuade us that no transition burden should be imposed.

Second, tax reform will reduce the value of owner-occupied homes to some extent even if they are spared the transition burden. Although exempting homes from the transition burden allows their values to remain equal to their replacement cost, their values will still decline because the replacement cost of homes will fall. By lowering the effective tax rate on new business investment to zero, while keeping the tax rate on new home construction at its current value of zero, reform will prompt (an efficient and highly desirable) reallocation of new investment away from housing and into the business sector. Like most other assets, the replacement costs of homes rise as more of them are produced and fall as fewer are produced.

Accordingly, the reduction in the demand for homes in the wake of reform will drive down the replacement cost of homes and hence the values of existing homes. Note that this decline is due not to the introduction of the X tax but to the repeal of the income tax system that has given homes their tax advantage.

The magnitude of the price decline is uncertain. Diamond and Zodrow (1998, 27; 2008, 233–34) note that studies have reached a variety of conclusions about the impact of switching to a consumption tax on the value of existing homes, ranging from a 20 percent decline to almost no decline. The large price declines are unrealistic, however, because they assume extremely high adjustment costs. In their own simulations, Diamond and Zodrow (2008, 241–44) estimate a decline of 1.9 percent with no adjustment costs, 2.7 percent under moderate adjustment costs, and 3.3 percent with larger adjustment costs. As Diamond and Zodrow (1998) and the Congressional Research Service (1996) note, the most expensive homes will experience the largest price declines, because their high-tax-bracket purchasers receive the largest housing tax preferences today, and the end of those preferences will therefore have the largest impact on their demand.

In any case, existing homes will decline in value to some extent due to the reduction in housing demand. Because the value of mortgage debt will not decline, the percentage impact on homeowner equity will be larger than the price decline. For example, Diamond and Zodrow (2008, 241–44) assume that homeowners initially carry debt equal to 35 percent of home value and note that their estimated home price declines of 1.9, 2.7, and 3.3 percent translate into reductions of 2.9, 4.2, and 5.1 percent, respectively, in homeowner equity. Of course, homeowners who are more heavily leveraged would be harder hit.

As we discussed in chapter 8, the situation is quite different for most business capital. Even as reform reduces housing investment, it increases business investment, except perhaps for a few types of business capital that receive highly favorable treatment under today's tax system. Because the replacement costs of business capital rise as more is produced, reform will increase the replacement costs of most business capital, which would boost the value of most types of business capital were it not for the transition burden. We mentioned another reinforcing factor in chapter 8; many types of business capital are taxed on a deferred basis under the current tax system and their deferred tax liabilities make their current values less than replacement cost. In the absence of the transition burden, the forgiveness of the deferred tax liabilities would push their value up to replacement cost, causing further appreciation beyond that caused by the rise in replacement cost. In contrast, there are no significant deferred tax liabilities for owner-occupied homes.

In short, in the absence of the transition burden, reform would boost the value of most business capital but lower the value of homes. It is reasonable to impose a transition burden, softened by relief, to block an increase in the value of existing business capital while dispensing with a transition burden that would amplify a decline in home values.

Third, homeowners are generally less affluent than equity holders of business firms, who, as discussed in chapter 8, will bear the transition burden on business capital. Fourth, on a related note, it would be politically difficult to impose the transition burden on homeowners.

The change in the treatment of mortgage debt under the X tax does not represent a tax increase on housing, at least in principle, because the denial of a deduction for the borrower is accompanied by a removal of the tax on the lender. As Hall (1996, 84) notes, though, there may be a net tax increase in practice, because not all interest income is actually taxed under the current system. Existing mortgages would be subject to the transition policy discussed in chapter 8, with current-law treatment (taxation of the lender and deduction by the borrower) continuing to apply until and unless the debt was renegotiated.

Possible Homeownership Preference. There may be strong political pressure to maintain some type of preferential treatment for homeownership under the X tax. As discussed above, a preference may be justified if homeownership promotes social stability. But any such preference should encourage homeownership rather than the purchase of more expensive homes. If a subsidy is provided, it should take the form of a flat tax credit for the purchase of a home. Although the credit could be conditioned on purchasing a home with some minimum value (perhaps regionally adjusted), it should not otherwise rise with home value. One possible model is the current federal income tax credit, which is essentially equal to a flat $5,000, for first-time District of Columbia homebuyers with moderate incomes.[26] Unlike this credit, however, any homeownership preference under the X tax should not be limited to first-time homebuyers, confined to a particular geographical area, or vary with income. The preference should also not depend on the extent to which the home purchase is debt financed.

Consumer Durables. Under current law, consumer durables are generally taxed similarly to owner-occupied housing. Owners cannot deduct purchases and are not taxed on imputed service flows. Capital gains are theoretically taxable, but rarely occur and are even more rarely reported. Capital losses are not deductible, except that an itemized deduction can be claimed for theft and casualty losses exceeding 10 percent of adjusted gross income. Unlike home mortgage interest, interest on durables loans is not deductible.

Under the X tax, the prepayment method should apply to consumer durables in the same manner as to owner-occupied housing. Because the only changes from current law are repeal of the (theoretical) tax on capital gains and the deduction for theft and casualty losses, the switch to the new tax system should be straightforward. Like owner-occupied housing, consumer durables will escape the transition burden, but the value of existing durables will still decline due to income tax repeal; production of new durables will fall due to the loss of their current tax advantage over business capital, which will lower replacement costs and the value of existing durables.

Production by Governments, Nonprofits, and Households

Production by governments, nonprofits, and households can and should be subject to the wage tax, but the cash-flow tax generally cannot be applied to these institutions.

Application of Wage Tax. Employees of the federal, state, local, and tribal governments and nonprofit organizations should be subject to the household wage tax on the same terms as other workers. This policy would be similar to current law, as those employees now pay income tax on their wages on the same terms as other workers.[27]

We begin by considering the application of the wage tax to federal government employees. This case is slightly more complex than the others, because the entity that pays these workers' wages also collects the tax imposed on the wages. If the household wage tax was strictly proportional, say at a 20 percent flat rate, it would be economically irrelevant whether the tax applied to federal employees. Exempting federal employees from the 20 percent tax would, in equilibrium, cause a 20 percent reduction in their before-tax wages. For all actual and potential federal employees, the exemption and the before-tax wage reduction would be exactly offsetting, leaving unchanged their after-tax wages and the federal government's net-of-tax cost of employing them.

Because the wage tax is progressive, though, budgetary balance and economic efficiency are improved by taxing federal government employees. Although an exemption would still allow the government to pay lower before-tax wages in equilibrium, the reduction in the government's wage costs would be outweighed by its loss of tax revenue. While the equilibrium wage reduction would be linked to the tax bracket of the marginal federal employee, workers with tax brackets higher than that of the marginal worker would disproportionately move to federal employment because they would receive the largest tax savings from the exemption. Because their tax savings would be greater than the reduction in before-tax wages, the exemption would raise their after-tax wages and increase the federal government's net-of-tax cost of employing them. In short, exempting federal employees from the wage tax would distort the allocation of labor in the economy by artificially drawing high-tax-bracket workers into federal employment and would provide windfall gains to those workers at the federal government's expense.

Economic neutrality also requires the application of the wage tax to employees of state, local, and tribal governments and nonprofit organizations. If these entities' employees were exempt from the wage tax, the entities would be able to pay significantly lower before-tax wages in equilibrium. As a result, in-house production by these entities would enjoy a large cost advantage over production by business firms, including production contracted out to firms by these entities. There is little case for providing a tax subsidy to production by these entities, at least not one limited to their in-house production.

Moreover, even if a subsidy was desired, a wage tax exemption would be an inefficient way to provide it. The analysis parallels the above analysis for federal employees. While the reduction in before-tax wages would be linked to the marginal employee's tax bracket, high-bracket workers would flock to work for state, local, and tribal governments and nonprofits, and the average employee's tax savings would exceed the reduction in before-tax wages. So, the exemption would distort labor allocation by drawing high-tax-bracket workers into this sector. Only part of the federal government's revenue loss would translate into reductions in employment costs for these entities; the remainder would show up as windfall gains to high-bracket workers employed by these entities. A wage tax exemption would have the same flaw as the current income tax exemption for municipal bond interest, which artificially entices high-bracket investors to hold municipal bonds and provides windfall gains to those investors at the federal government's expense.

Employees hired by households, such as babysitters, lawn-care workers, and so on, should also be subject to the wage tax. Tax compliance by such employees would presumably be no worse, and no better, than under the current tax system.

Exemption from Cash-Flow Tax. We recommend that the federal, state, local, and tribal governments and nonprofit organizations be exempt from the tax on business cash flow. Their production activities would effectively be subject to the same prepayment method that we have recommended for owner-occupied housing and consumer durables.

To begin, application of the cash-flow tax to the federal government would be pointless, as the same entity would both pay and receive the tax. And, for all these institutions, application of the cash-flow tax would be administratively infeasible, because the "cash" flow would consist of the imputed value of the services these entities provide. Although we have judged the measurement of imputed rent on owner-occupied homes to be impractical, the task could be attempted with the aid of real estate professionals and, as discussed above, has been attempted in some other countries. But measurement of the imputed value of police and fire production and environmental regulation transcends the impractical and enters the realm of the impossible.

The economic implications of exempting these entities from the cash-flow tax are similar to the implications, discussed above, of the corresponding exemption for owner-occupied housing and consumer durables. Because the cash-flow tax imposes a zero effective marginal tax rate on new investment, exemption gives these entities no competitive advantage. The exemption has the same three effects it did for owner-occupied homes; it causes these entities' above-normal returns to escape tax, spares these entities' existing assets on the reform date from the transition burden, and prevents the federal government from spreading the risk of these entities' returns.

Each of these effects is either unavoidable or desirable, or both. Because the returns generated by these entities' operations are impossible to measure, there is no hope of detecting and taxing above-normal returns or spreading risk. And there seems little reason to impose the transition burden on these entities. Imposing the transition burden on state, local, and tribal governments would merely transfer wealth from the American people in their capacity as state, local, and tribal taxpayers and service recipients to the American people in their capacity as federal taxpayers and service recipients. Imposing the transition burden on nonprofit organizations might burden the recipients of their services, an unappealing result.

If desired, the cash-flow tax could be applied to commercial enterprises operated by governments and nonprofits, because the cash flows of these enterprises can be easily measured. Some of these enterprises currently pay the unrelated business income tax. Nevertheless, we recommend that tax not be imposed on these enterprises. There is little reason to impose the transition burden on these entities, and it may be difficult to separate the commercial enterprises from the entities' other operations.

Similarly, the cash-flow tax would obviously not apply to household employers. For example, the purchase of a lawn mower would be treated as the purchase of a consumer good, even if the purchaser actually hires neighboring children to use it to mow the lawn; the purchaser would *not* file a business tax return on which he would expense the purchase of the mower, deduct the wage payments, and pay tax on the imputed value of the mowing services. As a result, existing mowers owned by household employers would escape the transition burden, an outcome that seems eminently satisfactory.

Patrolling the Boundaries of the Business Cash-Flow Tax

Under the above recommendations, different sectors of the economy will operate under different tax rules. The business sector will be subject to the cash-flow tax, whereas the nonbusiness sector, consisting of owner-occupied homes, consumer durables, governments, nonprofit organizations, and households will be exempt from it. We now discuss the complications that arise when assets cross the boundary between the two sectors.

General Principles. Because the cash-flow tax imposes a zero marginal effective tax rate on new investment, there is generally no tax incentive for investments to migrate from one sector to the other. It may seem at first glance that such an incentive exists for assets with above-normal returns. If such an asset is initially held by a business firm, wouldn't there be a tax incentive to sell it to, say, a nonprofit organization? Because the nonprofit, unlike the firm, is exempt from the business cash-flow tax, moving the asset into the nonprofit's hands appears to allow the subsequent above-normal returns to escape the tax that they would have faced if the asset remained in the firm's hands.

This analysis is flawed, though, because it overlooks the fact that the firm also pays cash-flow tax on the full proceeds of asset sales, including sales to nonprofits. If the firm retains the asset, it is taxed on the asset's future cash flows as they arise; if the firm sells the asset, it is taxed on the asset's sales price at the time of sale. Because the asset's price is equal in expected market value to its future cash flows, there is no tax incentive to sell. Although cash flows arising after the sale to the nonprofit are not taxed when they arise, that result is perfectly appropriate because the cash flows were pretaxed (in expected present value) at the time of the sale.

For the same reason, there is no tax *disincentive* to a firm purchasing an asset with above-normal returns from a nonprofit. To be sure, such a sale causes subsequent cash flows to be taxed as they arise, which they would not have been if the asset had remained in the nonprofit's hands. But the firm is allowed to deduct the asset's full purchase price at the time of purchase. The tax savings from that deduction offset the future taxes because the purchase price is equal, in expected market value, to the future cash flows. So, if such a purchase is desirable for nontax reasons, the X tax does nothing to inefficiently preclude it from occurring.

We need to consider a few special cases where things are a little more complicated.

Sales in Anticipation of Reform. The above analysis demonstrates the importance of an asset's location on the day that reform takes effect. If the asset is in the business sector on the effective date, its future cash flows are irrevocably subject to tax. If the asset stays in the business sector, the cash flows are taxed as they arise; if the asset is sold to the nonbusiness sector, the future cash flows are pretaxed at the time of sale. On the other hand, if the asset is in the nonbusiness sector on the effective date, its future cash flows are irrevocably shielded from tax. If the asset remains in the nonbusiness sector, the cash flows are not taxed; if the asset is sold to the business sector, the cash flows are taxed as they arise, but the taxes are fully offset by the purchaser's up-front deduction at the time of sale. In short, the transition burden applies to those assets, and only those assets, that are in the business sector on the effective date, regardless of subsequent sales. As explained above, there are no tax incentives for sales between the two sectors after the reform takes effect.

Without special rules, though, there would be an incentive for assets to migrate into the nonbusiness sector *before* reform takes effect. Fortunately, one of the transition rules specified in chapter 8 addresses this concern. During a transition period beginning on the date at which reform becomes a serious possibility, firms are allowed to expense asset purchases and are fully taxed on asset sales.

The next situation cannot be resolved quite as easily as this one.

Sales between Related Parties. The above analysis relied heavily on the asset's price being equal to the expected market value of its future cash flows. That equality holds for the market price, which is the price at which transactions between unrelated parties can be expected to occur. But it may not hold for the prices at which related parties choose to contract with each other, and still less the price at which a party transacts with itself.

For example, there is no net tax incentive or disincentive for a homeowner to sell his house at a market price to an unrelated company that will convert it to rental use; as explained above, the tax savings from the rental company's expensing of the purchase is equal to the expected market value of the taxes on the future cash flows that the home will generate as a rental property. But what happens if a taxpayer moves out of his house and begins renting it to other parties? The conceptually correct treatment is to allow the taxpayer to deduct the market value of the house, which his rental business has effectively purchased from his homeowner alter ego, and to tax the subsequent cash flows generated by the rental business. The problem, of course, is that the taxpayer has an incentive to overstate market value, which cannot be readily observed. Conversely, a taxpayer who ceases to rent out a house and begins living in it should pay tax on the full market value of the house, which his rental business has effectively sold to his homeowner alter ego. Here, the taxpayer has an incentive to understate market value.

Strict rules, strictly enforced, will be necessary to prevent abuse. In the first situation described above, the taxpayer should be required to use valuations that are commensurate with the past purchase price of the house and should also be required to retroactively adjust the valuation upward if subsequent cash flows are high relative to the valuation initially used. In the second situation described above, the value should be commensurate with the past rental cash flows. Although such rules may be too harsh in some cases and may deter some legitimate transactions, stringency is necessary to prevent abuse.[28]

Fiscal Federalism under the X Tax

We now discuss the interaction of the X tax with state, local, and tribal tax systems and the municipal bond market.

Deductibility of State, Local, and Tribal Taxes. The current federal income tax allows an itemized deduction for income and property taxes paid to state, local, and tribal governments. Taxpayers may elect to deduct sales taxes in lieu of income taxes. Firms may generally deduct their tax payments as business expenses. The propriety of this treatment continues to be debated, with some proposing to repeal the itemized deduction and some proposing limits on it, such as a ceiling or a floor on the amount deducted.

The appropriate federal tax treatment of such taxes may depend on how they are used. Allowing a deduction for taxes that finance a municipal golf course may be as inappropriate as allowing a deduction for fees paid to a private golf course. On the other hand, a deduction for taxes that finance productive infrastructure may be as appropriate as a deduction for business purchases. Taxes that finance transfer payments should probably not be deductible if the recipients are not taxed on the transfer payments, as they are not under the proposals we outlined in chapter 4.

We need not resolve these issues. The various treatments for these taxes that have been adopted, or proposed, under the current income tax could be adopted, with little change, under the X tax. Accordingly, this issue can, for the most part, be addressed separately from the question of whether to adopt our proposed tax reform.

It would be difficult, however, to allow a deduction for state and local individual income taxes imposed on investment income, given that such income would not be subject to individual tax under the X tax system. This issue would not arise if state and local governments conformed to the federal X tax design, as discussed below, and therefore ceased to impose individual income taxes on investment income.

Conformity of State and Local Tax Systems. Today, most states have an individual income tax. The state income tax base is usually defined, at least in part, by reference to either the current or a lagged version of the federal income tax base. A generally similar pattern prevails with respect to state corporate income taxes. It would be difficult for states to continue taxing corporate income or individual capital income after the X tax was adopted at the federal level. In view of the inefficiency of such taxes, that is all to the good. State taxes on capital income make even less sense than federal taxes on capital income. To maximize the simplicity and efficiency advantages of reforms, states should be offered financial incentives to reconfigure their taxes as household wage taxes and business cash-flow taxes. Of course, states would be free to set their own rate schedules and to choose which personal tax deductions and credits to allow on household wage tax returns.

Municipal Bonds. Under the current federal income tax, interest income on bonds issued by state, local, and tribal governments ("municipal bonds") is generally tax exempt. Some restrictions apply to bonds issued by these governments for private use. This exemption is obsolete under the X tax, because all interest is exempt from tax.

The removal of the tax on interest income throughout the economy should cause interest rates to decline in equilibrium, which would benefit all borrowers, including municipal bond issuers. Nevertheless, these issuers would lose the tax advantage that they have over other borrowers and would capture a smaller share of the pool of savings.

As mentioned above, however, the exclusion of municipal bond interest is an inefficient subsidy because it provides windfalls to high-bracket investors. If Congress wishes to continue subsidizing municipal borrowing, it can adopt a more efficient subsidy by making direct payments to issuers, as was done for the Build America bonds issued in 2009 and 2010.

Conclusion

The nonbusiness sector poses few difficult issues for the X tax. Exempting production in this sector from the business cash-flow tax promotes simplicity and is consistent with consumption tax principles.

Box
TAXATION OF HOME RESALES

Under the prepayment method, there is no deduction for home purchases and no tax on home sales. One implication of this treatment is that home resales have no tax implications. In contrast, the ex post method would tax the seller on the full sales price and would allow a corresponding deduction for the purchaser.

Some proposals, such as those of Poddar (2010) and Conrad (2010), would modify the prepayment method to include a tax on home resales. The tax would apply only to the gain on the sale, although some proposals, such as Poddar's and Conrad's, would treat the entire sale proceeds as taxable gain on the first resale after reform of a home purchased before reform. The proposals vary in their treatment of resales that generate losses. No deduction would be provided for the purchaser.

The goal of such a policy is to tax above-normal and lucky returns on homes while avoiding the complications of taxing imputed rent. If imputed rents on a home were higher than normal and were expected to remain so, the home price would appreciate to an unusual extent. Under these proposals, the government would tax away part of this price appreciation if and when the homeowner sells the home. These proposals are undesirable, however, for two reasons.

First, because this policy does not measure above-normal and lucky returns correctly, it can overtax imputed rents. The fact that a home experiences a capital gain does not mean that the owner has received an above-normal or lucky return. If a home's imputed rent rises over time, its price also rises over time, even if the owner receives only a marginal return. For example, assume that the marginal rate of return is 5 percent, and consider a home for which the imputed rent is $10,000 today and rises 1 percent per year. This home sells for $250,000 today, and the price rises by 1 percent per year. Each year, the homeowner receives imputed rent equal to 4 percent of the home value and experiences a 1 percent capital gain, thereby earning the 5 percent marginal return. Under consumption tax principles, no tax should be imposed on these returns. The original $250,000 sale price, which the prepayment method taxes at the time of construction, fully reflects the present value of the future imputed rents; note that a stream of rents that begins at $10,000 today and rises 1 percent per year has a present value of $250,000 when discounted at 5 percent per year. Any additional tax would overtax the imputed rents and violate the neutrality of consumption taxation.

In fact, there is no way to accurately measure the size of the above-normal or lucky returns without measuring imputed rents, precisely the problem that this policy is meant to sidestep. A cautious version of the policy might tax only the appreciation in excess of the normal rate of return; assuming that imputed rent cannot be negative, a homeowner with a capital gain greater than the normal rate of return must have received an above-normal or lucky return. But if some lucky returns are to be taxed, neutrality requires that there be some offsetting relief for unlucky returns. Of course, providing a deduction to homeowners who sell at a loss would introduce further complications.

Another problem is that the tax would generate a lock-in effect similar to that induced by capital gains taxation today. Because lucky homeowners would pay this tax only if and when they sold their homes, many of them would be deterred from selling, disrupting efficient allocation of the housing stock and impeding mobility. If a deduction was provided for homeowners who sell at a loss, owners whose homes have declined in value would have the opposite incentive; they would be prompted to sell in order to claim the loss deduction, even if a sale would otherwise not be beneficial. Of course, any policy to tax gains would introduce administrative complications, particularly because home improvement costs would then need to be tracked and capitalized.

As discussed above, Congress has exempted the first $250,000 ($500,000 for couples) of capital gains on homes from tax under the current system. It would be peculiar to expand taxation of gains on homes when switching from the income tax to the X tax, given that such taxation has far less of a useful role to play under X tax principles than under income tax principles.

10

The VAT Alternative

For the reasons that we set forth in chapter 2 and have elaborated throughout this book, we believe that the X tax is the best way to tax consumption. The X tax has many of the advantages of, and can exploit the experience gained from, the VAT while achieving sufficient progressivity to allow it to serve as a complete replacement of the income tax system.

As we explained in chapter 2, distributional concerns make it more likely that any retail sales tax or VAT will be adopted as a partial, rather than a complete, replacement for the income tax system. In this chapter, we discuss how such a partial-replacement VAT should be structured if one is adopted, drawing on our analysis of the X tax in the earlier chapters.

Subtraction and Credit-Invoice VATs

Our discussion in chapter 2 focused on a subtraction-method VAT. As noted by Duncan and Sedon (2009, 1368), the VATs in most countries take the form of a credit-method VAT, also known as a credit-invoice method VAT. Although the credit method and subtraction method differ in administration, they are economically similar.

Recall that under a subtraction-method VAT, the tax base for each firm is receipts from sales of real goods and services minus purchases of real goods and services (including capital goods) from other businesses. For the economy as a whole, the base of a VAT is sales of real goods and services to consumers, because sales from one business to another are subject to offsetting inclusion and deduction and do not make up part of the net tax base.

The credit method works in a slightly different manner. Instead of deducting its purchases from other firms, each firm claims a credit against the tax on its sales for tax paid on its purchases from other firms. This method uses invoices to show the VAT paid on purchases and charged on sales, which creates a paper trail that aids enforcement. Again, there is no tax relief for the payment of employee compensation. Like the subtraction method, the credit method results in a consumption tax base.

An important administrative difference between the subtraction- and credit-method VATs is that a subtraction-method VAT is period based, whereas the credit-method VAT is transaction based. Under a subtraction-method VAT, a firm files a periodic return, perhaps annually, that tabulates business receipts and business purchases and applies the VAT rate to the difference. In this administrative respect, the subtraction-method VAT resembles the corporate income tax, although it has a quite different base than that tax. Under a credit-method VAT, tax is imposed on each sale with credit for VAT paid on business purchases, which is administratively similar to a retail sales tax.

To illustrate how the two methods work, consider the example in table 10-1, taken from Carroll and Viard (2010). A manufacturer purchases nothing from other firms, sells its output ($300) to a wholesaler, who sells all of its output ($700) to a retailer, who then sells final products to consumers ($1,000).

If a 10 percent retail sales tax were imposed, it would apply to the $1,000 of final sales to consumers, and $100 in tax would be collected. If the VAT rate is 10 percent, $100 in total VAT is collected on the sale of the product under either the subtraction or the credit method. However, unlike the sales tax, a portion of the VAT is collected at each stage of the production process.

Under the subtraction method, each firm subtracts its pretax purchases from its pretax sales and pays tax on the difference. The manufacturer pays $30 (10 percent of the difference between $300 of sales and $0 of purchases), the wholesaler pays $40 (10 percent of the difference between $700 of sales and $300 of purchases), and the retailer pays $30 (10 percent of the difference between $1,000 of sales and $700 of purchases). Under the credit method, $30 tax is collected from the manufacturer ($30 tax on sales minus $0 tax on purchases), $40 from the wholesaler ($70 tax on sales minus $30 tax on purchases), and $30 from the retailer ($100 tax on sales minus $70 tax on purchases).

In this example, the VAT collected at each stage of production is exactly the same under the subtraction and credit methods. Under the

TABLE 10-1

DIFFERENT BUT ECONOMICALLY EQUIVALENT WAYS TO TAX CONSUMPTION

Economic Activity	Manu-facturer	Whole-saler	Retailer	Total
1. Sales	$300	$700	$1,000	
2. Purchases	$0	$300	$700	
3. Labor	$0	$200	$300	
4. Value added (sales–purchases)	$300	$400	$300	$1,000
Retail Sales Tax				
5. Retail sales tax (10% of retailer sales)	**$0**	**$0**	**$100**	**$100**
Subtraction-Method VAT				
6. Subtraction-method VAT (10% of line 4)	**$30**	**$40**	**$30**	**$100**
Credit-Method VAT				
7. Tax on sales (10% of line 1)	**$30**	**$70**	**$100**	
8. Less: input tax on purchases	**$0**	**$30**	**$70**	
9. Net VAT liability	**$30**	**$40**	**$30**	**$100**

SOURCE: Example drawn from Carroll and Viard (2010).

credit method, the VAT at each stage equals the difference between the tax on sales and the tax on purchases; under the subtraction method, the VAT at each stage equals the VAT rate multiplied by the difference between sales and purchases. The two computations are conceptually and arithmetically equivalent.

This equivalence breaks down under other circumstances. As Metcalf (1996, 94–97), Duncan and Sedon (2009, 1369–70), Carroll and Viard (2010, 1119–20), and Carroll et al. (2010, 5–7) explain, the two methods yield different results when multiple tax rates apply to various products or when some products are exempt from tax.

One fallacy about the retail sales tax and the VAT should be noted. Some supporters of those taxes claim that sellers of illegal drugs and other participants in the underground economy will pay sales tax or VAT when they spend their illegal income, thereby ending their tax advantage over legal businesses. As Bradford (1986, 71–72), Metcalf (1996, 98), Auerbach (2005), and Hines (2004) observe, this claim is squarely incorrect. Drug dealers would actually retain their tax advantage under a VAT or sales tax because they, unlike legal businesses, would not collect tax from their customers. Tax is therefore evaded in either case. Although it appears that it is the drug seller who evades income tax whereas it is the drug buyer who evades sales tax or VAT, even that difference is largely illusory. The equilibrium price of the drugs actually adjusts so that the buyer and seller share the profits from tax evasion in roughly the same way under each tax system.

The Superiority of the VAT to the Retail Sales Tax

As we noted in chapter 2, the differences between the sales tax and the VAT are essentially administrative. Many experts on tax administration argue that a retail sales tax is difficult or impossible to enforce at high tax rates, sometimes mentioning 10 percent as a threshold at which enforcement becomes particularly difficult (see the references cited by Gale [2005, 898]).

Some of the arguments about the sales tax's enforcement difficulties may be overstated. Moreover, it seems unlikely that a tipping point occurs at 10 percent or any other particular tax rate. Nevertheless, because the sales tax is collected only at the retail level, it is probably more vulnerable to evasion than the VAT, which is collected throughout the production chain. And the enforcement difficulties surely become more severe as the tax rate rises to the levels that would be required to replace a substantial part of the federal income tax system.

As Zodrow (1999) noted, if a high-rate tax labeled as a retail sales tax is adopted at the federal level, compliance concerns make it likely that it will be administered, at least partly, in accordance with VAT principles; in his phrase, it is likely to be "a VAT in drag." Even the FairTax plan illustrates this point to some extent. Although the plan generally follows the retail-sales-tax approach of exempting business-to-business sales from tax, it makes an exception for items that are readily susceptible to consumer use. For those items, the proposal adopts the credit-method VAT approach; it taxes all sales, whether to businesses or consumers, but then allows business purchasers to claim credit for the tax.

In any case, there is no doubt that the VAT can be successfully enforced at relatively high rates, because more than 145 countries currently do so. There is no comparable experience to provide the same reassurance about the retail sales tax. Because the VAT and the sales tax are otherwise so similar, it is foolhardy to use the latter if there are any serious doubts about its enforceability. The sales tax has no evident countervailing advantage, relative to the VAT, other than that it spares firms with no retail sales the burden of filing returns and remitting tax.

In practice, the sales tax may have other disadvantages, relative to the VAT, besides compliance. It is imperative that a consumption tax avoid tax cascading, in which a single final consumption item is taxed multiple times. VATs generally avoid cascading because a deduction or credit for business purchases is built into the basic design of the tax. An ideal textbook retail sales tax avoids cascading by simply not taxing business-to-business transactions. Under most state and local retail sales tax systems in the United States, however, business purchases are often taxed. As discussed by Cline et al. (2005), Mikesell (1997), Durner and Bui (2010, 983–84), and Viard (2010), a substantial portion, perhaps roughly 40 percent, of state retail sales taxes are collected on purchases of business inputs. Although a federal sales tax might be able to avoid political pressure to tax business-to-business transactions, the state experience is not encouraging. Smart and Bird (2009) found evidence that investment increased when Canadian provinces switched from retail sales taxes that included significant taxation of business purchases to VATs that did not tax such purchases.

State and local retail sales tax systems in the United States typically suffer from another serious flaw. As Mikesell (1997), Durner and Bui (2010, 984–85), and Viard (2011d) note, these tax systems tax the sales of many goods to consumers but generally do not tax sales of services. In contrast, VATs around the world generally apply to a wide range of services to consumers, although some services, such as medical care and financial services, remain untaxed. Once again, it is possible that a federal retail sales tax might be able to avoid political pressure to exempt consumer purchases of services, but it seems safer to adopt the VAT with its proven track record.

One potential difficulty would arise under either a federal sales tax or a VAT. In practice, both types of taxes tend to exclude a substantial portion of consumption to address distributional concerns. The Organisation for Economic Co-operation and Development (2008, 53) reports that standard

VAT exemptions among OECD countries include health care, education, and financial services and that most of these VATs could more accurately be termed "partial VATs." Food consumed at home also often receives preferential treatment. Viard (2011e) discusses the corresponding experience under state and local sales taxes in the United States.

Because this base narrowing tends to occur under VATs as well as under sales taxes, structuring a federal consumption tax as a VAT is unlikely to avert the problem. As Carroll et al. (2010) emphasize, the exclusion of a substantial fraction of consumption from the tax base distorts consumption decisions and reduces the economic benefits of a VAT. Stelzer (2010) provides humorous details of the arbitrary distinctions that the British VAT has drawn in its definition of tax-exempt food and clothing.

The X tax appears to have an advantage over the VAT in this regard. Under an X tax system, it is highly unlikely that workers in, say, the food or health care industries would be exempted from the household wage tax or that firms in those industries would be exempted from the business cash-flow tax. To be sure, tax deductions or credits for purchases of such items might be offered under the household wage tax. Even so, the X tax is probably less vulnerable to this base narrowing than a sales tax or VAT.

In view of the above considerations, we follow Mikesell (1997, 86), Cnossen (2009, 697), and others in concluding that a federal VAT would be superior to a federal retail sales tax. We therefore refer throughout this chapter to a potential federal VAT rather than to a potential federal sales tax. Given the similarity of the two taxes, though, our analysis below can be applied to either type of levy.

Recent Discussion of VAT

As Thorndike (2009) notes, the possibility of a U.S. VAT has been discussed since at least 1921, when it was proposed by tax economist Thomas S. Adams. In the last few years, the VAT has drawn renewed interest. The U.S. Department of the Treasury, Office of Tax Policy (2007, 19–42) analyzed three corporate tax reform options, one of which would have replaced the corporate income tax with a 5 or 6 percent VAT. The Roadmap for America's Future proposal, which Rep. Paul Ryan (R-Wisconsin) unveiled in January 2010, would have similarly replaced the corporate income tax with an 8.5 percent VAT. Prominent commentators such as Bartlett (2009), Zakaria (2010), and Barro (2011) have called for a VAT to address the long-run fiscal imbalance. Two prominent tax reform plans, by Graetz (2008) and Burman (2008), call for the adoption of a VAT accompanied by reduction, but not elimination, of individual and corporate income taxes.

As detailed by Carroll and Viard (2010, 1117) and Goldfarb (2009, 2010), a number of current and former government officials alluded to the possibility of a VAT in 2009. Recommendations that a VAT be considered were much more common than outright endorsements of the tax. Most or all of the comments envisioned the VAT as an addition to, or partial replacement for, the income tax rather than as a complete replacement. On November 17, 2010, the Bipartisan Policy Center, chaired by Alice Rivlin and Pete Domenici, offered a deficit-reduction plan that included a 6.5 percent credit-invoice VAT, accompanied by reductions in individual and corporate income tax rates.

In contrast, the deficit-reduction plan approved by a majority of the President's National Commission on Fiscal Responsibility and Reform on December 3, 2010, did not include a VAT. The plan instead emphasized reforming the individual and corporate income taxes through base broadening and rate reduction. In the wake of that plan, discussions of a VAT generally gave way to discussions of income tax reform. For example, when Representative Ryan revised his Roadmap plan in April 2011, he dropped the provision for replacing the corporate income tax with a VAT.

The discussion of a VAT in 2009 and 2010 triggered a backlash. On April 15, 2010, the Senate voted 85–13 to adopt Senate Amendment 3724, a nonbinding resolution stating, "It is the sense of the Senate that the Value Added Tax is a massive tax increase that will cripple families on fixed income and only further push back America's economic recovery." The resolution was supported by Democrats 43–12, Republicans 40–1, and independents 2–0. History suggests, however, that this resolution may be an unreliable guide to the VAT's ultimate prospects. Although the Senate voted 98–0 on July 14, 1981, to adopt a nonbinding resolution stating that Social Security benefits should not be subject to income tax, partial income taxation of benefits was included in the bipartisan Social Security reform package adopted less than two years later. Overwhelming support for symbolic resolutions that condemn an unpopular measure in isolation does not always preclude subsequent enactment of the measure as part of a bipartisan response to a widely recognized problem.

Using the VAT to Replace Other Taxes

If the VAT is to serve as a partial replacement of the individual income tax, it is necessary to decide how to scale back the income tax. Graetz (2008) would eliminate income tax liability for a large number of low- and moderate-income households, in addition to lowering tax rates, whereas Burman (2008) would reduce income taxes across the board. The Graetz approach would provide greater simplification, but might exacerbate the problem of voters not perceiving the cost of government.

While much of the VAT revenues would probably go to reduce the individual income tax, a VAT could also be used to replace other taxes. On both efficiency and simplicity grounds, the corporate income tax is a prime candidate for replacement, as urged by Viard (2011c). As mentioned above, the U.S. Department of the Treasury (2007) considered this approach, which was also taken in Representative Ryan's 2010 proposal. The U.S. Department of the Treasury (2007, 27) estimated that replacement of the corporate income tax with a VAT would increase long-run output by 2.0 to 2.5 percent. Another prime candidate for replacement is the Unearned Income Medicare Contribution tax, slated to take effect in 2013.

Distributional concerns may provide an impetus to replace part or all of the payroll and self-employment taxes. That approach would offer significantly smaller efficiency gains than income tax replacement. As we discussed in chapter 4, payroll taxes do not distort the saving decision. Also, the replacement of the Social Security tax by a VAT would create significant difficulties for the design of the Social Security system. As we explained in chapter 4, Social Security benefits and taxes are linked at the individual level because each worker's monthly benefits depend on AIME, a measure of the lifetime earnings on which the worker has paid Social Security tax. Workers with higher lifetime earnings receive higher monthly benefits, although the increase is less than proportional. The link between benefits and taxed earnings is intended to give the program a contributory feature.

In chapter 4, we rejected replacement of the Social Security tax by the X tax because it would be harder to maintain this contributory link under the latter. This objection applies with far greater force to a VAT, which, unlike the household X tax, does not directly base tax payments on workers' earnings. If a VAT was used to finance Social Security, the current benefit formula would lose its contributory rationale because there would be little visible link between the earnings on which benefits are based and the VAT payments that would pay for the benefits. Of course, budget constraints imply that workers with higher lifetime earnings make higher lifetime VAT payments, but that link may be too subtle to carry political weight. The current benefit formula would probably come under serious political pressure after its contributory rationale was undermined. Why pay higher monthly benefits to workers with higher lifetime earnings (who presumably have *less* need for benefits) when there is little visible indication that they have paid more into the program? The payment of a flat monthly benefit to all retirees, or even means testing of benefits, might be viewed as more appropriate. Of course, the transition to any new benefit formula would pose severe political complications.

In view of these considerations, replacement of the Social Security tax by a VAT seems impractical, as Viard (2011c) noted. As discussed below, a VAT will require some adjustments to Social Security taxes and benefits in any event, but it is best to avoid the disruption arising from an attempt to replace the Social Security tax.

Replacement of the Medicare payroll and self-employment tax by a VAT, as proposed by Burman (2008), would pose fewer difficulties, because there is almost no link at the individual level between taxes and benefits in the Medicare program.[29]

The "Easy" Stuff

As we explained in chapter 2, the X tax differs from a VAT only by taxing labor compensation at the household level rather than at the firm level. The other difference between the X tax that we have discussed in this book and the VAT considered in this chapter is that the income tax system is assumed to remain in place alongside the latter but not the former. As a result, much of the analysis, and many of the recommendations, in this book can be applied to a partial-replacement VAT, with some revisions to reflect these two differences.

Some issues can be handled quite similarly under the VAT as under the X tax. One example is the financial sector. As we recommended for the X

THE VAT ALTERNATIVE 165

tax in chapter 6, the VAT should use the R+F cash-flow method to tax the provision of financial services to households. No tax should be imposed on the provision of financial services to firms, and firms should not deduct the cost of such services. Another example is the treatment of owner-occupied housing and consumer durables. As we recommended for the X tax in chapter 9, the VAT should apply to the production of new housing and durables, with no tax on resales.

In some areas, a partial-replacement VAT can escape difficulties encountered by a complete-replacement X tax.

Because the VAT does not impose a separate tax on labor compensation, special rules for the taxation of fringe benefits and pensions would be unnecessary. Also, because the income tax would remain in place, adoption of a partial-replacement VAT would cause no administrative complications for current means tests. It would still be desirable, though, to replace the income-based means tests for Medicare premiums with the AIME-based provisions that we recommended in chapter 4; indeed, this change would be desirable if neither a VAT nor an X tax was adopted.

Because the VAT does not distinguish between wages and business cash flow, there would also be no need for the reasonable-compensation rules that we discussed in chapter 5. Another complication discussed in that chapter, the treatment of firms with negative cash flows, would also largely disappear. To begin, negative value added is much less common than negative cash flow, because wages are not deducted in computing value added. Also, as we noted, there is generally little political resistance to the policy of providing refunds for negative value added, although restrictions on refunds are sometimes imposed.

A decision on whether to exempt small firms from the VAT would need to be made. Although small-firm exemptions are common in VAT systems, the case for exemption is uncertain. Because small firms should find VAT compliance no more difficult, and probably easier, than income tax compliance, it can be argued that the case for a small-firm exemption is no stronger under a VAT than under the income tax. It may be desirable, however, to provide some administrative simplification for small firms.

The VAT would undoubtedly be border adjusted, as it is in other countries and as permitted by international trade rules. Indeed, the competitiveness fallacy that we discussed in chapter 7 has played an important role in the political promotion of the VAT. As a result, the VAT enjoys a political advantage—the illusory improvement in competitiveness—that the X tax lacks. The border adjustment should be relatively easy to design, given the extensive international experience on which to draw. From a political and administrative perspective, international issues can be handled at least as easily under the VAT as under the X tax.

The economic effects are a different matter. By itself, the illusory nature of the competitiveness advantage is not an affirmative argument against border adjustment; it merely means that border adjustment will fail to deliver the gains some are hoping for. As we explained in chapter 7, though, border adjustment will result in a wealth transfer from Americans to foreigners by removing from the tax base the consumption of foreigners financed by their existing American assets. Moreover, simple calculations suggested this transfer, even in the presence of transition relief, is large, although it would be smaller for a partial-replacement VAT than for a complete-replacement tax. Border adjustments therefore carry substantial disadvantages to countries considering implementing a VAT.

Several important issues are actually more complicated under a partial-replacement VAT than under a complete-replacement X tax.

Monetary Policy and Other Transition Issues

Although the monetary policy reaction to the introduction of a VAT is sometimes overlooked in discussions of tax reform, it is quite important. As explained below, a monetary policy dilemma arises, because the VAT is a firm-level tax that reduces the market-clearing level of the real wage paid by firms to workers. As a result, it is likely that the Federal Reserve will partially or fully accommodate the VAT by allowing the consumer price level to rise. For previous discussions of this issue, see Tait (1988, 193), Joint Committee on Taxation (1993, 53–59), Bull and Lindsey (1996, 362), Hall (1996, 77; 1997, 150), Metcalf (1996, 97), and Bradford (1996b, 135).

Monetary Policy Dilemma. Following Carroll and Viard (2010), consider a worker who produces 100 apples. With no taxes, the worker is paid a wage equal to the consumer price of 100 apples; if apples sell for $1, the worker is paid a wage of $100. The worker continues to receive the same

$100 wage in a world with a 20 percent individual income tax. In that case, however, the worker pays $20 income tax on the $100, reducing disposable income to $80, which is enough to buy 80 apples. Note that although the individual income tax reduces the worker's real after-tax wage from 100 to 80 apples, it does not reduce the real wage paid by the firm to the worker, which remains equal to 100 apples. The wage paid by the firm is unaffected because the tax is collected from the worker *out of* the wage payment that he receives from the firm.

Now, suppose that the 20 percent income tax is replaced by a 20 per-cent (tax-inclusive rate) VAT. Also, assume that the Federal Reserve pursues monetary policy that keeps the tax-inclusive consumer price of apples unchanged at $1. Then, the firm clears only 80 cents for each apple sold, with the other 20 cents paid in VAT. Because the 100 apples produced by the worker are now worth only $80 to the firm, the market-clearing wage falls to $80. Of course, with the income tax removed, the worker now keeps the entire $80 wage. Because apples still cost $1 (with tax included), the worker receives the same real disposable income of 80 apples that she enjoyed under the 20 percent income tax.

There is, or should be, no real difference between the two cases. Either way, the firm pays 100 apples to obtain the services of the worker, with the worker receiving 80 of the apples and the government receiving the other 20 apples. The only difference is the manner of tax collection. The income tax is collected from the worker and is taken out of the wage after it is paid to the worker; the firm gives 100 apples to the worker, who then turns 20 of them over to the government. The VAT is collected from the firm and is effectively taken out of the wage before the worker receives it; the firm gives 80 apples to the worker and 20 apples to the government. In a frictionless textbook economy, none of this makes any difference.

Unfortunately, the difference may be significant in the real world because it may be difficult to reduce nominal wages. Continuing to assume that the Federal Reserve keeps the consumer price of apples at $1, suppose now that the worker's nominal wage remains rigid at $100 rather than falling to the new market-clearing level of $80, which means that firms must pay 100 apples to workers. In order to pay this wage and satisfy its VAT obligations, the firm must reduce its hiring until the marginal product of labor rises to 125 apples; with the worker producing 125 apples, each of which sells for $1, the firm can pay the $100 wage and $25 VAT (20 percent of $125). The hiring reduction causes high unemployment, which presumably drives wages down to the $80 market-clearing level after some period of time.

In practice, the Federal Reserve is likely to alter monetary policy to avert these adverse developments. If the Fed accommodates the VAT by allowing the consumer price of apples to rise to $1.25, real wages can fall without reducing nominal wages. Such accommodation seems likely; regardless of whether nominal wages would actually be rigid under these circumstances, the Fed would probably be reluctant to take the chance. It should be noted that the accommodation results in a one-time increase in the price level, not a lasting acceleration of the rate of price increases.

A survey by Carroll et al. (2010, 36–38) finds that central banks have often accommodated increases in VAT tax rates. Although central banks have not always accommodated introductions of new VATs, those VATs were often accompanied by offsetting reductions of other indirect taxes that also taxed labor at the firm level, making accommodation unnecessary; that experience would not be relevant for a U.S. VAT that replaced part of the individual income tax. Tait (1988, 194–212) finds mixed evidence on whether introductions of VATs and rate increases have been accommodated in various countries. More recently, the Bank of England (2011, 30–31) explained that the increase in British inflation in early 2011 was partly due to a January 2011 increase in the VAT rate. On the whole, this evidence indicates that accommodation is possible but not certain.

For commonly proposed VAT rates, the price increase would be quite large if the tax was completely or largely accommodated, causing significant disruption in an economy in which many contracts are written in nominal terms. For example, the Graetz and Burman plans call for a VAT on the order of 15 percent, and the average VAT rate among member nations of the OECD is about 17.7 percent. Phasing in the VAT over time would make the price increase more gradual, causing less disruption than an abrupt increase. Of course, such a phase-in would provide an incentive to acceler-ate consumption and reduce saving; recall that the neutrality of a consump-tion tax depends on the tax rate being constant over time.

One way to further reduce the necessary accommodation seems not to have been considered. The introduction of the VAT could be accompanied by the conversion of the employer payroll tax into an employee payroll tax. Such a shift would provide a further reduction in firm-level labor taxes and would have the side effect of making Social Security financing more transparent by showing employees the full tax imposed on their earnings.

In any event, the decision of whether to accommodate the VAT should be agreed on by the Federal Reserve and the political branches. Although the Fed must retain some flexibility on how to implement any accommodation, the issue of whether the country should experience a double-digit one-time increase in consumer prices is not a technocratic issue that can be left solely to that institution. As Bull and Lindsey (1996, 373) stress, the chosen approach should be publicly announced, and if a decision not to accommodate the VAT is made, steps should be taken to facilitate the necessary nominal wage reductions.

As Bradford (1996b, 137) and Hall (1996, 77–78) note, the fact that the X tax imposes its wage tax at the household level allows it to avoid these difficulties, removing any need for the Fed to accommodate.

Impact of Accommodation. In some respects, the burden of the VAT would be little affected by whether or not the Federal Reserve accommodated the tax. (For purposes of this discussion, we assume that if the Fed did not accommodate, nominal wages would fall to their market-clearing level, so that labor markets would not be disrupted.) As explained above, the same decline in real wages would occur, with or without accommodation. Moreover, accommodation would not change the aggregate transition burden on existing wealth, as the proportional burden would remain equal to the tax rate.

In other respects, though, accommodation would change how the VAT burden is distributed. For example, accommodation would change the allocation of the transition burden on existing wealth. As we explained in chapter 8, the transition burden of an X tax would fall on equity holders, as there would be no change in the real value of debt, and equity holders would therefore bear the full burden in their capacity as residual claimants. The same impact would occur under a VAT that was not accommodated. But if the VAT was accommodated, part of the burden would be transferred from equity holders to debt holders, as accommodation would cause the real value of bonds to decline, assuming that the bonds were not indexed against inflation. If the tax was fully accommodated, the real values of both debt and equity would decline by a proportion equal to the tax rate.

Accommodation would also affect loans between households, reducing the wealth of lenders and increasing the wealth of borrowers.

Regardless of whether the VAT was accommodated, many transfer payment recipients would escape any VAT burden on their benefits. Despite initial appearances, for example, there would be no VAT burden on Social Security recipients who became eligible for benefits before the VAT was adopted. (As explained below, there would be an impact on new Social Security recipients, an impact that would not depend on whether the VAT was accommodated.) While it may seem that a Social Security recipient would pay VAT at the cash register when she used her benefits to pay for consumer goods, she would actually suffer no net burden. If the Fed did not accommodate, there would be no rise in consumer prices and no change in her benefits. If the Fed did accommodate, consumer prices would rise, but her benefits would automatically increase to offset the price increase, due to the cost-of-living adjustment prescribed by current law. The same analysis would apply to recipients of other inflation-indexed transfer payments.

Recipients of transfer payments that are not inflation-indexed might bear a VAT burden, however, depending on whether the Fed accommodated. If the Fed did not accommodate, an alimony recipient would bear no VAT burden, as there would be no change in prices and no change in the alimony payment. But if the Fed accommodated, prices would rise and there would, in most cases, be no automatic compensatory increase in the alimony payment. Accommodation would then impose a burden on the alimony recipient while providing relief to the alimony payer. The same analysis would apply to other transfer payments that are not inflation-indexed, such as child support and Temporary Assistance to Needy Families benefits. In each of these cases, though, it is possible that courts or legislatures would eventually adjust the benefits to account for the price increase, thereby eliminating the recipients' burdens.

For further discussion of the impact of accommodation, see Joint Committee on Taxation (1993, 53–54).

Transition Relief. Like the X tax, the VAT faces the question of whether and how to offer relief for the transition burden. We recommended in chapter 7 that relief for existing business capital be provided at the firm level under the X tax. Because firms also remit VAT payments, it might seem natural to provide firm-level transition relief under the VAT as well. Household-level relief would be more appropriate, however, due to the allocation of the transition burden under the VAT.

Firm-level transition relief generally accrues to the benefit of individuals, both foreign and American, holding equity in firms operating in the United States. That is appropriate under our proposed X tax because it is those equity holders who bear the transition burden, given that the tax is not border adjusted and does not prompt the Federal Reserve to increase the consumer price level. But the transition burden would be distributed quite differently under the VAT. Because the tax would be border adjusted, the transition burden would fall on American wealth holders. And if the VAT is accommodated by the Fed, part of the transition burden is shifted from equity holders to debt holders, as discussed above. Transition relief at the firm level would therefore be misaligned with the incidence of the transition burden. Instead, it would be appropriate to provide relief to American consumers at the household level. It would be straightforward to provide such relief through the income tax system that we assume will remain in place alongside the VAT.

Governments and Nonprofits

One challenge confronting a sales tax or VAT is the treatment of state, local, and tribal governments and nonprofits. The logical solution, which is embedded in the FairTax plan, is to impose an employer payroll tax, with a rate equal to the sales tax or VAT rate, on these institutions. Unfortunately, the payroll tax proposal has drawn strong objections, which are based on an optical illusion.

The common, but erroneous, perception expressed by Graetz (2008, 187–88) and others is that the payroll tax would be a new burden on these governments and that it would provide an incentive for them to contract out functions to private enterprises. In reality, the payroll tax would restore neutrality by eliminating the disincentive to contracting that would otherwise arise from the imposition of VAT on private contractors.

State, local, and tribal governments and nonprofits would obtain the money to pay the payroll tax from the reduction in their wage costs. As noted above, adoption of the VAT would cause real wage payments to fall for employers throughout the economy. For business firms, the lower payments would be offset by the new VAT; for governments and nonprofits, they would be offset by the new employer payroll tax. For all employers, there would be no net change in the cost of hiring employees. Without the payroll tax, governments and nonprofits would enjoy a massive windfall, with the magnitude of the windfall arbitrarily based on the extent to which they produce in-house rather than contracting with business firms.

Nobody objects today to the application of federal income tax to the wages earned by employees of state, local, and tribal governments and nonprofits. Moreover, under the X tax, which splits the VAT into separate taxes on wages and business cash flow, nobody objects to imposing the household tax on the wages of these employees, as we recommended in chapter 9. Yet, when the wage tax and business cash-flow tax are combined into a VAT, the continued inclusion of these wages in the tax base is inexplicably viewed as an unacceptable burden.

Ideally, therefore, the VAT should be accompanied by an employer payroll tax on state, local, and tribal governments and nonprofits. Unfortunately, political pressure may prevent this neutral solution from being adopted.

It makes no real economic difference whether a similar employer payroll tax is imposed on the federal government, given that the government would pay this flat-rate tax to itself. It would probably be simpler to dispense with such a tax. Still, imposing the tax would maintain continuity in budget accounting. Today, the federal government pays wages gross of individual income tax, which are recorded as outlays, and collects income tax on those wages, which are recorded as receipts. Without an employer payroll tax, the government would pay net-of-VAT wages and collect no VAT on its own production, artificially reducing both recorded outlays and recorded receipts.

Household employers should similarly be taxed on the wages they pay. For example, the hiring of a lawn-care worker should be treated as a consumption purchase subject to VAT. Compliance would presumably be no better, and no worse, than under the current income tax system.

Implications for Social Security

As Viard (2011c) detailed, the adoption of a VAT would pose complications for the Social Security system, even if Social Security payroll and self-employment taxes were maintained, as we recommended above. The complications arise from the same source as the monetary policy dilemma: the fact that a VAT reduces the real wage paid by the firm to the worker rather than being paid by the worker from the wages. Moreover, these complications would be present regardless of whether the real wage reduction occurred through consumer price increases (if the Federal Reserve accommodated the tax) or nominal wage reductions (if the Fed did not accommodate).

The introduction of a 10 percent VAT would reduce the real wages paid to workers by firms by 10 percent, thereby shrinking the Social Security payroll tax base by the same proportion. This impact is often referred to as the "excise tax offset" because it arises under excise taxes as well as VATs. Note that any individual income tax reductions that accompanied the introduction of the VAT would do nothing to counteract the payroll tax base reduction, because income taxes are not deducted in computing the payroll tax base. Real payroll tax revenues could be maintained by increasing the statutory payroll tax rate.

Similar complications would arise on the benefit side. As noted by Viard (2011c) and Toder, Nunns, and Rosenberg (2011), the detailed mechanics of the AIME computation imply that each annual cohort's real Social Security benefits are proportional to the real value of the Social Security Administration's National Average Wage Index in the year that the cohort attains age sixty. The introduction of a permanent 10 percent VAT in 2013 would therefore reduce real benefits by 10 percent for cohorts born in or after 1953, while leaving untouched the real benefits paid to cohorts born in or before 1952.

As explained above, the VAT does not alter real benefits for transfer payments that are inflation-indexed, such as Social Security benefits for past retirees, whether or not the Fed accommodates the tax. Also, as explained above, the VAT reduces real benefits for transfer payments that are fixed in nominal terms if, and only if, the Fed accommodates the tax. Social Security benefits for new recipients are in a third category, because real benefits are proportional to real wages. The VAT reduces the real values of these benefits, whether or not the Fed accommodates the tax, because the VAT reduces real wages.

Real benefits for cohorts born in or after 1953 could be maintained by increasing the parameters that enter the benefit formula. An alternative solution would be to apply payroll taxes to, and compute benefits in terms of, VAT-inclusive wages. With a 10 percent VAT, for example, if a worker was paid $90 in wages by the firm, payroll taxes could be imposed on $100, consisting of the $90 wage plus the $10 VAT that the worker effectively paid at the firm level. The full $100 amount would then also be included in the worker's benefit computation, and the National Average Wage Index would be defined in terms of VAT-inclusive wages. It is unclear whether this approach has any political or other advantages over simply increasing the payroll tax rate and the benefit formula parameters.

In any case, it would be irresponsible to simply leave the wage definition, payroll tax rate, and benefit parameters unchanged while introducing a VAT. Even if a reduction of Social Security taxes and benefits is desired, it should not be done in this backdoor manner. Moreover, such inaction would cause a worsening of the Social Security system's finances, as the revenue reduction would immediately take full effect for all workers, while the benefit reduction would take effect only as new retirees began to draw benefits. Also, the disparate treatment of those turning sixty in the year of VAT introduction and those who turned sixty in the preceding year would be widely and correctly perceived as capricious.

Another concern relates to the nominal bonds held by the Social Security trust funds, which are claims against the remainder of the federal government. If the Federal Reserve accommodated the VAT and consumer prices rose, the real value of these bonds would fall. Although this would not alter the federal government's overall finances, it would reduce the resources available to Social Security while increasing the resources available to the remainder of the government. If desired, this reallocation could be undone through a general-revenue transfer to the trust fund. This issue would not arise if the Fed did not accommodate the VAT.

Also, if individual income tax rates were reduced as part of the reform, less revenue would be raised from the income taxation of Social Security benefits. As we discussed in chapter 4, the revenue from such taxation is earmarked to the Social Security and Medicare Part A trust funds. If the reduction in trust fund revenue was considered undesirable, a small portion of the VAT revenue could be earmarked to the trust funds.

Combating the "Money Machine"

Another concern about the VAT, vividly expressed by Christian and Robbins (2011), is that it may function as a money machine, fueling the growth of federal spending. Pierson (2011) reports that members of the National Commission on Fiscal Responsibility and Reform identified this concern as the decisive factor dissuading them from recommending a VAT. Going further back, President Ronald Reagan criticized the VAT on this ground at a February 21, 1985, press conference, as noted by Tait (1988, 226). In this regard, a complete-replacement X tax has an advantage over a partial-replacement VAT because the complete replacement of the income tax is likely to restrain efforts to expand government in the future.

It is difficult to determine the extent, if any, to which the VAT actually functions as a money machine. Although countries with VATs tend to have larger public sectors than those without, this correlation does not necessarily establish that the VAT *causes* an expansion of government. Keen and Lockwood (2006, 917) find evidence that increases in VAT rates do not predict subsequent increases in the size of government, after controlling for other relevant variables, casting doubt on a causal effect. In contrast, Holtz-Eakin and Smith (2010) find that increases in VAT rates do have such predictive power, supporting a causal effect. Tait (1988, 226–28) argues that the VAT has not had a significant effect on the size of government.

This evidence indicates that it is possible, though not certain, that the VAT will stimulate the growth of government. Accordingly, we now discuss ways to combat this possibility.

Visibility. A specific concern about the VAT relates to its visibility, as it is easier to raise a tax when voters have little awareness of it. If the VAT were not listed on customer receipts, it would be a highly invisible tax. But the VAT could be separately listed on customer receipts, as is currently done for state and local retail sales taxes in the United States. The full VAT liability, including the portion collected earlier in the production chain, could and should be listed.

Edwards (2005) notes that Canada, unlike most European nations, requires that the VAT be listed on customer receipts. In a historical survey of the Canadian VAT, Sullivan (2010) argues that its visibility has had important political consequences. After being pushed through Parliament by a Conservative government and taking effect at a 7 percent rate in 1991, the tax drew immediate public opposition, prompting pledges by the Liberal Party to work for repeal. After winning power, however, the Liberal

Party decided to keep the tax. In 2006, a Conservative government reduced the national tax rate to 5 percent. Sullivan notes that, far from inexorably rising, the VAT rate has actually fallen, and the introduction of the tax has not sparked an increase in total revenue or spending. He attributes these outcomes to the visibility of the tax.

Tax visibility is relative. As Sullivan notes, Canada's VAT replaced a manufacturing tax that was almost completely invisible to the average voter. The relevant question for the United States is how the visibility of the VAT compares to that of the income tax. One argument holds that even a VAT listed on receipts is relatively invisible because it is collected in numerous small increments throughout the year, whereas income tax liability is prominently displayed on an annual tax return. Although this argument may have some merit, it is not fully convincing. The typical worker's income tax is fully collected through withholding, which is relatively invisible; when taxpayers file their returns, they may focus on the refunds they will receive rather than on the annual tax liability shown on the return. Moreover, 46 percent of all households did not pay individual income tax in 2011 (as estimated by Urban-Brookings Tax Policy Center [2011]), so the individual income tax was presumably not visible to them. In contrast, all households would be subject to the VAT. Burman (2008) argues that a VAT earmarked to pay for federal health care programs would make the cost of those programs more visible to voters, particularly those who do not pay individual income tax, and thereby create pressure to restrain their growth.

Still, because even a visible VAT gives the government an additional revenue source to exploit, other measures to restrain spending may be desirable.

Measures to Restrain Spending. One possibility is to adopt budget procedures to restrain spending at the same time that a VAT is introduced. For example, Burman (2008) suggests that the introduction of a VAT be accompanied by entitlement spending caps and super-majority voting requirements for new entitlements. Such measures should be considered, although their effectiveness is unclear.

Still another approach is to completely replace an existing revenue source at the time a VAT is introduced, because reintroducing a revenue source is likely to be more difficult than increasing one that remains in place. As we have noted, complete replacement of the individual income tax is unlikely, for distributional reasons, and replacement of the Social Security payroll and self-employment tax would complicate the operation of the Social Security program. It might be possible, though, to completely replace other taxes, such as the corporate income tax, the Unearned Income Medicare Contribution tax, or the Medicare payroll and self-employment tax.

Conclusion

A VAT is more likely to be adopted as a partial than as a complete replacement for the income tax. Some issues can be handled as easily, or more easily, under the VAT as under the X tax, but other issues are more difficult. Monetary policy, Social Security, and state and local governments and nonprofits pose particular challenges. To combat a potential money machine, the VAT should be listed separately on customer receipts, and its enactment should be accompanied by measures to restrain federal spending.

Conclusion

In this book, we have outlined how a progressive consumption tax, in the form of the Bradford X tax, can be used to completely replace the income tax system and end its inefficient penalty on saving and investment without adverse distributional consequences.

As outlined in chapters 3 through 9, we propose an X tax, consisting of a flat-rate firm-level tax on business cash flow and a graduated-rate household tax on wages. The tax would completely replace the individual and corporate income taxes, the estate and gift taxes, and the Unearned Income Medicare Contribution tax slated to take effect in 2013. We have used 35 percent as an illustrative top tax rate on wages and 38.8 percent as an illustrative flat tax rate on business cash flow, while noting that the actual rate could be higher or lower, depending on various decisions about the details of the tax.

In those chapters, we outlined a number of design features that the X tax should employ. We recommend that the tax generally ignore public and private transfer payments, except for tax relief for charitable contributions. To distinguish wages from business cash flow when owners work for firms, we recommend a unified reasonable-compensation rule that applies to firms organized in different ways and governs both the X tax and the payroll tax. To prevent the tax on investment that would arise if firms could not receive tax relief for negative cash flows, we recommend a carryback period of at least five years and unlimited carryforward with interest.

We propose that transactions between financial intermediaries and household customers be taxed under a cash-flow method that integrates real and financial transactions, and that transactions between intermediaries and business customers not be taxed. To prevent a wealth transfer from Americans to foreigners, we recommend that the tax not be border adjusted. To mitigate transfer-pricing problems that can arise in the absence of border adjustment, we propose to tax transactions between firms and related foreign parties on a cash-flow method similar to the method we recommend for financial intermediaries.

We recommend that firms receive transition relief for the unclaimed cost basis of their capital stock, including inventory, and propose transition rules for a variety of other situations. We recommend that owner-occupied homes and consumer durables be taxed under a prepayment method that effectively exempts these assets from the business cash-flow tax. We similarly recommend that governments and nonprofit institutions be exempt from the business cash-flow tax.

As we explained in chapter 1, the removal of the income tax penalty on saving should promote economic efficiency and long-run growth. A number of simulation models have been used to estimate the magnitude of the economic gains. Space precludes a full discussion of this issue, but we highlight results from leading studies and discuss some of the uncertainty surrounding these estimates.

Auerbach (1996, 62) estimated a long-run output increase of 2.0 to 8.9 percent from various proposals to replace the income tax with a consumption tax, and Altig et al. (2001) estimated long-run output gains of 1.9 percent to 9.4 percent for various proposals. Diamond and Zodrow (2008, 239) estimate a 4.9 percent long-run output gain from switching to a Hall-Rabushka flat tax with no transition relief. A significant part of the long-run gains come at the expense of short-run consumption. Because these simulation models are stylized, they can yield only rough and uncertain estimates of the effects of the reforms. Nevertheless, the results indicate that moving to consumption taxation can produce sizable economic benefits.

Two patterns emerge clearly from the studies. First, the long-run output increase is diminished if the consumption tax is more progressive; as with an income tax, greater progressivity pushes up marginal tax rates for many taxpayers and tends to reduce labor supply. Second, the long-run output increase is also diminished if the tax on old capital is lower, due to either the application of a lower tax rate to business cash flow or the provision of transition relief. These two factors have conflicting implications for the gains from moving to the X tax. While the progressivity of the X tax tends to diminish the output gain, the relatively high tax rate on business cash flow tends to increase the output gain.

Altig et al. (2001, 587, 591) offer a more concrete perspective on this question because they specifically examine an X tax option involving a 30 percent tax rate on cash flow and high-wage workers. For this option, they estimate a long-run output gain of 6.4 percent, resulting from a 21 percent increase in the capital stock and a 2 percent increase in labor supply, with a 4.4 percent increase in hourly wages. Households throughout the income distribution share in the long-run gains. Because our proposal includes transition relief, whereas the option specified by Altig et al. apparently does not, the gains from our proposal could be somewhat smaller. The President's Advisory Panel on Federal Tax Reform (2005, 190) estimated that the Progressive Consumption Tax Plan that it considered, which featured a switch to an X tax with transition relief, would yield a long-run output gain of "up to 6.0 percent."

As federal spending grows in upcoming decades, pressure for additional revenue will intensify. Turning to the income tax system for this revenue will place heavier marginal tax rates on saving and investment, an outcome that can be averted by moving to consumption taxation. Yet, the most prominent potential consumption taxes, the retail sales tax and value-added tax, have the drawback of regressivity. In this book we have argued that the Bradford X tax is a progressive consumption tax that can be used to completely replace the income tax system and its economic flaws. In short, we have sought to point the way forward to an efficient, fair, and simple tax system that will ensure a prosperous future for the American people.

Notes

1. The trade-off fallacy is embraced by, among others, Zelenak (1999, 1183–84), Gravelle (1994, 31), McMahon (2006), Congressional Research Service (2010, 3), and Seidman (2009, 237).

2. The list includes employer pension plans, traditional IRAs, nondeductible IRAs, nonworking spousal IRAs, Roth IRAs, rollover IRAs, SIMPLE IRAs, 401(k) plans, profit-sharing plans, employee stock ownership plans, money purchase plans, defined benefit plans, Simplified Employee Pensions, SARSEPs, SIMPLE 401(k) plans for small employers, 403(b) tax-sheltered annuity plans for 501(c)(3) organizations and public schools, 457(b) deferred compensation plans for state and local governments, Archer medical savings accounts, and health savings accounts.

3. Algebra reveals that the difference between the tax-exclusive and tax-inclusive rates is equal to their product. In this example, the difference between .25 and .2 is .05, which is equal to $(.25)*(.2)$.

4. The Medicare payroll tax rate is 2.9 percent through 2012, but is slated to rise to 3.8 percent in 2013 for the highest earners. See note 6, below, and associated text.

5. Treasury's new methodology also accounts for above-normal returns and for the fact that part of the corporate income tax is actually a tax on cash flow rather than on net income.

6. These taxes have been modified by recent legislation. Three laws adopted in December 2010, December 2011, and February 2012 lowered the Social Security tax rate from 12.4 to 10.4 percent for 2011 and 2012 as a temporary stimulus measure. The 0.9 percent Medicare surtax, which is slated to take effect in 2013, was added by the health care reform law adopted in March 2010.

7. The only link is that, to receive Medicare Part A coverage without paying premiums, an individual must have paid at least a minimal amount of Medicare payroll or self-employment taxes for at least ten years. Provided that this threshold is met, the benefits received under Medicare Part A are independent of the amount of taxes paid.

8. One potential problem is that it may be unconstitutional to provide a refundable tax credit, as opposed to a deduction, for contributions to religious organizations. The refundable credit could be viewed as too similar to a direct spending program that benefits religion, potentially triggering a violation of the establishment clause of the

First Amendment to the U.S. Constitution. We believe, however, that the application of the credit to religious contributions will withstand constitutional challenge.

9. It is far from clear, however, that such a transfer would be desirable. Viard (2011b) argues that the revenue from taxation of Social Security benefits should be paid to the general treasury, rather than the trust funds, under the current tax system. If that perspective is adopted, there would be no reason to compensate the trust funds for the loss of this revenue under the X tax system.

10. Social Security beneficiaries younger than the normal retirement age (currently 66, but slated to rise to 67) also face an earnings test under current law. This provision requires recipients to delay part or all of their benefits if they earn more than a small amount of labor income; receiving other types of income has no effect on benefits. As Biggs (2008) explains, the earnings test creates an unnecessary work disincentive, because many of the affected recipients believe that the benefits they are denied due to work are permanently lost, although they are actually offset by higher monthly benefits, starting when the recipient stops working or attains the normal retirement age. The earnings test should be abolished, under either the current system or the X tax system. Nevertheless, if desired, the earnings test can be maintained under the X tax; because the test applies only to labor income, the necessary information can be obtained from household tax returns.

11. Limited partners potentially face incentives to understate wages similar to those of S shareholders because they are also not subject to self-employment taxes on their partnership income. Historically, this has not been a problem because limited partners have not been allowed to work for, or otherwise actively participate in, the firm's operations, although this may be changing in some states. In any case, the income of high-income limited partners will be subject to the Unearned Income Medicare Contribution tax, which is slated to take effect in 2013. The 3.8 percent rate of this tax matches the marginal payroll tax rate for many of these partners, eliminating any incentive to understate wages.

12. The same logic applies to VATs. Perhaps for this reason, many VATs allow full refunds for negative tax bases, which arise when a firm's purchases from other firms exceed its sales. (Also, such refunds may avoid the "corporate welfare" stigma because the VAT is deemed to be borne by consumers rather than firms.) Even so, as Ernst and Young (2010) note, the rules applicable to refunds of negative VAT tax bases are sometimes more stringent than for refunds of VAT tax payments, reflecting fears of abuse and manipulation. Tait (1988, 307–8) and Keen and Smith (2006, 867–68) discuss various types of VAT refund fraud. Of course, negative tax bases under the X tax are considerably more common than under the VAT because the X tax allows a deduction for wages.

13. In a possible variant, firms could be allowed to elect to have the interest rate on their carryforwards measured by the return on the stock market (or some other risky investment) rather than by the Treasury rate. Of course, in any year with negative market returns, the firm's carryovers would shrink accordingly. Obviously, no firm would

be allowed to change its election retroactively. Firms should be indifferent in choosing between "investing" their carryforwards at the two rates because they, or their owners, can freely move their other investments between Treasury debt and the stock market.

14. A number of papers, including Chia and Whalley (1999), Grubert and Mackie (2000), Jack (2000), Auerbach and Gordon (2002), and Rousslang (2002), have discussed whether financial services should be taxed. Their apparently conflicting conclusions may reflect differences in terminology and in the nature of the consumption tax being considered, but we do not attempt to reconcile their results here.

15. The financial services are taxed if the income tax disallows an interest expense deduction, as the current tax system does for most consumer loans other than home mortgages. This treatment introduces a different problem, though, because pure interest expense should be deductible under an income tax. Bradford (1996a, 458–60) notes that the current system also taxes financial services embedded in short-term insurance contracts, because consumers do not deduct their net payments on such contracts.

16. An exemption approach is commonly adopted under VAT systems, as documented by Merrill (1997, 20–25). Due to the way in which actual credit-invoice VATs work, this policy is actually worse than the tax exemption described above, because it results in tax cascading for business customers.

17. Wang (2003) and Wang, Basu, and Fernald (2008) outline a general-equilibrium method of measuring bank output, which modifies the spread method to incorporate a risk premium.

18. Because exporting firms would have consistently negative tax liabilities, an effective border adjustment requires that they be able to obtain prompt refunds. Such refunds are routinely provided under VATs.

19. Although the authors embracing this fallacy are too numerous to list, a few examples are Brys (2010, 104), Tonelson and Kearns (2010), Hartman (2004), and Westin (2004).

20. The analyses include Auerbach (2005; 2008, 17–20), Weisbach (2008, 81–84), Shaviro (2007a, 104–6), Bradford (2004, 5–17), Viard (2004a, 2004b, 2009a), Grubert and Newlon (1997, 8–10), Hines (1996, 478–79), Metcalf (1996, 97–99), and Whalley (1988, 39). For more technical discussions, see Feldstein and Krugman (1990), Grossman (1980), Dixit (1985, 319), and Lockwood, De Meza, and Myles (1994).

21. Shaviro (2004, 107–8) observes that the distinction between origin and destination is separate from the distinction between residence and source. An origin-based tax can apply to the value added that is produced inside the United States (a source concept) or to the value added that is produced by United States residents (a residence concept). Similarly, a destination tax can apply to consumption that occurs inside the United States (a source concept) or to consumption by United States residents (a residence concept). The residence basis is conceptually better, but the tax is likely to be imposed partly on a source basis, for administrative reasons. Miller (2009a, 2009b) notes that VATs generally employ a mixture of residence and source concepts.

22. Of course, destination tax systems must draw an *administrative* distinction between domestic and foreign firms, requiring the former to collect and remit tax on their sales while collecting tax directly from consumers on purchases from the latter.

23. The "new view" of dividend taxation pioneered by King (1974), Auerbach (1979), and Bradford (1981) implies that dividend taxes also impose deferred taxes on investment. These taxes, which are modest, given today's preferential dividend tax rates, have implications similar to the firm-level deferred taxes considered in the text. Other deferred taxes also exist at the individual level. As Lyon and Merrill (2001) and Viard (2000) note, pensions and conventional IRAs also face deferred tax liabilities under the current income tax system because contributions are deducted and withdrawals are taxed. Appreciated assets also face deferred tax liabilities because capital gains tax is imposed only on realization. Pension recipients and holders of conventional IRAs and appreciated assets therefore enjoy a gain in value from income tax repeal, due to the forgiveness of deferred tax liabilities.

24. As we discussed in chapter 1, wage tax rates might still be higher under the X tax than under the income tax, although the higher rates would not necessarily imply larger work disincentives.

25. This approach is not exact. Capital that received an up-front credit gets off easy unless its basis was reduced by *the deduction equivalent of the credit,* a practice that current law does not follow (basis is generally reduced by the face value of the credit). By using the regular-tax depreciation schedules, we also ignore the potential effect of the alternative minimum tax on deferred tax liabilities.

26. In the unlikely event that the homebuyer purchases a home for less than $5,000, the credit is limited to the purchase price.

27. As we mentioned in chapter 4, though, some state and local government employees and long-time federal government employees are exempt from the Social Security payroll tax, and some long-time state and local employees are also exempt from the Medicare payroll tax.

28. In chapter 7, we recommended that an R+F cash-flow method be applied to transactions between U.S. firms and foreign affiliates to prevent transfer pricing abuse. In principle, that same method could also be applied to the transfer pricing problems now under consideration, obviating the need for the strict rules discussed in the text. As we discussed in chapter 6, however, the R+F cash-flow method is too counterintuitive to apply to households and ordinary firms, so we do not recommended its use in this context.

29. If the Medicare payroll and self-employment tax were replaced by a VAT, the current requirement that a worker have paid a modest amount of Medicare taxes for at least ten years (discussed in note 7, above) could be revised to require ten years of residence in the United States.

References

Altig, David, Alan J. Auerbach, Laurence J. Kotlikoff, Kent A. Smetters, and Jan Walliser. 2001. Simulating fundamental tax reform in the United States. *American Economic Review* 91 (3): 574–95.

Andrews, William D. 1974. A consumption-type or cash flow personal income tax. *Harvard Law Review* 87 (6): 1113–88.

———. 1980. A supplemental personal expenditure tax. In *What should be taxed: Income or expenditure?* ed. Joseph A. Pechman, 127–51. Washington, D.C.: Brookings Institution.

Atkinson, Anthony B., and Joseph E. Stiglitz. 1976. The design of tax structure: Direct versus indirect taxation. *Journal of Public Economics* 6 (1-2): 55–75.

Auerbach, Alan J. 1979. Wealth maximization and the cost of capital. *Quarterly Journal of Economics* 93 (3): 433–36.

———. 1996. Tax reform, capital allocation, efficiency and growth. In *Economic effects of fundamental tax reform*, ed. Henry J. Aaron and William G. Gale, 29–73. Washington, DC: Brookings Institution.

———. 1997. The future of fundamental tax reform. *American Economic Review* 87 (2) (papers and proceedings issue): 143–46.

———. 2005. A consumption tax. *Wall Street Journal*, August 25, A8.

———. 2007. Tax reform in the 21st century. In *Fundamental tax reform: Issues, choices, and implications*, ed. John W. Diamond and George R. Zodrow, 27–59. Cambridge, MA: MIT Press.

———. 2008. The choice between income and consumption taxes: A primer. In *Institutional foundations of public finance: Economic and legal perspectives*, ed. Alan J. Auerbach and Daniel Shaviro, 13–46. Cambridge, MA: Harvard University Press.

———. 2010. A modern corporate tax. Center for American Progress/Hamilton Foundation. Available at http://www.americanprogress.org/issues/2010/12/pdf/auerbachpaper.pdf.

Auerbach, Alan J., and Roger H. Gordon. 2002. Treatment of financial services under a VAT. *American Economic Review* 92 (2): 411–16.

Auerbach, Alan J., and Laurence J. Kotlikoff. 1987. *Dynamic fiscal policy*. Cambridge: Cambridge University Press.

Auten, Gerald, and Geoffrey Gee. 2009. Income mobility in the U.S.: New evidence from income tax data. *National Tax Journal* 62 (2): 1–28.

Avi-Yonah, Reuven S. 2010. Déjà vu all over again? Reflections on Auerbach's "modern corporate tax." University of Michigan Law School Paper 29. Available at http://law.bepress.com/cgi/viewcontent.cgi?article=1139&context=umichlwps.

Bank of England. 2011. *Inflation report, May 2011.* Available at http://www.bankof england.co.uk/publications/inflationreport/ir11may.pdf.

Bankman, Joseph, and David A. Weisbach. 2006. The superiority of an ideal consumption tax over an ideal income tax. *Stanford Law Review* 58 (5): 1413–56.

Barro, Robert J. 1997. *Determinants of economic growth: A cross-country empirical study.* Cambridge, MA: MIT Press.

———. 2011. How to really save the economy. *New York Times*, September 11, WK8.

Bartlett, Bruce. 2009. *The new American economy: The failure of Reaganomics and a new way forward.* New York: Palgrave-Macmillan.

Batchelder, Lily L., Fred Goldberg, and Peter Orszag. 2006. Efficiency and tax incentives: The case for refundable tax credits. *Stanford Law Review* 59 (1): 23–76.

Biggs, Andrew. 2008. The Social Security earnings test: The tax that wasn't. *Tax Policy Outlook.* July.

———. 2011. Means testing and its limits. *National Affairs* 9: 97-112.

Bradford, David F. 1981. The incidence and allocation effects of a tax on corporate distributions. *Journal of Public Economics* 15 (1): 1–22.

———. 1986. *Untangling the income tax.* Cambridge, MA: Harvard University Press.

———. 1988. What are consumption taxes and who pays them? *Tax Notes* 39 (3): 383–91.

———. 1996a. Treatment of financial services under income and consumption taxes. In *Economic effects of fundamental tax reform*, ed. Henry J. Aaron and William G. Gale, 437–60. Washington, DC: Brookings Institution.

———. 1996b. Consumption taxes: Some fundamental transition issues. In *Frontiers of Tax Reform*, ed. Michael J. Boskin, 123–50. Stanford, CA: Hoover Institution Press.

———. 1998. Transition to and tax-rate flexibility in a cash-flow-type consumption tax. In *Tax Policy and the Economy*, vol. 12, ed. James M. Poterba, 151–72. Cambridge, MA: MIT Press.

———. 2003. Addressing the transfer pricing problem in an origin-basis X tax. *International Tax and Public Finance* 10 (5): 591–610.

———. 2004. *The X tax in the world economy: Going global with a simple, progressive tax.* Washington, DC: AEI Press.

Brill, Alex, and Alan D. Viard. 2008. Effective marginal tax rates, part 2: Reality. *Tax Notes* 120 (3): 327–32.

Brys, Bert. 2010. Making fundamental tax reform happen. In *Making reform happen: Lessons from OECD countries.* Paris: Organisation for Economic Co-operation and Development.

Bull, Nicholas, and Paul Burnham. 2008. Taxation of capital and labor: The diverse landscape by entity type. *National Tax Journal* 61 (3): 397–419.

Bull, Nicholas, and Lawrence B. Lindsey. 1996. Monetary implications of tax reforms. *National Tax Journal* 49 (3): 359–79.

Burman, Leonard E. 2008. A blueprint for tax reform and health reform. *Virginia Tax Review* 28 (2): 287–323.

Carroll, Robert, Robert Cline, Tom Neubig, John Diamond, and George Zodrow. 2010. *The macroeconomic effects of an add-on value added tax: Prepared for the National Retail Federation.* Ernst and Young Report. October. Available at http://www.nrf.com/modules.php?name=Pages&sp_id=1406.

Carroll, Robert, and Alan D. Viard. 2010. Value added taxation: Basic concepts and unresolved issues. *Tax Notes* 126 (9): 1117–26.

Carroll, Robert, Alan D. Viard, and Scott Ganz. 2008. Is the X tax the progressive consumption tax America needs? *Tax Policy Outlook.* December.

Chia, Ngee-Choon, and John Whalley. 1999. The tax treatment of financial intermediation. *Journal of Money, Credit, and Banking* 31 (4): 704–19.

Christian, Ernest S., and Gary A. Robbins. 2011. A value-added tax fuels big government. *Wall Street Journal,* August 24, A13.

Cline, Robert, John Mikesell, Tom Neubig, and Andrew Phillips. 2005. Sales taxation of business inputs: Existing tax distortions and the consequences of extending the sales tax to business services. *State Tax Notes* 35 (7): 457–70.

Cnossen, Sijbren. 2009. A VAT primer for lawyers, economists, and accountants. *Tax Notes* 124 (7): 687–98.

Congressional Budget Office. 2011a. *Options for changing the tax treatment of charitable giving.* Available at http://www.cbo.gov/ftpdocs/121xx/doc12167/CharitableContributions.pdf.

———. 2011b. *CBO's 2011 long-term budget outlook.* Available at http://www.cbo.gov/ftpdocs/122xx/doc12212/06-21-Long-Term_Budget_Outlook.pdf.

———. 2011c. *Trends in the distribution of household income between 1979 and 2007.* Available at http://www.cbo.gov/ftpdocs/124xx/doc12485/10-25-Household Income.pdf.

Congressional Research Service (James M. Bickley). 2010. Tax reform: An overview of proposals in the 111th Congress. Report R40414. Washington, DC.

Congressional Research Service (Jane G. Gravelle). 1996. Effects of flat taxes and other proposals on housing. Report 96-379. Washington, DC.

Conrad, Robert F. 2010. Commentary on Poddar. *Tax Law Review* 63 (2): 471–76.

Desai, Mihir A., C. Fritz Foley, and James R. Hines, Jr. 2007. Labor and capital shares of the corporate tax burden: International evidence. Unpublished manuscript. Available at http://www.people.hbs.edu/mdesai/PDFs/Labor%20and%20Capital.pdf.

Diamond, John, and George R. Zodrow. 1998. Housing and intergenerational redistributions under a consumption tax reform. *Proceedings of the 91st Annual Conference of National Tax Association,* 25–31.

———. 2008. Consumption tax reform: Changes in business equity and housing prices. In *Fundamental Tax Reform: Issues, Choices, and Implications,* ed. John W. Diamond and George R. Zodrow, 227–60. Cambridge, MA: MIT Press.

Dixit, Avinash. 1985. Tax policy in open economies. In *Handbook of public economics,* vol. 1, ed. Alan J. Auerbach and Martin S. Feldstein, 313–74. Amsterdam: North-Holland.

Duncan, Harley, and Jon Sedon. 2009. How different VATs work. *Tax Notes* 125 (12): 1367–74.

Durner, Leah, and Bobby Bui. 2009. Comparing value added and retail sales taxes. *Tax Notes* 126 (8): 983–87.

Durner, Leah, Bobby Bui, and Jon Sedon. 2009. Why VAT around the globe? *Tax Notes* 125 (8): 929–34.

Edwards, Chris. 2003. A primer on replacing the corporate income tax with a cash-flow tax. *Tax Notes* 100 (10): 1293–1306.

———. 2005. Options for tax reform. *Tax Notes* 106 (13): 1529–56.

Ernst and Young. 2010. *VAT and GST: Multiple burdens for multinational companies.* Available at http://www.ey.com/GL/en/Services/Tax/Indirect-Tax/Services---Tax---Indirect-Tax---VAT-and-GST---multiple-burdens-for-multinational-companies.

———. 2011. *VAT and GST: Managing the multinational burden.* Available at http://www.ey.com/GL/en/Services/Tax/Indirect-Tax/VAT---GST---Sales-tax/VAT-and-GST-Managing-the-multinational-burden.

European Coal and Steel Community, High Authority. 1953. *Report on the problems raised by the different turnover tax systems applied within the Common Market.* Luxembourg.

Feldstein, Martin S., and Paul Krugman. 1990. International trade effects of value-added taxation. In *Taxation in the global economy,* ed. Assaf Razin and Joel Slemrod, 263–82. Chicago: University of Chicago Press.

Fixler, Dennis J., Marshall B. Reinsdorf, and George M. Smith. 2003. Measuring the services of commercial banks in the NIPAs: Changes in concepts and methods. *Survey of Current Business* 83 (9): 33–44.

Frank, Robert H. 2005. Progressive consumption taxation as a remedy for the U.S. savings shortfall. *Economists' Voice* 2 (3).

———. 2008. Progressive consumption tax. *Democracy Journal.org* 8: 21–23.

Gale, William G. 2005. The national retail sales tax: What would the rate have to be? *Tax Notes* 107 (7): 889–911.

Gentry, William M., and R. Glenn Hubbard. 1997. Distributional implications of introducing a broad-based consumption tax. In *Tax policy and the economy,* vol. 11, ed. James M. Poterba, 1–47. Cambridge, MA: MIT Press.

Goldfarb, Sam. 2009. Policy experts revisit VAT as debt crisis looms. *Tax Notes* 124 (7): 644–46.

———. 2010. Grim budget picture grows grimmer faster. *Tax Notes* 126 (1): 31–32.

Graetz, Michael J. 2008. *100 million unnecessary returns: A simple, fair, and competitive tax plan for the United States.* New Haven, CT: Yale University Press.

Gravelle, Jane G. 1994. *Taxing capital income.* Cambridge, MA: MIT Press.

Grossman, Gene M. 1980. Border adjustments: Do they distort trade? *Journal of International Economics* 10 (1): 117–28.

Grubert, Harry, and James Mackie. 2000. Must financial services be taxed under a consumption tax? *National Tax Journal* 53 (1): 23–40.

Grubert, Harry, and T. Scott Newlon. 1997. *Taxing consumption in a global economy.* Washington, DC: AEI Press.

Hall, Robert E. 1996. The effects of tax reform on prices and asset values. In *Tax Policy and the Economy,* vol. 10, ed. James M. Poterba, 71–88. Cambridge, MA: MIT Press.

———. 1997. Potential disruption from the move to a consumption tax. *American Economic Review* 87 (2) (papers and proceedings issue): 147–50.

Hall, Robert E., and Alvin Rabushka. 1983. *Low tax, simple tax, flat tax.* New York: McGraw Hill.

———. 1995. *The flat tax.* 2nd ed. Stanford, CA: Hoover Institution Press.

Harberger, Arnold. 2008. The corporate income tax: Reflections on what is known, unknown, and unknowable. In *Fundamental tax reform: Issues, choices, and implications,* ed. John W. Diamond and George R. Zodrow, 283–307. Cambridge, MA: MIT Press.

Harris, Tameka R. L., William A. Jolliff, Amanda S. Lyndaker, and Matthew B. Schroeder. 2011. Annual industry accounts: Revised statistics for 2007–2009. *Survey of Current Business* 91 (1): 9–29.

Hartman, David A. 2004. The urgency of border-adjusted federal taxation. *Tax Notes* 104 (10): 1075–88.

Heritage Foundation. 2011. *Saving the American dream: The Heritage plan to fix the debt, cut spending, and restore prosperity.* Available at http://www.savingthedream.org/about-the-plan/plan-details/SavAmerDream.pdf.

Hines, James R., Jr. 1996. Fundamental tax reform in an international setting. In *Economic effects of fundamental tax reform,* ed. Henry J. Aaron and William G. Gale, 465–93. Washington, DC: Brookings Institution.

———. 2004. Might fundamental tax reform increase criminal activity? *Economica* 71 (283): 483–92.

Hoffman, Lorey Arthur, S. N. Poddar, and John Whalley. 1987. Taxation of banking services under a consumption type, destination basis VAT. *National Tax Journal* 40 (4): 547–54.

Holtz-Eakin, Douglas, and Cameron Smith. 2010. Leviathan unbound: The VAT? American Action Forum. Available at http://americanactionforum.org/files/Leviathan%20Unbound.pdf.

Hubbard, R. Glenn. 2011. Tax reform is the swiftest path to growth. *Wall Street Journal,* August 12, A15.

Hubbard, R. Glenn, Jonathan Skinner, and Stephen P. Zeldes. 1995. Precautionary saving and social insurance. *Journal of Political Economy* 103 (2): 360-99.

Hufbauer, Gary Clyde, assisted by Carol Gabyzon. 1996. *Fundamental tax reform and border adjustments.* Washington, DC: Institute for International Economics.

Jack, William. 2000. The treatment of financial services under a broad-based consumption tax. *National Tax Journal* 53 (4), pt. 1: 841–51.

Jenn, Brian H. 2008. The case for tax credits. *Tax Lawyer* 61 (2): 549–97.

Johansson, Sven-Erik. 1969. Income taxes and investment decisions. *Swedish Journal of Economics* 71 (2): 104–10.

Joint Committee on Taxation. 1993. *Methodology and issues in measuring changes in the distribution of tax burdens.* JCS-7-93. Available at http://www.jct.gov/publications. html?func=startdown&id=2857.

———. 2001. *Study of the overall state of the federal tax system and recommendations for simplification, pursuant to section 8022(3)(B) of the Internal Revenue Code of 1986, volume 2: Recommendations of the staff of the Joint Committee on Taxation to simplify the federal tax system.* JCS-3-01. Available at http://www.jct.gov/publications. html?func=startdown&id=2090.

———. 2011. *Present law, data, and analysis relating to tax incentives for homeownership.* JCX-50-11. Available at http://www.jct.gov/publications.html?func=start down&id=4366.

Kaldor, Nicholas. 1955. *An expenditure tax.* London: Allen and Unwin.

Kaplow, Louis. 2008a. Capital levies and transition to a consumption tax. In *Institutional foundations of public finance: Economic and legal perspectives,* ed. Alan J. Auerbach and Daniel Shaviro, 112–46. Cambridge, MA: Harvard University Press.

———. 2008b. *The theory of taxation and public economics.* Princeton, NJ: Princeton University Press.

Keen, Michael, and Ben Lockwood. 2006. Is the VAT a money machine? *National Tax Journal* 59 (4): 905–28.

Keen, Michael, and Stephen Smith. 2006. VAT fraud and evasion: What do we know and what can be done? *National Tax Journal* 59 (4): 861–87.

King, Mervyn A. 1974. Taxation and the cost of capital. *Review of Economic Studies* 41 (1): 21–35.

Laffer, Arthur. 2010. A growth agenda for the new Congress. *Wall Street Journal,* November 12, A19.

Landsburg, Steven E. 2011. How the death tax hurts the poor. *Wall Street Journal,* October 29–30, A15.

Lockwood, Ben, David De Meza, and Gareth D. Myles. 1994. When are origin and destination regimes equivalent? *International Tax and Public Finance* 1 (1): 5–24.

Lyon, Andrew B. 1990. Invariant valuation when tax rates change over time: Confirmations and contradictions. *Journal of Political Economy* 98 (2): 433–37.

Lyon, Andrew B., and Peter R. Merrill. 2001. Asset price effects of fundamental tax reform. In *Transition costs of fundamental tax reform,* ed. Kevin A. Hassett and R. Glenn Hubbard, 58–92. Washington, DC: AEI Press.

McCaffery, Edward. 2002. *Fair not flat: How to make the tax system better and simpler.* Chicago: University of Chicago Press.

McMahon, Martin J., Jr. 2006. An income tax is superior to a wage or consumption tax. *Tax Notes* 110 (12):1353–55.

Merrill, Peter R. 1997. *Taxation of financial services under a consumption tax.* Washington, DC: AEI Press.

Merrill, Peter R., and Chris R. Edwards. 1996. Cash-flow taxation of financial services. *National Tax Journal* 49 (3): 487–500.

Metcalf, Gilbert E. 1996. The role of a value-added tax in fundamental tax reform. In *Frontiers of tax reform*, ed. Michael J. Boskin, 91–109. Stanford, CA: Hoover Institution Press.

Mikesell, John L. 1997. Is the retail sales tax really inferior to a value-added tax? In *The sales tax in the 21st century*, ed. Matthew N. Murray and William F. Fox, 75–87. Westport, CT: Praeger.

Miller, Rebecca. 2009a. Echoes of source and residence in VAT jurisdictional rules. University of Sydney Law School Legal Studies Research Paper 09/44. June.

———. 2009b. Intentional and unintentional double non-taxation issues in VAT. University of Sydney Law School Legal Studies Research Paper 09/45. June.

Mintz, Jack M. 1996. The thorny problem of implementing new consumption taxes. *National Tax Journal* 49 (3): 461–74.

National Taxpayer Advocate (Nina E. Olson). 2004. *2004 annual report to Congress*, vol. 1. Available at http://www.irs.gov/pub/irs-utl/ntafy2004annualreport.pdf.

Nguyen, Elena L. 2011. The international investment position of the United States at year end 2010. *Survey of Current Business* 91 (7): 113–23.

Organisation for Economic Co-operation and Development. 2008. *Consumption tax trends, 2008*. Paris: OECD.

Organisation for Economic Co-operation and Development, Center for Tax Policy and Administration. 2007. *Survey on the taxation of small and medium-sized enterprises: Draft report on responses to the questionnaire*. Paris: OECD.

Pierson, Drew. 2011. Fiscal commission looked closely at a VAT, members say. *Tax Notes* 130 (11): 1251–53.

Poddar, Satya. 2010. Taxation of housing under a VAT. *Tax Law Review* 63 (2): 443–70.

Poddar, Satya, and Morley English. 1997. Taxation of financial services under a value-added tax: Applying the cash-flow approach. *National Tax Journal* 50 (1): 89–111.

Pollack, Sheldon D. 1997. Gross revenue from gambling: Some unintended consequences. *Tax Notes* 76 (11): 1455–65.

President's Advisory Panel on Federal Tax Reform. 2005. *Simple, fair, and pro-growth: Proposals to fix America's tax system*. Washington, DC: Government Printing Office. Available at http://govinfo.library.unt.edu/taxreformpanel/final-report/index.html.

Raby, Burgess J. W., and William L. Raby. 2001. Offsetting gambling gains with losses not always possible. *Tax Notes* 90 (11): 1515–19.

Randolph, William C. 2006. International burdens of the corporate income tax. Congressional Budget Office Working Paper 2006-09. Washington, DC.

Rousslang, Donald J. 2002. Should financial services be taxed under a consumption tax? Probably. *National Tax Journal* 55 (2): 281–91.

Samuelson, Paul. 1964. Tax deductibility of economic depreciation to ensure invariant valuations. *Journal of Political Economy* 72 (6): 604–6.

Sandmo, Agnar. 1979. A note on the neutrality of the cash flow corporate tax. *Economics Letters* 4 (2): 173–76.

Seidman, Laurence S. 2009. *Public finance*. New York: McGraw Hill/Irwin.

———. 2011. How to clean up tax expenditures: Terminate or 'credify.' *Tax Notes* 133 (2): 217–19.

Seidman, Laurence S., and Kenneth A. Lewis. 2009. Two ways to tax very-high-income households. *Tax Notes* 123 (12): 1466–71.

Shaviro, Daniel N. 2000. *When rules change: An economic and political analysis of transition relief and retroactivity*. Chicago: University of Chicago Press.

———. 2004. Replacing the income tax with a progressive consumption tax. *Tax Notes* 103 (1): 91–113.

———. 2007a. Simplifying assumptions: How might the politics of consumption tax reform affect (impair) the end product? In *Fundamental tax reform: Issues, choices, and implications,* ed. John W. Diamond and George R. Zodrow, 75–124. Cambridge, MA: MIT Press.

———. 2007b. Beyond the pro-consumption tax consensus. *Stanford Law Review* 60 (3): 745–88.

Sheppard, Lee A. 2011. The corporate tax: Victim of changes? *Tax Notes* 133 (2): 20–21.

Shoven, John. 1996. Comment. In *Economic effects of fundamental tax reform,* ed. Henry J. Aaron and William G. Gale, 461–62. Washington, DC: Brookings Institution.

Slemrod, Joel. 1995. The simplification potential of alternatives to the income tax. *Tax Notes* 66 (9): 1331–38.

Smart, Michael, and Richard M. Bird. 2009. The impact on investment of replacing a retail sales tax with a value-added tax: Evidence from Canadian experience. *National Tax Journal* 62(4): 591–609.

Smith, Adam. 1976. (1776). *An inquiry into the nature and causes of the wealth of nations*. Chicago: University of Chicago Press.

Sorensen, Peter. 2009. Dual income taxes: A Nordic tax system. Department of Economics, University of Copenhagen.

Stelzer, Irwin. 2010. Small bras and the value-added tax. *Wall Street Journal*, April 5, A19.

Steuerle, Gene. 1997. Taxing the elderly on their Medicare benefits. *Tax Notes* 76 (4): 551–52.

———. 2005a. Taxing the capital income of only the poor and the middle class. *Tax Notes* 107 (2): 239-40.

———. 2005b. When is it best to tax the wealthy? (Part 1 of 2). *Tax Notes* 109 (11): 1451–52.

Sullivan, Martin A. 2010. VAT lessons from Canada. *Tax Notes* 103 (5): 493–96.

Summers, Lawrence H. 1981. Capital taxation and accumulation in a life-cycle growth model. *American Economic Review* 71 (4): 533–44.

Tait, Alan A. 1988. *Value added tax: International practice and problems*. Washington, DC: International Monetary Fund.

Tax Executives Institute. 1992. *Value-added taxes: A comparative analysis.* Washington, DC: Tax Executives Institute.

Thorndike, Joseph J. 2009. Early proposals for an American VAT. *Tax Notes* 124 (1): 75–77.

Thuronyi, Victor. 2011. Progressive corporate tax reform. *Tax Notes* 130 (11): 1303–12.

Toder, Eric, Jim Nunns, and Joseph Rosenberg. 2011. Methodology for distributing a VAT. Urban Institute Research Paper. April. Available at http://www.urban.org/UploadedPDF/1001533-Methodology-Distributing-VAT.pdf.

Toder, Eric, and Kim Reuben. 2007. Should we eliminate taxation of capital income? In *Taxing capital income,* ed. Henry J. Aaron, Leonard E. Burman, and C. Eugene Steuerle, 89–141. Washington, DC: Urban Institute Press.

Tonelson, Alan, and Kevin L. Kearns. 2010. Trading away the stimulus. *New York Times,* September 10.

Urban-Brookings Tax Policy Center. 2010. Table T10-0186: Distribution of business income by statutory marginal tax rate, 2011. Available at http://www.taxpolicycenter.org/numbers/Content/PDF/T10-0186.pdf.

———. 2011. Table T11-0173: Tax units with zero or negative tax liability, 2004–2011. Available at http://www.taxpolicycenter.org/numbers/Content/PDF/T11-0173.pdf.

U.S. Department of the Treasury, Office of Tax Policy. 2007. *Approaches to improve the competitiveness of the U.S. business tax system for the 21st century.* Available at http://www.treas.gov/press/releases/reports/hp749_approachesstudy.pdf.

Viard, Alan D. 2000. The transition to consumption taxation, part 1: The impact on existing capital. *Economic and Financial Review,* no. 3, 2–22. Available at http://dallasfed.org/research/efr/2000/efr0003a.pdf.

———. 2004a. Border adjustments won't promote competitiveness. *Tax Notes* 105 (1): 122–24.

———. 2004b. Why attacks on analysis of border adjustment were unsuccessful. *Tax Notes* 105 (8): 1153–55.

———. 2006. McMahon off base on consumption tax. *Tax Notes* 111 (2): 247–49.

———. 2008. The Fairtax: A response to Adler's critique. *Tax Notes* 118 (4): 567–68.

———. 2009a. Border tax adjustments won't stimulate exports. *Tax Notes* 122 (9): 1139–43.

———. 2009b. Review of *Institutional foundations of public finance. National Tax Journal* 62 (2): 367–74.

———. 2009c. Two cheers for corporate tax base broadening. *National Tax Journal* 62 (3): 399–412.

———. 2010. Sales taxation of business purchases: A tax policy distortion. *State Tax Notes* 56 (12): 967–73.

———. 2011a. Tax policy and growth. In *Rules for growth: Promoting innovation and growth through legal reform.* The Kauffman Task Force on Law, Innovation, and Growth, 179–207. Kansas City, MO: Marion Ewing Kauffman Foundation.

———. 2011b. Social Security and the general treasury: Who's raiding whom? *Tax Notes* 130 (8): 943–51.

———. 2011c. VAT replacement: Concurrent tax and Social Security reforms. In *The VAT reader: What a federal consumption tax would mean for America*, 123–29. Washington, DC: Tax Analysts.

———. 2011d. Goods versus services: A call for sales tax neutrality. *State Tax Notes* 60 (7): 511–18.

———. 2011e. Should groceries be exempt from sales tax? *State Tax Notes* 61 (4): 241–46.

Wang, J. Christina. 2003. Loanable funds, risk, and bank service output. Federal Reserve Bank of Boston Working Paper 03-4. Available at http://www.bos.frb.org/economic/wp/wp2003/wp034.htm.

Wang, J. Christina, Susanto Basu, and John G. Fernald. 2008. A general-equilibrium asset-pricing approach to the measurement of nominal and real bank output. National Bureau of Economic Research Working Paper 14616. December.

Weisbach, David A. 2000. Ironing out the flat tax. *Stanford Law Review* 52 (3): 599–664.

———. 2007. Comment on Toder and Reuben. In *Taxing capital income*, ed. Henry J. Aaron, Leonard E. Burman, and C. Eugene Steuerle, 143–51. Washington, DC: Urban Institute Press.

———. 2008. Implementing income and consumption taxes. In *Institutional foundations of public finance: Economic and legal perspectives*, ed. Alan J. Auerbach and Daniel Shaviro, 59–93. Cambridge, MA: Harvard University Press.

Westin, Richard A. 2004. Modifying the federal tax framework to stimulate employment without violating GATT principles. *Tax Notes* 103 (3): 335–45.

Whalley, John. 1988. Lessons from general equilibrium models. In *Uneasy compromise: Problems of a hybrid income-consumption tax*, ed. Henry J. Aaron, Harvey Galper, and Joseph A. Pechman, 15–53. Washington, DC: Brookings Institution.

Yin, George K. 1995. Accommodating the "low-income" in a cash-flow or consumed income tax world. *Florida Tax Review* 2 (8): 445–91.

Zakaria, Fareed. 2010. Defusing the debt bomb. *Newsweek*, March 8.

Zelenak, Lawrence. 1999. The selling of the flat tax: The dubious link between rate and base. *Tax Notes* 85 (9): 1177–95.

Zodrow, George R. 1999. The sales tax, the VAT, and taxes in between—or, is the only good NRST a VAT in drag? *National Tax Journal* 52 (3): 429–42.

Index

About the Authors

Robert Carroll is a principal with Ernst & Young LLP's Quantitative Economics and Statistics group. Before joining Ernst & Young, he was deputy assistant secretary for tax analysis at the U.S. Treasury Department, a visiting scholar with the Congressional Budget Office, and a senior economist with the President's Council of Economic Advisers. He was also recently on the faculty of American University's School of Public Affairs and a senior fellow with the Tax Foundation. Mr. Carroll has written on a wide variety of tax issues.

Alan D. Viard is a resident scholar at the American Enterprise Institute (AEI). Previously, he was a senior economist at the Federal Reserve Bank of Dallas and an assistant professor of economics at Ohio State University. He has also worked for the Treasury Department's Office of Tax Analysis, the President's Council of Economic Advisers, and the Joint Committee on Taxation. Mr. Viard has written on a wide variety of tax and budget issues.